International regimes have been a major focus of research in International Relations for over a decade. Three schools of thought have shaped the discussion: realism, which treats power relations as its key variable; neoliberalism, which bases its analysis on constellations of interests; and cognitivism, which emphasizes knowledge dynamics, communication, and identities. Each school articulates distinct views on the origins, robustness, and consequences of international regimes. This book examines each of these contributions to the debate, taking stock of, and seeking to advance, one of the most dynamic research agendas in contemporary International Relations. While the differences between realist, neoliberal, and cognitivist arguments about regimes are acknowledged and explored, the authors argue that there is substantial scope for progress towards an inter-paradigmatic synthesis.

CAMBRIDGE STUDIES IN INTERNATIONAL RELATIONS: 55

Theories of international regimes

Cambridge Studies in International Relations is a joint initiative of Cambridge University Press and the British International Studies Association (BISA). The series will include a wide range of material, from undergraduate textbooks and surveys to research-based monographs and collaborative volumes. The aim of the series is to publish the best new scholarship in International Studies from Europe, North America, and the rest of the world.

CAMBRIDGE STUDIES IN INTERNATIONAL RELATIONS

55 *Andreas Hasenclever, Peter Mayer, and Volker Rittberger*
Theories of international regimes

54 *Miranda A. Schreurs and Elizabeth C. Economy (eds.)*
The internationalization of environmental protection

53 *James N. Rosenau*
Along the domestic–foreign Frontier
Exploring governance in a turbulent world

52 *John M. Hobson*
The wealth of states
A comparative sociology of international economic and political change

51 *Kalevi J. Holsti*
The state, war, and the state of war

50 *Christopher Clapham*
Africa and the international system
The politics of state survival

49 *Susan Strange*
The retreat of the state
The diffusion of power in the world economy

48 *William I. Robinson*
Promoting polyarchy
Globalization, US intervention, and hegemony

47 *Roger Spegele*
Political realism in international theory

46 *Thomas J. Biersteker and Cynthia Weber (eds.)*
State sovereignty as social construct

45 *Mervyn Frost*
Ethics in international relations
A constitutive theory

44 *Mark W. Zacher with Brent A. Sutton*
Governing global networks
International regimes for transportation and communications

Series list continues after index

Theories of international regimes

Andreas Hasenclever

Peter Mayer

Volker Rittberger

University of Tübingen

PUBLISHED BY THE PRESS SYNDICATE OF THE UNIVERSITY OF CAMBRIDGE
The Pitt Building, Trumpington Street, Cambridge CB2 1RP, United Kingdom

CAMBRIDGE UNIVERSITY PRESS
The Edinburgh Building, Cambridge CB2 2RU, United Kingdom
40 West 20th Street, New York, NY 10011–4211, USA
10 Stamford Road, Oakleigh, Melbourne 3166, Australia

First published 1997

Printed in the United Kingdom at the University Press, Cambridge

Typeset in 10/12½pt Palatino [SE]

A catalogue record for this book is available from the British Library

Library of Congress Cataloguing in Publication data

Hasenclever, Andreas.
Theories of international regimes / Andreas Hasenclever, Peter Mayer, Volker Rittberger
p. cm. – (Cambridge Studies in International Relations: 55)
Includes bibliographical references and index.
ISBN 0 521 59145 7 (hc) – ISBN 0 521 59849 4 (pb)
1. International relations.
I. Mayer, Peter, 1961– . II. Rittberger, Volker, 1941– . III. Title.
IV. Series.
JX1395.H365 1997
327.1'01–dc21 96-46493 CIP

ISBN 0 521 59145 7 hardback
ISBN 0 521 59849 4 paperback

Contents

Figures and tables

Acknowledgments

If books can be written by accident, then this is one of them. It all began when Margaret Hermann challenged us to write a review essay on regime theory for the *Mershon International Studies Review* which she edits. Somehow this request must have been wrongly interpreted by us – or should we say it was received all too well? In any case, after missing several deadlines and trying Peg's patience the best we could, we produced a manuscript which was about four or five times longer than the sixty pages we had been allotted.

Then came a few months of silence – time enough to get a little nervous. Would the editors of the *Mershon International Studies Review* decide that they had seen enough of our opinion on international regimes? Or would they send us the manuscript back with some ideas on how to cut it down by four-fifths? Fortunately, neither happened. Instead they did two things which took us by surprise, and for which we are most grateful. First, they themselves went to the trouble of producing an abridged version of our ridiculously oversized "article," making it, after all, possible for it to appear in the journal in October 1996 under the title "Interests, Power, Knowledge: The Study of International Regimes" (*Mershon International Studies Review* 40 (supp. 2): 177–228). Sections of this article are reprinted in this book with the permission of the Mershon Center, The Ohio State University, and the International Studies Association. Since then it has come to our attention that Robert Woyach was in charge of this laborious task of abridgement, which until now has been an unacknowledged one. So we do not wish to miss this opportunity to express our gratitude for his excellent work. Second, they encouraged us to seek a publisher for the complete manuscript. We followed their advice and were fortunate enough to find Cambridge University Press interested in bringing out this heavily revised version of the original review essay.

In writing and rewriting this book we received support and encouragement from various people and institutions besides those already mentioned. Heike Brabandt, Markus Müller, Gudrun Schwarzer, Marit Schweiker, Wolfgang Wagner, and Michael Zürn read and commented on earlier versions of the manuscript. Special thanks are due to Frank Schimmelfennig who not only read the manuscript particularly carefully, but also wrote an extensive and most useful critical comment, highlighting numerous opportunities for improving the text. We have benefitted a great deal from the criticism and advice of several anonymous reviewers. Andrea Falke and Monique Youssef allowed us to share in their privilege of speaking English as their first language. Christina Schrade advised us on matters of PC. (Naturally, the authors accept full responsibility for any remaining errors.) Heike Brabandt, Dirk Peters, Susanne Riegraf, and Stefan Stampfer spent countless hours preparing the index. Last but not least, we gratefully acknowledge the financial support of the Deutsche Forschungsgemeinschaft, which enabled us to do the research necessary to write this book.

We would like to dedicate this book to our friends and colleagues in the Center for International Relations/Peace and Conflict Studies at the University of Tübingen. It is a pleasure to work with you!

Andreas Hasenclever
Peter Mayer
Volker Rittberger

1 Introduction: three perspectives on international regimes

More than twenty years after students of international relations began to ask questions about "international regimes" (Ruggie 1975), scholarly interest in the "principles, norms, rules, and decision-making procedures" (Krasner 1983c: 2) that govern state behavior in specific issue-areas of international relations continues to be strong. It may be the case that the term "regime" has lost some of its earlier charm (Milner 1993: 494). But the substantive questions that define the regime-analytical research agenda – whether couched in terms of "regimes," "institutions" or otherwise – still count among the major foci of International Relations scholarship in both Europe and North America. What accounts for the emergence of instances of rule-based cooperation in the international system? How do international institutions (such as regimes)[1] affect the behavior of state and non-state actors in the issue-areas for which they have been created? Which factors, be they located within or without the institution, determine the success and the stability of international regimes? Is it possible to come up with non-idiosyncratic explanations for the properties of particular institutional arrangements (such as the extent to which they are formalized)?

Various theories have been proposed to shed light on at least some of these questions. According to the explanatory variables that these theories emphasize, they may be classified as power-based, interest-based, and knowledge-based approaches, respectively. In fact, we may talk of three *schools of thought* within the study of international regimes: realists, who focus on power relationships; neoliberals, who base their

[1] As we shall see in the next chapter, most students of regimes agree that international regimes can be seen as a special case of international institutions. Hence, we will often use the generic term "institution" in lieu of "regime," except where the specifics of regimes or their status as institutions are at issue.

analyses on constellations of interests; and cognitivists, who emphasize knowledge dynamics, communication, and identities. The use of the term "schools" does not imply that there are no significant differences among the positions taken by members of the same school with respect to international regimes. As we shall see in the chapters that follow, there are many such differences. It does imply, though, that the disagreements between members of different schools of thought are of a more fundamental nature.

One major difference separating the three schools of thought is the degree of "institutionalism" that power-based, interest-based, and knowledge-based theories of regimes tend to espouse. By "institutionalism" we mean the view that (international) institutions matter. Such a view may be, and actually is, held in minimalist and maximalist versions. To see just what this view involves, a basic distinction, to which we will return repeatedly throughout this book, is helpful. Analytically, institutions can be significant in two respects: they may be more or less *effective*, and they may be more or less *robust* (or resilient). While effectiveness involves a static perspective in the sense that it can be determined at and for any given point in time, resilience (robustness) is essentially a dynamic measure of the significance of regimes, the application of which presupposes a relevant change in the regime's environment (Powell 1994: 340f.).

To be more precise, regime *effectiveness* comprises two overlapping ideas (Underdal 1992; Young 1994: ch. 6). First, a regime is effective to the extent that its members abide by its norms and rules. (This attribute of regimes is sometimes also referred to as "regime strength.") Second, a regime is effective to the extent that it achieves certain objectives or fulfills certain purposes. The most fundamental and most widely discussed of these purposes is the enhancement of the ability of states to cooperate in the issue-area. In contrast, regime *robustness* (resilience) refers to the "staying power" of international institutions in the face of exogenous challenges and to the extent to which prior institutional choices constrain collective decisions and behavior in later periods, i.e. to the extent to which "institutional history matters" (Powell 1994: 341). In other words, institutions that change with every shift of power among their members or whenever the most powerful participants find that their interests are no longer optimally served by the current regime, *lack* resilience. "Change" in this context may mean either a fundamental alteration of the regime's normative content or a drastic change (usually, a decline) in the exent to which the regime's prescriptions are actually complied with by its members (or both). At least in principle, therefore, a regime may turn out brittle, even though it continues to exhibit a high degree of effectiveness: compliance with the new norms and rules may be just as high as it was with the previous ones. The two dimensions of regime significance are conceptually independent (although they may be correlated empirically), i.e. a regime's robustness cannot be inferred from its effectiveness nor vice versa.[2]

None of the theories that we review in this book denies international regimes any impact whatsoever on world politics, but the degree of "institutionalism" implicit in these theories varies considerably. This variance can, to a large measure, be attributed to the "behavioral models" (Young 1989a: 209–13) upon which realists, neoliberals, and cognitivists tend to base their analyses, i.e. to the assumptions they make about the nature of state actors and their motivation. *Power-based theories of regimes*, which assume that states care not only for absolute, but for relative gains as well, are least inclined to ascribe a considerable degree of causal significance to international institutions, although they acknowledge that regime-based inter-state cooperation is a reality that is in need of explanation. In a sense, power theorists of regimes face this need even more than others, since sustained international cooperation which is not readily reduced to a form of external balancing represents a major "puzzle" to the realist research program. Realists who take international institutions seriously[3] argue that power is no less central in cooperation than in conflict between nations. According to these authors, the distribution of power resources among actors strongly affects both the prospects for effective regimes to emerge and persist in

2 This is not to say that the two dimensions are completely unrelated at the conceptual level: (time series) data about effectiveness are relevant (though not sufficient) for determining the level of a regime's robustness. For illuminating discussions of the meaning and implications of an institutionalist position see Krasner (1983b; 1988) and Powell (1994: 340–2). The distinction between effectiveness and resilience/robustness is also implicit in Young's (1989a: ch. 3) analysis of the "power of institutions." See also Rittberger and Zürn (1990: 46–9), Young (1994: 72–7) as well as Hasenclever, Mayer, and Rittberger (1996: 4–6).

3 Of course, not all of them do. Many realists stick to the "orthodox" position arguing that the causal significance of regimes and other international institutions is too slight to warrant extensive efforts to come to grips with them analytically. For a recent forceful attempt to expose the "false promise of institutions" in international relations theory and in particular in security studies see Mearsheimer (1995). Several institutionalists from different schools of thought have responded to Mearsheimer's criticisms; see Keohane and Martin (1995), Kupchan and Kupchan (1995), Ruggie (1995), and Wendt (1995).

an issue-area and the nature of the regimes that result, especially as far as the distribution of the benefits from cooperation is concerned. Other realists have stressed the way in which considerations of relative power – forced upon states by the anarchical environment in which they struggle for survival and independence – create obstacles for international cooperation that tend to call into question the effectiveness of international regimes (at least on the assumption that the leading school of thought in regime analysis, neoliberalism, has stated the functions that regimes may perform correctly).

Neoliberal or *interest-based theories of regimes* have been extraordinarily influential in the past decade and have come to represent the mainstream approach to analyzing international institutions. Though not completely insensitive to the effects of power differentials, they emphasize the role of international regimes in helping states to realize common interests. In so doing, they portray states as rational egoists who care only for their own (absolute) gains. Neoliberals have drawn heavily on economic theories of institutions focusing on information and transaction costs. Game-theoretic models have been applied to characterize the constellations of interests that underlie different types of regimes and also affect the likelihood of a regime being created in the first place. Deliberately appropriating essential elements of the realist approach to world politics, neoliberals have challenged the rationality of orthodox realism's skepticism *vis-à-vis* international institutions by attempting to show that this skepticism cannot in fact be based on the assumptions realists make about the nature of states and the international system. Whereas power-based theories may well be regarded as a borderline case of institutionalism, interest-based theories of regimes adopt an unequivocally institutionalist perspective, i.e. they portray regimes as both effective and resilient. Regimes help (self-interested) states to coordinate their behavior such that they may avoid collectively suboptimal outcomes, and states can be shown to have an interest in maintaining existing regimes even when the factors that brought them into being are no longer operative. Nevertheless, the institutionalism of neoliberals is a bounded one. This is implicit in the rational choice models upon which their theories are based. For these models treat actors' preferences and identities as exogenously given and thus as essentially unaffected by rule-governed practices or institutions.

Realists have taken up the neoliberal challenge by pointing out that their opponents' argument is flawed because it fails fully to appreciate the meaning of those realist assumptions that neoliberals claim to have incorporated into their theory, including assumptions about the basic motivation of states dwelling in anarchy.[4] Members of the third school of thought in regime analysis, cognitivism, have subjected interest-based theorizing to a similarly thorough criticism. Yet, the thrust of this criticism is directly opposed to that of the former one: from the cognitivist point of view, the problem with neoliberalism is not that it has misconstrued some of the realist assumptions about the nature of world politics. Rather, its limits as a theory of international institutions can be traced back directly to three realist "heritages" still operative in interest-based theories: (1) the conception of states as rational actors, who are atomistic in the sense that their identities, powers, and fundamental interests are prior to international society (the society of states) and its institutions; (2) the basically static approach to the study of international relations, which is ill-equipped to account for learning (at the unit level) and history (at the system level); and (3) the positivist methodology that prevents students of international institutions from understanding central aspects of the workings of social norms (including norms at the inter-state level).

Hence, *knowledge-based theories of regimes* have focused on the origins of interests as perceived by states and, in this connection, have accentuated the role of causal as well as normative ideas. Part of their contribution may thus be seen as complementary to the rationalist neoliberal mainstream in regime analysis, attempting to fill a gap in interest-based theorizing by adding a theory of preference formation. This strand of knowledge-based theorizing will be referred to here as "weak cognitivism." But the criticism of some cognitivists runs deeper, suggesting that an institutionalism that is informed by a sociological rather than a rational choice perspective is appropriate for the international system as well. Thus, "strong cognitivists" have pointed out that interest-based theories have provided a truncated picture of the sources of regime robustness by failing to take adequate account of the repercussions of institutionalized practices on the identities of international actors. At least in a great many situations, it is suggested, states are better understood as role-players than as utility-maximizers. Consequently, knowledge-based theories of regimes tend to embrace an institutionalism that

[4] This realist counter-attack, delivered in particular by Grieco (1988a; 1990) and directed mainly at the neoliberal work of Keohane (1983; 1984), set off the latest round of the longstanding debate between realism and liberalism in international relations theory. The controversy is documented in Baldwin (1993b) and has been lucidly reviewed by Powell (1994).

Table 1. *Schools of thought in the study of international regimes*

	Realism	Neoliberalism	Cognitivism (especially "strong cognitivism")
Central variable	power	interests	knowledge
"Institutionalism"	weak	medium	strong
Meta-theoretical orientation	rationalistic	rationalistic	sociological
Behavioral model	concerned with relative gains	absolute gains maximizer	role-player

is much more pronounced than that which we find in either neoliberalism or realism.

One word of caution is in order at this stage. We use the term "school of thought" to refer to ideas, i.e. sets of theories, rather than to people: schools of thought, in our parlance, are constituted by contributions which share certain assumptions and emphases in making sense of regimes, rather than by contributors. They are intellectual, not sociological, entities. It is therefore not inconsistent with our claim that three schools of thought define the contemporary study of international regimes to find that, occasionally, individuals have contributed to more than one "school." A case in point is Robert Keohane who, although his work is most closely associated with neoliberalism, has also made notable contributions to the power- and knowledge-based research agendas (Keohane 1980; Goldstein and Keohane 1993a). This said, most authors whose works we discuss in this book can be unambiguously attributed to a particular school of thought. (In this sense, one can talk of "members" of a school.) And even those who, like Keohane, have straddled the lines are more strongly associated with one school (in Keohane's case, neoliberalism) than with others.[5]

In this book we review recent and not so recent contributions to all

[5] The distinctions among these three schools of thought within the study of regimes are not novel. Young and Osherenko (1993a: 8–20) distinguished power-based, interest-based, and knowledge-based hypotheses regarding the formation of regimes. P. Haas (1993: 174, 176) also made use of this typology (and terminology), applying it to "regime patterns," by which term he understands "styles of collective management and lesson-drawing associated with regime creation, persistence, and change." In the same context, he talked of three competing "schools of thought." By contrast, Haggard and Simmons (1987) distinguished *four* "theoretical approaches to regime change and variance": structural, game-theoretic, functional, and cognitive. However, the differ-

three schools of thought. Since interest-based theories represent the mainstream approach to analyzing international regimes and, consequently, have attracted criticism from opposed perspectives, we address their arguments first (ch. 3). Subsequently, we look at various power-based theories of regimes (ch. 4), before we discuss some of the work on international institutions that has been done from a cognitivist point of view (ch. 5). In each case, we pay special attention to the points of disagreement with neoliberalism as the leading school of thought in regime analysis. The conclusion (ch. 6) seeks to draw these threads together by focusing on the question of to what extent syntheses between two or even all three of these schools of thought appear possible and desirable. We begin, however, by addressing a set of very fundamental questions that cut across these paradigmatic divisions, although it would be naïve to assume that they are strictly prior to them: What exactly is an international regime? Is the concept of an international regime precise enough to guide potentially cumulative empirical research? Insofar as it is not, how can this problem be remedied? And how does the concept of international regime relate to cognate concepts such as international institution or international organization? It is these conceptual issues that are the subject of the following chapter.

ence between their classification and the one underlying this book is less great than it might seem at first sight and is largely one of terminology. Thus, the first and the last of Haggard and Simmons's four sets of theories of regimes are more or less identical to what we refer to as power-based and knowledge-based theories, respectively, while the remaining two classes, functional and game-theoretic approaches, collapse into our single category of interest-based theories. Keohane (1988: 382) suggested the term "reflective approaches" to denote the comparatively heterogeneous school of thought which we (following Haggard and Simmons) here refer to as "cognitivists" (particularly that group of scholars which we will call "strong cognitivists"). For a valuable recent survey of the regime literature organized along the substantive *research questions* that drive regime analysis, rather than along the schools of thought that have crystallized in the process, see Levy, Young, and Zürn (1995).

2 Conceptual issues: defining international regimes

More than a decade ago, Susan Strange (1983) directed a volley of criticisms against the study of international regimes, which has earned her the status of the almost ritually cited radical critic of this research program. One of the reasons why she saw regime analysis doomed to failure was the "imprecision" and "woolliness" of the concept of international regime. Much of the scholarly discussion revolving around this concept, she suspected, was attributable to the fact that "people mean different things when they use it" (Strange 1983: 343). Doubts about the utility of the concept in its present form have not been confined to radical critics, though. Scholars much more favorable to the study of regimes such as Friedrich Kratochwil and John Gerard Ruggie (1986: 763) have conceded Strange's point and called for efforts at conceptual development. Oran Young (1989a: 9) went so far as to complain that "the whole enterprise of regime analysis continues to rest on a shaky foundation," explaining that "[t]he concept of a regime itself is often used so loosely that critics have reasonably questioned whether the concept is anything but a woolly notion likely to produce more confusion than illumination." Hence, it comes as no surprise that during the last decade several attempts have been made to clarify, modify, or even supplant the so-called *consensus definition* of the term "international regime," which Strange had in mind when she formulated her skepticism concerning the regime concept. It is useful briefly to review this discussion in order to assess the extent to which the conceptual criticism made by Strange and others is still justified (if it ever was).

The consensus definition of "international regime" (which we have already cited at the beginning of chapter 1) was one of the results of a conference convened to prepare the 1982 special issue of *International Organization* on international regimes and it was later elaborated by

Stephen Krasner in his introductory essay to the same issue.[1] According to Krasner (1983c: 2; see also 1985: 4f.), regimes are

> implicit or explicit principles, norms, rules, and decision-making procedures around which actors' expectations converge in a given area of international relations. Principles are beliefs of fact, causation, and rectitude. Norms are standards of behavior defined in terms of rights and obligations. Rules are specific prescriptions or proscriptions for action. Decision-making procedures are prevailing practices for making and implementing collective choice.

The international regime for the prevention of nuclear proliferation may serve to illustrate this definition (Müller 1989: 282–90; 1993a: 135–43; see also Smith 1987). This regime can be regarded as resting upon four *principles*:

(1) a principle which links the proliferation of nuclear weapons to a higher likelihood of nuclear war
(2) a principle that acknowledges the compatibility of a multilateral nuclear non-proliferation policy with the continuation and even the spread of the use of atomic energy for peaceful purposes
(3) a principle stating a connection between horizontal and vertical nuclear proliferation (i.e. the notion that in the long run the proliferation of nuclear weapons can only be halted if the nuclear powers are ready to reduce their nuclear arsenals)
(4) a principle of verification.

A variety of *norms* serve to guide the behavior of regime members in such a way as to produce collective outcomes which are in harmony with the goals and shared convictions that are specified in the regime principles. In the case at hand, Harald Müller (1989: 283f.) identifies nine such norms, including the obligation of non-nuclear weapon states to refrain from producing or acquiring nuclear weapons, the obligation of all members not to assist non-nuclear weapon states in the production or acquisition of nuclear weapons, and the obligation of nuclear weapon states to enter into serious negotiations with the purpose of concluding nuclear disarmament treaties. A host of more specific *rules* convert the regime norms into concrete prescriptions or proscriptions, whereby the

[1] Bringing together a group of excellent scholars of different theoretical orientations, this impressive collection of papers, which was later published as a book (Krasner 1983a), has had a tremendous influence on the ensuing debate and is still worth studying today. Other important pioneering works in the study of regimes include Ruggie (1975), E. Haas (1975; 1980), Keohane and Nye (1977), and Young (1980).

rule-density (i.e. the number and specificity of rules that concretize a given norm) varies considerably by regime norm. Thus, the norms pertaining to nuclear exports and verification have given rise to very detailed regulations, which make it possible (at least in principle) to distinguish clearly between compliant and non-compliant behavior on the part of the member states. Other norms, however, particularly those that create obligations specifically for nuclear powers, remain vague owing to the failure of regime members to reach agreement on corresponding rules (e.g. rules regarding time-frames for disarmament). Finally, various types of *procedures* form an integral part of the non-proliferation regime, e.g. procedures for the collective review and revision of provisions of the Nuclear Non-proliferation Treaty (NPT). While this treaty forms the normative backbone of the regime, it must not be equated with the regime as such. Various other documents (formal and informal ones), including the London Suppliers' Guidelines, the Statute of the International Atomic Energy Agency (IAEA), the safeguard rules in INFCIRC/66 and /153, and the Tlatelolco and Rarotonga Treaties, spell out injunctions which, together with the NPT, constitute the content of the nuclear non-proliferation regime (Müller 1993b: 362).[2]

Before turning to some of the difficulties Krasner's definition has given rise to, it is worthwhile emphasizing two uncontroversial, yet important implications. First, international regimes are international institutions and should be studied as such (e.g. Keohane 1984: 57; 1989c: 3f.; Young 1986: 107). Second, the terms "international regime" and "international organization" are neither synonymous (i.e. have the same meaning) nor co-extensional (i.e. refer to the same entities), even though in many cases regimes will be accompanied by organizations designed or employed to support them in various ways (e.g. Young 1989a: 25–7). In the non-proliferation case for example, the IAEA has such a part, helping the member states, as it does, to put the verification principle into practice. Perhaps the most fundamental difference between regimes and organizations – both of which can be seen as

[2] It is fairly common among students of regimes to treat a particular agreement (or sequence of agreements) as the one "authoritative" source for the normative content of the regime under study. Thus, the ozone regime is defined by the Vienna Convention and the subsequent protocols, the Berlin regime by the Quadripartite Agreement, etc. But this practice is neither required or suggested by the definition of "regime" nor always appropriate. Indeed, as Müller (1989: 282) emphasizes, one of the advantages of the regime concept is that it calls upon scholars to go beyond treaty analysis and to envisage a "functional whole" which may be composed of a rather heterogeneous set of (formal and informal) agreements, practices, and institutions.

representing a type of international institution (Keohane 1989c: 3f.) – lies in the fact that regimes, being no more than sets of principles, norms, rules, and procedures accepted by states, do not possess the capacity to act, whereas organizations can respond to events (even when their political leeway, more often than not, is tightly circumscribed) (Keohane 1988: 384, n. 2). Moreover, as is most obviously exemplified by the United Nations, the sphere of activity of an international organization need not be restricted to a particular issue-area of international relations, whereas regimes are issue-specific institutions by definition. These analytical distinctions notwithstanding, regime theorists have warned against artificially separating the scholarly study of regimes from research on formal international organizations (Kratochwil and Ruggie 1986: 771–4). In fact, as will become obvious in the next chapter, some of the functions ascribed to regimes, e.g. collecting and disseminating information, can hardly be performed without the aid of some organizational structure embedded in the regime.

For all its alleged flaws, the consensus definition has significantly promoted research by providing practitioners of regime analysis with a valuable analytical tool or, at the very least, a salient, non-arbitrary point of departure for further specifying their object of study. At the same time, researchers could not help noticing a discomforting degree of vagueness associated with various elements of this definition, which might inhibit the cumulation of knowledge about regimes in the long run. Two aspects of this problem, in particular, have received attention among regime analysts and have prompted different and, in part, quite radical suggestions for conceptual revision. The *first* one concerns the precise meaning and the mutual relationship of the four regime components: what criteria do students of regimes have for distinguishing principles, norms, rules, and procedures of a regime reliably? And why is it that we need such a relatively complex construct at all? The *second*, more fundamental, problem of interpretation arises from the phrase "around which actors' expectations converge" and amounts to the question of when we may say that a rule (or any other regime component) *exists* in a given issue-area. The rest of this chapter is devoted to a consideration of these two problems.

A complex and a lean definition of "international regime"

In a review article, Young (1986: 106) criticized Krasner's definition of the term "international regime" on three counts: (1) The definition is "really only a list of elements that are hard to differentiate conceptually and that often overlap in real-world situations." (2) It "exhibits a disconcerting elasticity when applied to the real world of international relations." (3) It is "conceptually thin" in that it fails to "tie the concept into . . . [some] larger system of ideas that would help to solve the . . . ambiguities [inherent in the definition] . . ., and that would offer guidance in formulating key questions and hypotheses regarding international regimes." Leaving aside Young's third point for a moment, this criticism reflects a dissatisfaction with the consensus definition that has been expressed now and again by students of regimes and commentators on regime analysis (Haggard and Simmons 1987: 493f.): the definition, even when Krasner's careful explication is taken into account, does not seem to be precise enough to preclude fruitless disputes about the proper description of any given regime (the content of its principles, norms, etc.).

Consequently, some have suggested dropping the consensus definition altogether and replacing it by a more straightforward formulation, which would be less amenable to divergent interpretations. At one point, Robert Keohane (1989c: 4) defined the concept of regime as follows: "Regimes are institutions with explicit rules, agreed upon by governments, that pertain to particular sets of issues in international relations." Thus, the complex apparatus of principles, norms, rules, and procedures collapses into the single concept of rules. Scholars are relieved of the burden of justifying their decision to call a given injunction a "norm" rather than a "rule" (or perhaps even a "principle") of the regime concerned.

While the pragmatic gains of this move are obvious, it also involves costs which should not be overlooked. Not only does the consensus definition, by its very complexity, encourage the analyst to reflect thoroughly upon the mutual relationship of the various injunctions ("rules" in Keohane's terminology) in the issue-area in question, it also forces a certain structure upon descriptions of regimes, thus making comparison across issue-areas easier, which, in turn, is a prerequisite for inductive theory-building.[3] Last but not least, the hierarchy of regime components implied in the consensus definition had enabled Krasner

[3] This is not to say that accumulating empirical generalizations is the most promising, or even a viable, strategy of theory-building. Waltz (1979: ch. 1) and Dessler (1991) have provided good reasons to doubt this. On the other hand, many students of international relations do proceed that way, and it would be somewhat bold to claim that all of their results are worthless just because they do not add up to theory.

(1983c: 3f.) to categorize two kinds of regime change and, at the same time, specify the identity conditions of a regime in terms of these components: only if principles or norms are altered does a *change of the regime* itself take place; all other changes in regime content are *changes within a regime*. No such strategy is available to those who adopt Keohane's "lean" definition. It is therefore not surprising that the consensus definition has never run out of supporters.[4]

But what about Young's third point, the alleged "conceptual thinness" of the definition? The requirement of (sufficient) conceptual thickness can be understood as reflecting the view that no satisfactory definition of a social phenomenon can be formed independently of any theory about this phenomenon. This view is not uncommon in international relations theory. Kenneth Waltz (1979: 11) endorses it when, discussing the difficulties of defining the concept of power, he emphatically argues that "the question of meaning . . . [is] a problem that can be solved only through the articulation and refinement of theories." And Arthur Stein (1983: 115) applies it explicitly to the phenomenon under consideration, when he advocates a "theoretically rooted" conceptualization of regimes. Indeed, not only does there seem to be much truth in this view, it also has important consequences for the nature of our problem. Most significantly, it implies that we would be mistaken to think that we could *begin* research by devising a "valid" definition of "regime" that could not and should not be altered throughout the subsequent process of theory-building. Thus, in the absence of a well-articulated and highly developed theory of international regimes, all that we can reasonably be looking for is an appropriate *working definition*.

The question, then, is which of the two definitions we have discussed so far, the complex or the lean one, is preferable in this respect. The debate that we have just brought into focus suggests that unanimity may be very hard to achieve on this issue. But there is no reason to assume that progress in the study of regimes is seriously hampered

[4] For more or less explicit defenses of the definition and, more specifically, its four-part structure see Zacher (1987: 175–7; 1996: 13f.), Kohler-Koch (1989b: sect. 3), and Müller (1993a: ch. 3; 1994: 28f.). A quite substantial modification, which, however, still preserves the four regime components introduced by the consensus definition, is Aggarwal's (1985: 18–20) distinction between "meta-regimes" (principles and norms) and "regimes" (rules and procedures). German students of regimes, in their comparatively extensive empirical work, have generally found it useful to rely on the consensus definition for identifying their unit of analysis (Kohler-Koch 1989a; Rittberger 1990b; List 1991; Wolf 1991; Zürn 1992: ch. 3; Müller 1993a; Schrogl 1993).

until a new consensus has been established. On the one hand, the differences between the two definitions do not seem to be substantial enough to warrant suspicion that two students of regimes will talk at cross-purposes simply because one adheres to the complex definition and the other to the lean one. (Here we neglect the fact that Keohane wants to take into account only explicit rules, whereas Krasner's definition encompasses both explicit and implicit principles, norms, rules, and procedures – an issue which we are going to return to shortly.) On the other hand, in the longer run, the breakdown of the consensus, far from damaging the cause of regime analysis, may even lead to a better understanding of the nature and workings of regimes, provided that proponents of the complex definition take up the challenge of Keohane, Young, and others by doing two things: first, demonstrate that the four components can indeed be distinguished with reasonable precision, and second, come up with theoretical and/or empirical arguments to show that the complex structure makes an empirical difference as well, that – for example, in terms of effectiveness or resilience – full-blown "complex regimes" are indeed different from truncated "semi-regimes" which meet the requirements of the lean definition only.

Behavioral, cognitive, and formal approaches to conceptualizing international regimes

The value of the complex definition relative to its lean alternative has not been the only conceptual issue to divide students of regimes, however. Whether international regimes are best conceptualized as complex or simple regulatory structures, the question remains what it means for such a structure to exist in the first place. The vague reference Krasner's formulation makes to "actors' converging expectations" could not have settled this issue. Nor has the widely shared commitment to the view that regimes are social institutions proven able to secure easy agreement on that matter. In the ensuing debate three distinct positions have emerged, arguing that regimes are best conceptualized in (1) behavioral, (2) cognitive, or (3) formal terms, respectively.

(1) For Young (1989a: 12f.), social institutions are "practices consisting of recognized roles linked together by clusters of rules or conventions governing relations among the occupants of these roles." Consequently, he opts for a "behavioral approach to the empirical identification of regimes" (Young 1989a: 13, n. 5). This understanding of the nature of

institutions in general and regimes in particular has various implications. For one thing, no rule (whatever the basis of its existence) can be said to be part of a regime that does not shape the behavior of its addressees, at least to some degree, thus warranting the talk of a practice, i.e. a pattern of rule-governed behavior (Rawls 1955: 3, n. 1). In other words, if the "effectiveness" of a rule is defined technically as the extent to which the behavior of those subject to the rule conforms to it (Nollkaemper 1992: 49), the rules of regimes, by definition, are not ineffective. Since a social practice can coexist with a considerable measure of deviation, however, it does not follow that compliance must be perfect for a regime to be in place. Another implication of this approach is that the rules that govern practices and form part of regimes need not be formally stated, nor do they need to be stated at all (i.e. it is possible to think of *implicit regimes*). Moreover, even where a formal agreement has been concluded to deal with the issues in question, it is often misleading to simply equate the content of the regime with the terms of this agreement (Young 1989a: 15, n. 11).[5]

Other authors have taken a similar stance. Mark Zacher (1987: 174), for instance, suggests that the actual behavior of states is an essential criterion when it comes to establishing whether certain injunctions are accepted in an issue-area. In accordance with Young and other proponents of the behavioral approach to operationalizing regimes, Zacher perceives no need for requiring that all behavior conform to the prescriptions and proscriptions of the regime all the time. But

> occurrences of major or long-term noncompliance, particularly involving participation of or support by major actors in the system, bring into question the efficacy of regime injunctions. We must doubt the effectiveness of behavioral guidelines if glaring violations are allowed to persist[6] or if states tend to violate norms and rules on those few occasions when they would benefit from doing so. This view of the *preconditions for regime injunction* reflects that of international legal scholars on the preconditions for the existence of international customary law. [emphasis added]

[5] Young does not explictly refer to "implicit" or "tacit" regimes in this context, but we hold that the possibility of such regimes, which had also been accepted by the creators of the consensus definition, is implied by his "behavioral approach." For the distinction between informal and implicit rules see Kratochwil (1993a: sect. 3).

[6] In Axelrod's (1986: 1097) explication of the concept of norm, sanctioning behavior is brought to the fore: "A norm exists in a given social setting to the extent that individuals usually act in a certain way and are often punished when seen not to be acting this way."

Thus, the "effectiveness of behavioral guidelines," for Zacher, is not merely a contingent (empirical) property of regimes but part of their very nature. Similarly, Klaus Dieter Wolf and Michael Zürn (1986: 204f.) have suggested clarifying (or developing) the consensus definition by adding the attribute of rule-effectiveness (see also Rittberger and Zürn 1990: 16; Rittberger 1990a: 3).

(2) In their review of the study of international organization, Kratochwil and Ruggie (1986) adopted a different approach, one which may be called "cognitive" and which is characterized by a shift of emphasis away from "overt behavior" to intersubjective meaning and shared understandings. In fact, they reject a focus on compliance in assessing the existence and impact of norms and rules, arguing that "norms are counterfactually valid" (Kratochwil and Ruggie 1986: 767). As we have noted, proponents of a "behavioral approach" are aware of this. But their solution – requiring less than perfect compliance for a regime to exist – must appear insufficient from a point of view such as Kratochwil and Ruggie's. More significant than the fact of a rule having been violated is how such an incident is interpreted by the other members of the community (which is, in this case, a community of states), and the *communicative action* (reproaches, excuses, justifications, etc.) that it gives rise to. Kratochwil and Ruggie (1986: 766) do not deny that studying these phenomena requires an epistemology different from the one favored by mainstream regime analysts, one that is less positivist in orientation and much more open to the *Verstehen* school in the meta-theory of the social sciences.[7] Indeed, one of their central theses is that the current "practice of regime analysis is wracked by epistemological anomalies" (Kratochwil and Ruggie 1986: 764). Most fundamentally, students of regimes have failed to take seriously some salient implications of the consensus definition:

> International regimes are commonly defined as social institutions around which expectations converge in international issue-areas. The emphasis on convergent expectations as the constitutive basis of regimes gives regimes an inescapable intersubjective quality. It follows that we *know* regimes by their principled and shared understandings of desirable and acceptable forms of social behavior. Hence, the ontology of regimes rests upon a strong element of intersubjectivity. (Kratochwil and Ruggie 1986: 764)

[7] For an accessible description of this meta-theoretical stance see Hollis and Smith (1990: ch. 4); the classical analysis of the *Verstehen* approach in the social sciences is, of course, Weber's (1949 [1904]: 49–112).

Since the epistemology of positivism rests upon a "radical separation of subject and object"[8] and mainstream regime analysis is committed to it, regime analysis suffers from a serious cognitive dissonance, as it were: "epistemology fundamentally contradicts ontology."

(3) In a recent article, Keohane (1993a: 26–9) has subjected both approaches to conceptualizing the existence of regimes, the one stressing behavior as well as the one stressing intersubjective understandings and communicative action, to sharp criticism. In opposition to both of these "'thick' substantive definitions," he advocates a definition of "regime" that is more on the formal side, conceptualizing regimes primarily (but not exclusively) in terms of explicit rules, agreed upon by actors and pertaining to a specific issue-area in international relations.

Unlike the proponents of substantive definitions, Keohane (1993a: 27) rejects outright the notion of implicit regimes, which invites the logical fallacy of first identifying "regimes on the basis of observed behaviour, and then . . . [using] them to 'explain' observed behaviour." Thus, he endorses an observation, already made by Haggard and Simmons (1987: 494), that "[f]ocusing on 'implicit regimes' . . . begs the question of the extent to which state behavior is, in fact, rule-governed." Even when tacit regimes are not considered, however, requiring a measure of "effectiveness" for a regime to exist, as is characteristic of the behavioral approach, is highly problematic, as it amounts to inverting "the usual order of scientific investigation, in which description, and descriptive inference, precede explanation." This oddity is especially troublesome, because causal inference in International Relations is notoriously difficult. As a result, there is a considerable risk of investigators being "forever stuck at the first level: identifying the phenomenon to be studied" (Keohane 1993a: 28).

The cognitive approach as favored by Kratochwil and Ruggie faces equally daunting difficulties. Again, Keohane's (1993a: 27) point is a methodological one:

> [I]t is enormously difficult, indeed ultimately impossible, to determine "principled and shared understandings." To what extent principled, to what extent shared? How are we to enter into the minds of human beings to determine this? And which human beings will count? Even if we could devise a way to assess convergent expectations

[8] For a classic argument for why the essence of communicative action must escape a purely positivist approach see Searle (1969: ch. 2, especially 50–3).

> intersubjectively, what standard of convergence would we require to determine that a regime existed?

These criticisms of substantive approaches to conceptualizing regimes are certainly serious. But are they fatal as well? As to the *behavioral approach*, Keohane's argument can be weakened, though probably not refuted altogether by pointing out that "effectiveness" in this context is best understood as the degree of compliance with given rules, the assessment of which may often be difficult due to data problems, but does *not* require causal inference. (In practice this means that one has to focus on explicit regimes, as the rules of tacit regimes are usually not "given.") Keohane is right, however, in observing that a behavioral approach precludes an explanation in regime terms of the observable regularity in behavior. Valid scientific explanations are logical inferences, the premises of which include at least one *empirical* hypothesis (see also sect. 5.2 below). If, however, the term "regime" is defined behaviorally, the corresponding general statement in such an "explanation" of a given pattern of behavior is not empirical, but *analytic* (i.e. a tautology): given a behavioral understanding of regimes, the statement: "if a regime exists in the issue-area, states tend to act in accordance with its injunctions" is true by definition.

It does not follow, though, that a behavioral concept of regime is useless for social scientific purposes. On the one hand, the question can still be posed, and appears more significant than ever, of how (and when) regimes – understood as practices consistent with explicit rules – come about. On the other hand, patterned behavior is not the only dependent variable of interest in a regime-analytical research context. Others include regime robustness, the extent to which the regime attains the purposes for which it has been established (e.g. enhancing the overall welfare of the participants or improving environmental quality in a specific region), changes in the issue-area specific capabilities of regime members (and outsiders), and civilizing effects on the overall relationship of regime members (Krasner 1983b: 359–67; Mayer, Rittberger, and Zürn 1993: 424; Hasenclever, Mayer, and Rittberger 1996). None of these intriguing questions, however, is removed from the regime-analytical agenda simply because a behavioral approach to conceptualizing regimes has been adopted.

As to the *cognitive approach*, Keohane's criticism may overstate the concomitant data problems. A focus on communicative action no more requires the researcher to "enter into the minds of human beings" than successful communication is dependent on some mystical ability on the part of those exchanging messages and performing speech acts to do so. Communication is based on the knowledge of public rules, not on mutual access to private sensations or mental states. "Understanding rule-following differs from an exercise of empathy" (Kratochwil 1984: 706). Similarly, the validity of certain performative acts such as promising or contracting is only loosely connected to the actors' "thoughts and feelings" while performing these acts (Austin 1975: ch. 2). This is not to say that the phenomena to which Kratochwil and Ruggie draw attention are readily investigated within a positivist framework. Kratochwil and Ruggie are the first to deny this. Therefore, to the extent that objections to their approach presuppose the standards of this methodology (as at least the tenor of Keohane's criticism seems to do), they are merely begging the question as to how international regimes and, more generally, international norms are best studied. As we have already indicated in the introductory chapter, this question is a central issue in the ongoing debate between neoliberalism and strong cognitivism – a debate in which, consequently, we find Keohane and Kratochwil and Ruggie on opposite sides (see sect. 5.2 below).

Finally, the disadvantages of the alternative: a purely *formal conceptualization*, which equates regimes with explicit (issue-area specific) agreements, must not be overlooked. One problem with this solution is that it is not well attuned to the conceptual and theoretical linking up of regime analysis with the study of social institutions which is now taken for granted by most students of regimes. Rules written down on a piece of paper do not constitute social institutions, nor do (particular) promises or contracts (even though both promising and contracting *are* social institutions). While inter-state agreements may frequently help *bring about* rule-governed practices and thus social institutions,[9] there is no logically necessary connection between agreements and institutions. Of course, nothing in the term "regime" forces us to use it to refer to a social institution. On the other hand, as we have noted, it has become almost a commonplace among students of regimes that regimes *are* institutions, and therefore, unless one is

[9] As Wendt and Duvall (1989: 63) have pointed out, institutions and practices are co-determined: "all practices presuppose institutions (otherwise they would be mere 'behaviors' rather than 'practices'), and all institutions presuppose practices (otherwise they would not exist at all)."

willing to bear the risk of considerable linguistic and intellectual confusion, sooner or later, either this usage has to be explicitly rejected (and eventually abandoned) or the definition of regime has to be made to conform to it.

It may be objected that the use of the word "institution" is less homogeneous than we are assuming, and indeed Keohane's (1989c: 3) own definition of "institution," stipulating that institutions are "persistent and connected sets of rules (formal and informal) that prescribe behavioral roles, constrain activity, and shape expectations," makes no overt reference to actual behavior. Yet even this formulation can hardly legitimize a purely formal conceptualization of regimes. The following consideration may show this. It is not unusual even for agreed-upon rules to become obsolete sometime, even though they have never been explicitly suspended. New technologies and material opportunities may undermine existing institutions, leading to new social practices. (The rule that marriage is for life – "till death us do part" – may be a case in point.) Under such circumstances these rules will no longer shape actors' expectations, *even though they could still be rules of an existing regime* (as long as we assume a formal understanding of this term). Thus, even in Keohane's own terms and contrary to his explicit conceptual intentions, it would seem to be *not* necessary for (formally defined) regimes to be institutions.

Difficulties such as these may have led Keohane (1993a: 28) to amend his preferred definition of "regime" by adding "thin" substantive content. He now proposes defining

> *agreements* in purely formal terms (explicit rules agreed upon by more than one state) and . . . [considering] *regimes* as arising when states recognize these agreements as having continuing validity. . . . [A] set of rules need not be "effective" to qualify as a regime, but it must be recognized as continuing to exist. Using this definition, regimes can be identified by the existence of explicit rules that are referred to in an affirmative manner by governments, even if they are not necessarily scrupulously observed.

Ironically, this definition does not seem to differ all that much from Kratochwil and Ruggie's cognitive approach. Performative acts such as accusing a government of violating certain rules, justifying one's behavior in terms of higher-order rules, or even apologizing for a breach of certain rules, which are the primary material of this approach, all involve references, made "in an affirmative manner," to rules and thus are the kind of data that are also needed for identifying regimes in terms of this modified formal definition.[10]

Concluding remarks

As our discussion has shown, choice among these various approaches to conceptualizing the existence of a regime is less than straightforward. Differing research objectives and strategies, incongruent conceptual schemes, and divergent epistemological stances on the part of students of regimes may make universal agreement unlikely. As always in such cases, much will depend on scholars being clear and explicit about their usage. Unfortunately, theories of regimes are often not sufficiently definite (let alone explicit) as to which approach to conceptualizing regimes they opt for. It is probably fair to say, though, that interest-based and power-based theories lean toward either a formal or, less frequently, a behavioral approach, whereas knowledge-based theories, not surprisingly, favor a cognitive definition of regime. If, as seems to be the case, the formal approach (whether or not enriched by "thin substantive content") enjoys the approval of a majority of scholars in the field today, this is largely for pragmatic reasons. This approach is not burdened with the problem of defining a threshold of compliance (or convergence of expectations) separating regime from non-regime situations. Moreover, it directs research squarely to the question of what it is that accounts for variation in the effectiveness of agreed-upon rules. To be sure, the notion of implicit regimes drops out, but this is perhaps not too great a loss for regime analysis given the notorious difficulties involved in establishing the existence of such phenomena in concrete cases. Finally, downplaying behavioral aspects in the concept of regime does not preclude studying regimes under an institutionalist perspective, even if it had to be conceded that regimes *per se* do not constitute social institutions: the task then would become one of determining when and how regimes as agreements can form the basis of international institutions.

10 A formulation very similar to Keohane's modified formal definition of "regime" is Rittberger's (1993b: 10f.). This similarity is not coincidental, but resulted from extended discussions among proponents of different approaches to operationalizing regimes, which were consciously conducted with the view to re-establish a consensus on this central issue. As we shall see in the next chapter, parts of this revised definition are not unproblematic, either, especially when used in the context of Keohane's contractual theory of regimes.

Has this discussion demonstrated that Strange's rejection of the concept of regime as "woolly" and "imprecise" was unfounded? Perhaps not altogether so. But the arbitrariness involved in the use of this concept certainly is much smaller than she suggested. Moreover, as Kratochwil and Ruggie (1986: 764f.) have reminded us, the concept of regime shares this fate of being contested with many other, more famous social science concepts, including concepts, such as "power" and "state," which are fairly close to the hearts of many radical critics of regime analysis (see also Müller 1989: 290). As indicated above, we believe that, ultimately, the best hope for overcoming arbitrariness and ambiguity in definitional matters lies in the development of strong theories. In the following three chapters we take stock of neoliberal, realist, and cognitivist approaches to constructing such theories.

3 Interest-based theories: political market failure, situation and problem structures, and institutional bargaining

It is appropriate to begin our discussion of theories of international regimes with those contributions which can be referred to as interest-based or neoliberal. This school of thought has come to represent the mainstream approach to analyzing international regimes, and the other two schools, realism and cognitivism, regularly make reference to its arguments in order to give their own positions a clear profile. This is not to say that the neoliberal account of regimes owes nothing to the ideas that are fundamental to power- and knowledge-based theories. Realism in particular provides central assumptions which leading interest-based theories of regimes such as Keohane's "contractualism" and those contributions which we call "situation-structural" have consciously adopted. Before turning to individual interest-based theories, we therefore highlight major commonalities and differences between realism and neoliberalism.

The rationalist (or utilitarian) approach to international regimes

A most important point of agreement between realist and neoliberal theories of international regimes is their shared commitment to rationalism, a meta-theoretical tenet which portrays states as self-interested, goal-seeking actors whose behavior can be accounted for in terms of the maximization of individual utility (where the relevant individuals are states). Foreign policies as well as international institutions are to be reconstructed as outcomes of calculations of advantage made by states. These calculations, in turn, are informed, though not exclusively determined, by the preferences (utility functions) of actors.

Rationalists assume that actors' preferences are fairly stable over time. This assumption is best understood as an epistemologically motivated rule of theory construction, the purpose of which is to discourage all too easy and therefore empty (pseudo-)explanations of social behavior. Duncan Snidal (1986: 43) has made this point succinctly: "If preferences change too quickly, the [rationalist mode of explanation] degenerates to a generalized *post hoc* revealed-preference exercise, where actions are assumed to reflect prevailing fluctuations in preferences" (see also Harsanyi 1969: 518–21). Note that assuming stable preferences – by which is meant here stable *preferences over outcomes* – does not preclude explanation of a change in behavior (reflecting a change in "preferences over policies"). As we shall see shortly, neoliberals in particular have argued that international regimes may redistribute states' expected utilities over options, thus turning previously too risky cooperative strategies into rational means for reaching states' *unchanged* goals of welfare and security.[1]

The strongest form of rationalist theory of social behavior goes beyond this minimal requirement, assuming that preferences are stable not only over time but also across actors. In theories of this type the source of variation in individual and collective behavior lies in the decision environment of "like units," i.e. in the *external* constraints on their action. These constraints may include the distribution of capabilities among states (Waltz 1979), the nature of the technology of warfare (Powell 1991), the degree of institutionalization in the international system (Keohane 1989c), or other features of the international environment. Both realists and neoliberals have been attracted to this strong form of rationalism, which at the same time represents a strong version of *systemic* theorizing.

The qualifier "strong" is apt here, because systemic theories are sometimes defined simply as non-reductionist, i.e. as accounts of behavior that make reference to how actors "stand in relation to one another" (Waltz 1979: 80). By this less demanding criterion, however, theories which attribute different preference orderings to different actors and indeed theories which locate most of the explanatory action at the *domestic* (subsystemic) level can be systemic, if only in a "weak" or minimalist sense. By contrast, in a strongly systemic theory "the internal attributes of actors [including their preferences over outcomes] are given by assumption rather than treated as variables" (Keohane 1989d: 40f.). Note that the difference between strongly and weakly systemic theories is not just one of form or style of presentation: strongly systemic

[1] For the important distinction between preferences over outcomes and preferences over policies (or actions), see Powell (1994: 318).

theories of international politics are committed to the substantive view that domestic politics is negligible, at least when it comes to explaining Waltz's (1986: 329) famous "small number of big and important things" in international life, whereas weakly systemic ones are not.[2]

If preferences are generally assumed not to be amenable to sudden and frequent change this assumption holds specifically for the interaction among states. In rationalist models, interaction (including cooperation) does *not* affect actors' utility functions or identities (in the language of cognitivists). Preferences help to explain interaction but not vice versa. This is another way of saying that rationalist analyses treat states as basically atomistic actors and deny (more often implicitly than explicitly) the existence of an international society as emphasized by some knowledge-based theories of regimes (see sect. 5.2 below).[3]

Another characteristic of rationalist and, therefore, of both neoliberal and realist theories of regimes is that they usually do not problematize actors' perceptions or causal beliefs. This can mean either of two things: (1) scholars implicitly assume that states have objectively adequate knowledge of the situation at hand, or (2) scholars use the perceptions of actors (e.g. those concerning the gains to be expected from a particular

[2] A weakly systemic theory in this sense is Moravcsik's (1992: 10–13) reconstruction of the liberal theory of international politics. In light of this reconstruction "neo*liberalism*" is a misnomer, precisely because neoliberalism aspires to be a strongly systemic theory, bracketing the influence of domestic structures and hence those factors which, according to Moravcsik, are highlighted by liberalism. In fact, in Moravcsik's (1992: 30–6) version of liberalism international institutions are assumed to affect state behavior only on the margin such that talk of a "neoliberal institutionalism" comes close to a contradiction in terms (see also Stein 1990: 25f.). It should be noted that other characterizations of the essence of the liberal perspective on world politics provide more justification for using this label for interest-based theories of regimes (Keohane 1990: 179–82; Nye 1993: 4; Zacher and Matthew 1995: 133–7). We adopt the language of "neoliberalism" here mainly because it has become conventional.

[3] In the words of Wendt (1987), rationalist theories of regimes adopt an individualist ontology (the relevant individuals being states). To him as well as other cognitivists, individualism is unsatisfactory because it ignores the *social* dimension of states' identities, i.e. their basic powers and interests, which, at least to a large extent, are "generated" or "constituted" by *international* society. From this point of view, even strongly systemic theories – theories which reject "explanatory reductionism" – can still be reductionist in another, more fundamental sense, viz. with regard to their underlying ontology. Consequently, for Wendt (1987: 341), it is important not to conflate systemic (whether strong or weak) and what he refers to as "structural" theories of international phenomena and finds exemplified in Wallerstein's (1974; 1980; 1989) world systems theory. In particular, both realism and neoliberalism are systemic, but not structural theories (but see now Wendt 1995: 72, n. 6). For a controversy about these and related issues see Hollis and Smith (1991; 1992) as well as Wendt (1991; 1992b).

instance of cooperation) as their basic data without inquiring into their origin. (Neither of these strategies is found acceptable by cognitivists.) This point must not be pushed too far, though. Both neoliberals and realists emphasize (as do cognitivists) the importance of various forms of *uncertainty* for any adequate account of international politics in general and of international regimes in particular. However, they focus on uncertainties which may be regarded as objective attributes of the social situation at hand as opposed to uncertainty that reflects individual dispositions or a lack of knowledge of cause – effect relationships as studied by science. For both realists and neoliberals a most important source of uncertainty of this kind is international anarchy. The most famous example of an implication of such objective uncertainty is John Herz's (1950) "security dilemma."

Differences between neoliberalism and realism

Where interest-based and power-based theories of regimes part company is in their respective specifications of the utility functions that states seek to maximize, i.e. in the behavioral models they base their analyses upon. Neoliberals depict states as rational egoists who are concerned only with their own gains and losses. By contrast, realists insist that the utility functions of states are (at least) partially interdependent such that the gains from mutual cooperation that a state's partners achieve may diminish considerably the utility of this state and consequently its willingness to cooperate in the first place. This is closely connected to another difference between the two schools of thought: much more than neoliberals realists stress the importance of power for the formation, the (normative) content, and the impact of international regimes. A general consequence of this difference in emphasis (which is also reflected in the choice of the behavioral model) is that realists tend to regard the effectiveness and the robustness of regimes as more narrowly circumscribed than neoliberals.

Conversely, neoliberals propose to analyze regimes as strictly interest-based phenomena the creation, maintenance, and demise of which can and must be accounted for from the perspective of strategically rational but otherwise mutually indifferent actors. Neoliberals readily concede that cooperation is affected by power relationships, but argue that constellations of interests (which are not readily reduced to configurations of power) and prevailing expectations – which, in turn, are strongly influenced by the presence and content of international institutions – are at least as important.

In the following we look into various interest-based approaches to the study of international regimes. We begin with two approaches which may be regarded as the purest representatives of the kind of rationalist theorizing about international regimes that we have just outlined. Relying heavily on modern economic theories of institutions, *contractualism* studies the effects of international regimes on the ability of actors to cooperate in situations resembling the Prisoner's Dilemma and develops a functional argument to explain the creation and maintenance of regimes (sect. 3.1). *Situation-structuralism* broadens the perspective adopted by contractualism by taking into account the full spectrum of strategic situations in which actors might cooperate through regimes, and analyzes the implications of different constellations of interests (or "games") for the likelihood of regime formation as well as for the institutional form of regimes (sect. 3.2).

We then move on to two approaches whose status as neoliberal-rationalist theories is less clear, but which nevertheless are best subsumed under the category of interest-based theories of regimes. Section 3.3 is concerned with the so-called *problem-structural approach* which regards the nature of issues as an important variable affecting the likelihood and the ease of regime formation in given conflict situations. Finally, we conclude our review of the leading school of thought in regime analysis with a discussion of Young's *model of institutional bargaining* (sect. 3.4). This theory of regime formation is avowedly interest-based in that it is based on the premise that "social institutions, including international regimes, arise from the interaction of self-interested parties endeavoring to coordinate their behaviour to reap joint gains" (Young and Osherenko 1993d: 249). On the other hand, Young is sharply critical not only of power-based approaches, but also of mainstream rationalist accounts of regime formation. In particular, he rejects the view (implicit in both contractualism and situation-structuralism) that actors are always fully aware of their interests and that preference formation is a process that is prior and exogenous to inter-state bargaining. In this way, he not only attempts to rectify the rationalist tendency to give structure priority over process but also echoes important concerns of the knowledge-based approach to international regimes.

3.1 Keohane's contractualist (or functional) theory of international regimes

Robert Keohane is the author of the most elaborate and also most widely discussed theory of international regimes to date. This so-called contractualist (or functional) theory of regimes is the backbone of a somewhat broader perspective on world politics, which focuses on the institutionalization of a growing sector of international behavior and for which the label "neoliberal institutionalism" has come into use (Keohane 1989c).[4] The influence of this formulation has been so strong that observers repeatedly were led to equate Keohane's approach with "regime theory" as such (e.g. Milner 1992: 475–8; Hurrell 1993). The grain of truth in this view is that the rational-choice perspective on regimes that Keohane and others (such as Arthur Stein, Charles Lipson, or Duncan Snidal) have first adopted has indeed left its stamp on the research program centering on the concept of regime. Keohane himself has made it clear on several occasions that he does not consider contractualism a comprehensive theory of regimes, let alone the only one (Keohane 1983: 143; 1993a: 37).

Realist premises and liberal institutionalist conclusions

The most conspicuous feature of Keohane's approach is that he deliberately adopts realist assumptions about the nature of international actors and their social environment to develop a theory which is opposed to orthodox realism in that it attributes international institutions a significant role in international politics. In doing so, he does not aim for a destruction of realism as a theoretical perspective, but at a "critique and modification" (Keohane 1984: 14), the main implication of which is that realism drops out as a major support for regime skepticism. Keohane, thus, acknowledges that states are "crucial actors" in world politics and that the fact of international anarchy has important repercussions on their interactions and, in particular, on their ability to cooperate (Keohane 1984: 25; Axelrod and Keohane 1986: 226). Following Waltz's (1979) example, he opts for a (strongly) systemic approach to theory, which focuses on the external structural conditions under which governments make foreign policy decisions, consciously neglecting the impact that the internal (domestic) attributes of the units may have on

[4] Apparently, Nye and Grieco have co-authored this term (see Grieco 1993b: 335, n. 1). Keohane (1993b: 272) is probably right that his perspective "borrows as much from realism as from liberalism" and that, consequently, its now conventional tag may be misleading. However, this argument has to be weighed against another: namely, that confusion may also arise (and does seem to have arisen with many readers) from too frequent renamings of theoretical perspectives. Moreover, a ready replacement does not seem to be at hand. Keohane (1993b: 298, n. 3) now prefers to refer to his position simply as "institutionalism." This, however, can be misleading, too, as long as two other schools of thought exist in the field.

the choices of actors. More specifically, he agrees that the distribution of power and wealth in the international system exerts a strong influence on state behavior.

Finally, he accepts (or appears to accept) realism's assumption about the fundamental motivation of states, expecting states to behave as rational egoists who act only to further their own interests. This last assumption is particularly important for a number of reasons. One is that it provides systemic theory-building with an indispensible "clue" as to how actors will react to varying environmental conditions. Moreover, since microeconomic theory uses the same clue, the egoistic-rationality assumption allows the study of international politics to pattern itself on this "prevailing model for systemic analysis" (Keohane 1984: 27). Last but not least, modeling states as rational egoists closes an open flank of earlier liberal work, which was less explicit in this respect and whose optimistic conclusions, therefore, to many scholars seemed to depend on illusory notions of the motivation of international actors (Keohane 1984: 66f.).[5]

Keohane (1984: 27) explains the two components of his motivational assumption as follows:

> Rationality means that [actors] have consistent, ordered preferences, and that they calculate costs and benefits of alternative courses of action in order to maximize their utility in view of those preferences. Egoism means that their utility functions are independent of one another: they do not gain or lose utility simply because of the gains or losses of others.

Thus, egoists are *not* envious, or what Michael Taylor (1976) termed "negative altruists": they are simply indifferent to how well others do.[6]

[5] But note that at least one major representative of that earlier work took a stance on the motivational issue which seems very similar to Keohane's:

> We banish from our construct the notion that individual actors, groups or elites regularly and predictably engage in political pursuits for unselfish reasons. All political action is purposively linked with individual or group perception of interest. . . . We further reject the notion of conscience, good will, dedication to the common good, or subservience to a socially manipulated consensus on welfare questions, as possessing little consistent reality in living politics. Cooperation among groups is thus the result of convergences of separate perceptions of interest and not a spontaneous surrender to the myth of the common good. (E. Haas 1964: 34)

[6] As we shall see below (sect. 4.3), realists have denied that the motivational assumption they make in their analyses of international politics is correctly described as egoism, using this "misrepresentation" of their position as a lever to launch a sharp counter-attack on neoliberalism.

In chapter 7 of his major study of regimes, *After Hegemony*, Keohane, *after* having developed his central argument, explores the consequences of relaxing either of the two component assumptions. Thus, the classical, substantive (or objective), conception of rationality that he has relied upon up to this point is replaced by Herbert Simon's (1972: 162) notion of "bounded rationality," which takes into account "constraints on the information-processing capacities of the actor"; and egoism is contrasted with empathy, defined by Keohane as a broader conception of self-interest, which allows the well-being of others to enter positively into actors' utility functions. In both cases Keohane constructs a kind of *a fortiori* argument: his conclusions about regimes and cooperation, he suggests, do not depend on these relaxations; *if*, however, the modified motivational assumptions should turn out to be more in line with reality, the plausibility of those conclusions would only be enhanced.

Common interests, cooperation, and regimes

Keohane (1984: 6, 247f.; 1989c: 2) makes it clear that the contractualist theory of regimes operates under a specific situational precondition: the states that are active in the issue-area concerned must share common interests which they can realize only through cooperation. It is important to note that, for Keohane, focusing on situations which meet this condition has *neither* of two consequences which might seem to follow immediately. First, the scope of the theory is *not* negligible (as orthodox realists might conclude in view of this precondition). States in many situations do have mutual interests; international politics is not a zero-sum game. In *After Hegemony* Keohane focuses on issues in the field of international political economy and on relations among the advanced industrialized countries of the West. However, he expects his theory to apply wherever and whenever common interests exist in a relationship with the explicit inclusion of security issues (Keohane 1984: 6f., 247; Keohane and Martin 1995: 43f.). Second, the theory is *not* trivial. It cannot be taken for granted that states with common interests will also cooperate. Indeed, the existence of such interests is a necessary, but not sufficient, condition for cooperation. To support the latter claim Keohane points to the Prisoner's Dilemma, which, in Keohane's (1984: 68) view, captures the essence of a wide range of situations in world politics and serves as an important model underlying much of the abstract reasoning that informs the contractualist theory of regimes.

		Actor B	
		C	D
Actor A	C	3,3	1,4
	D	4,1	2,2

Fig. 1. Prisoner's Dilemma. Number left (right) of comma refers to A's (B's) preference ordering (1=worst outcome; 4=best outcome).

The two-person Prisoner's Dilemma (PD) (figure 1) is a symmetrical game, where each player prefers mutual cooperation (CC) to mutual defection (DD), yet is even better off when she can benefit from the unrequited cooperation of her partner (DC). On the other hand, ending up as the one who behaves cooperatively without a response in kind (CD) is the outcome which is least desirable from either player's point of view. (Thus the preference ordering of both players from their respective points of view is: DC>CC>DD>CD.) In an isolated PD, cooperation is very unlikely, because each player will find it rational not to cooperate: whatever the other does, she will achieve a higher pay-off by defecting. As a result, however, both will do worse than they could have done had they not chosen this seemingly rational course of action. Thus, in single-play PD the two players have a *common interest* in achieving the CC outcome which, at the same time, they are *unlikely* to realize.[7]

Presupposing common interests, however, does have various other notable implications for Keohane's theory. To begin with, actors' interests

[7] This is the basic structure of the situation in which the two prisoners, from whose dilemma the name of the game has been derived, are trapped: Two criminals are held in custody charged with two offences they are suspected of having committed together, one of them less serious (say, a case of shoplifting), the other more so (say, a case of armed robbery). Unfortunately, the prosecutor has trouble providing conclusive evidence of their guilt in the latter case. So she decides to offer each of the suspects a deal: if he confesses the joint robbery, he will go free, whereas his accomplice, if he continues to deny his participation in the crime, will have to go to jail for both offences; in the case that both decide to confess, however, only the punishment for the theft will be remitted to them. The dilemma results from the fact that either prisoner has strong incentives to accept the prosecution's offer, since this is his best choice regardless of the decision of his former partner, while, *at the same time*, their mutual confession leads to a sentence which is stricter (being the penalty for robbery) than the one the prosecution would have been able to achieve (the penalty for shoplifting) had both of them refused to confess.

(or utility functions) are not explained within the theory, but are treated as exogenously given. This is a major reason why Keohane does not consider his theory a complete theory of cooperation and regimes. In particular, this theory does not, and is not meant to, account for the effects of learning and ideas on how actors define and understand their interests (Keohane 1984: 16, 132).[8]

Another implication of this theoretical point of departure is the need to specify the conceptual relationship between interests, cooperation, and regimes. Cooperation, Keohane never tires of emphasizing, "is not equivalent to harmony. Harmony requires complete identity of interests, but cooperation can only take place in situations that contain a mixture of conflicting and complementary interests. In such situations, cooperation occurs when actors adjust their behavior to the actual or anticipated preferences of others" (Axelrod and Keohane 1986: 226; see also Keohane 1988: 380). Cooperation, furthermore, is mutual adjustment that takes place "as the result of a process of policy coordination" (Keohane 1984: 52). If attempts to bring policies in line with one another are not made or fail, "discord" results. Thus, assuming "common interests" is not assuming that actors' interests are identical. Rather, it is to assume the presence of a mixed-motive situation (Schelling 1960: 89). It is also worth stressing that it is not interests (preferences over outcomes) that are adjusted when states cooperate, but policies (preferences over actions). Consequently, the means that states employ to help them realize these common interests do not (or need not) change those interests.

Contractualist theory focuses on one such instrument: the international regimes that states create in the pursuit of joint gains. The most general proposition of this theory is that regimes facilitate international cooperation (which would otherwise be difficult or impossible to achieve). They do so not (or not necessarily) by changing actors' interests or values but by altering their "incentives" for action, thus changing "the calculations of advantage that governments make" (Keohane 1984: 26). In game-theoretic terms, regimes do not operate by altering the payoff structure (although sometimes they may have such an effect as well), but by making a different strategy more rational for the actors. More

[8] In his more recent work, Keohane, together with Goldstein and others, has begun to fill this gap (Goldstein and Keohane 1993b). In doing so, however, he has transcended the confines of interest-based theorizing and moved closer to a knowledge-based approach to international institutions. Consequently, we address this segment of his thinking about regimes in the chapter on the cognitivist school in regime analysis (sect. 5.1).

specifically, states may still find themselves locked in a Prisoner's Dilemma, but, owing to the regime, mutual cooperation has become feasible even for egoistic utility-maximizers.

A theory which regards international regimes as catalysts of international cooperation needs to separate regimes (the "cause") and cooperation (the "effect") conceptually: regimes cannot be meaningfully hypothesized to *further* cooperation if all the cooperation that is involved in the situation is implicit in the regime as such. Contractualist theory takes account of this logical necessity by contrasting regimes with specific *agreements* (Keohane 1984: 61f.; 1993a: 23).

> It is crucial to distinguish clearly between international regimes, on the one hand, and mere *ad hoc* substantive agreements, on the other. Regimes . . . facilitate the making of substantive agreements by providing a framework of rules, norms, principles, and procedures for negotiation. A theory of international regimes must explain why these intermediate arrangements are necessary. (Keohane 1983: 153)

Within the conceptual framework of contractualism, international cooperation materializes in mutually beneficial agreements, not (or not only) in regimes. Regimes help to bring such agreements about.[9]

How regimes make a difference: the functions of regimes

Regimes further cooperation. But *how* is it that they can do so? Answering this question requires an analysis of the obstacles to cooperation that states are facing in the international system. To explore these obstacles Keohane, consistently with his assumption about actors' motivations, makes use of various *rational choice* models (Prisoner's Dilemma, theories of collective action, and theories of market failure). From slightly different vantage points, the analyses based on these models converge on the same central problem hampering, or downright discouraging, efforts at international cooperation: uncertainty (or lack of information). States are uncertain about their partners: can they be expected to keep their commitments, or would it be unwise to count on that? As a result, governments miss out opportunities of striking mutually beneficial bargains or withdraw from agreements already made.

[9] In light of this "crucial" distinction, Keohane's (1993a: 28) amended formal definition of regimes (quoted and discussed at the end of chapter 2 above) appears infelicitous, since this definition explicitly introduces regimes as a kind of international agreement and thus causes a disturbing ambiguity in the terminology of contractualism.

Regimes, on the other hand, facilitate cooperation just by providing states with information or reducing their information costs (Keohane 1984: 97, 245). This is their main *function*.

In situations resembling a Prisoner's Dilemma, states will often be disinclined to cooperate for fear of being double-crossed.[10] Regimes that include monitoring arrangements (making information about others' compliance more easily available) reduce this fear and in this way make it easier for states to cooperate. For one thing, the risks involved in cooperation are lower: provided that decisions to cooperate can be reversed, the exploitation that one may suffer will not last long. For another, the likelihood of being deceived in the first place is smaller: the greater probability of being "caught" reduces the expected utility of cheating. This effect is amplified by another feature of regimes and regime-based cooperation. Principles, norms, and rules, by their very nature, do not apply to a single case only, but to a variety of cases. Individual regimes, on their part, are often "nested" within larger, more encompassing frameworks of international principles and norms. In this way regimes produce connections or "linkages" between issues (and likewise between agreements dealing with particular issues). As a result, violating a particular agreement (or concluding an illegitimate one) has consequences beyond this particular issue and may affect the ability to achieve one's goals elsewhere (Keohane 1984: 89f.; Axelrod and Keohane 1986: 234). Moreover, institutions such as international regimes enhance the continuity of political relationships over time (*inter alia* by providing actors with valuable negotiation opportunities, which can be ignored only at a cost). Both properties of regimes work in the same direction: they increase the (perceived) "iterativeness" of the situation, thus allowing for a "shadow of future" to discourage defection. The significance of this fact is explained by the work of Robert Axelrod (1984) and others, who have shown that, in a Prisoner's Dilemma that is played over and over again by the same (egoistic) players, cooperation without central enforcement can be induced and maintained through a reciprocal strategy ("tit-for-tat") provided that future gains and losses are not too heavily discounted by the actors. (As Keohane [1984: 76] points out, the possibility of reversing decisions to cooperate "has an effect similar to that of iteration of the game, since it

[10] For a discussion of why, in the issue-area of international trade, "cheating" is indeed a potentially serious problem see Yarbrough and Yarbrough (1987: 6–9). See also Lipson (1984).

reduces the incentives to defect.") The contractualist theory incorporates this finding: regimes improve the conditions of application for the strategy of reciprocity through which cooperation is stabilized (Keohane 1984: 244; 1993a: 23; Axelrod and Keohane 1986: 250).

One difficulty plaguing the use of "tit-for-tat" in real-world situations is the so-called "sanctioning problem" (Axelrod and Keohane 1986: 255). This problem, the acuteness of which, other things being equal, increases with the number of actors involved, refers to the difficulties of meeting three preconditions for the successful operation of the strategy of reciprocity: (1) defections and defectors must be identified; (2) retaliation (if necessary) must punish the defector and only the defector; and (3) someone must be prepared to bear the costs of sanctioning. Contractualism suggests that regimes can mitigate all aspects of the sanctioning problem (Keohane 1984: 98; Axelrod and Keohane 1986: 237f.). It is noteworthy, though, that (at least in *After Hegemony*) Keohane emphasizes neither the monitoring capacities of regimes nor regime rules requiring states to retaliate against defectors (the latter being hardly mentioned). He is well aware that such rules would not be any more self-enforcing than the rules the respect for which they are intended to improve. The sanctioning problem involves a problem of collective action itself. Instead he focuses on the *reputational effects* of regimes: "International regimes help to assess others' reputations by providing standards of behavior against which performance can be measured, by linking these standards to specific issues, and by providing forums, often through international organizations, in which these evaluations can be made." (Keohane 1984: 94; see also 104–6)

Regimes in this way help to shape the reputations of their members. This raises the costs associated with non-compliance in any particular situation and, consequently, makes cooperation more likely. (Knowing that their partners have a reputation to lose by cheating, states' fear of being double-crossed diminishes.) The argument to show that their reputation is a matter of concern for rational actors is simple and runs as follows: actors with a reputation for trustworthiness are more easily accepted as partners in cooperative ventures for mutual benefit.[11] Yet,

[11] The most useful reputation is not that of a saint (or a fool, for that matter), who sticks to the cooperative course of action no matter what the others do. A reputed saint may find it easy to conclude agreements with others, but his partners are likely to test his "good nature," thus reducing his utility, even when, in fact, he is not a saint at all. The preferable reputation is that of a person who cooperates just *as long as* she sees her partners do the same (or maybe a little longer) (see Axelrod 1984: 138).

by reneging on their commitments under a regime states are likely to damage their reputation and thus to forfeit potential future gains from cooperation (which as rational actors they will seek to avoid). While these facts certainly do not guarantee compliance under all circumstances, they raise the threshold of opportunism for a rational egoist who is sensitive to her longer-term interests. (Note that this argument is fully compatible with the argument stressing the strategy of reciprocity: retaliation simply takes the form of others being less willing to cooperate with the defector in the future.)

In sum, international regimes serve various valuable functions for their members. Reduction of mutual uncertainty is the common denominator of most of these functions. Uncertainty being a major obstacle to international cooperation, international regimes therefore make it easier for states to work together for mutual advantage. Thus, they do make a difference in world politics.

Functional explanations for the emergence and persistence of regimes

Up to this point, our discussion of contractualism has been confined to certain *effects* of international regimes on state behavior. And indeed, the bulk of the theoretical analyses in *After Hegemony* deal with the consequences regimes have for their members and their ability to achieve certain goals. Still, it would be a false impression to believe that Keohane's theory has got nothing to say about the *causes* of regimes. What is more, in a sense, we have been talking about the origins of regimes all the while. Resolution of this seeming paradox comes from the fact that Keohane (1984: 80) proposes a *functional explanation* of regimes, i.e. an explanation that "account[s] for causes in terms of their effects."

As Keohane (1984: 81f.) points out, there are different ways of making sense of this aphoristic definition. Evolutionary theories explain causes in terms of their effects by specifying a mechanism (usually some sort of deadly competition) that chooses from among a variety of attributes a specific one such that the bearers of this attribute are best suited to meet a certain requirement set by the selection mechanism (e.g. the ability to defend oneself against aggressors). While their meeting this requirement is surely *caused* by this attribute (e.g. some physical property), the (eventual) predominance of this attribute in a given population can be explained with reference to this requirement: (most of) the units have this physical property *because* it helps them defend themselves. Noting that "states rarely disappear," Keohane quickly dismisses such a Darwinian type of explanation as inadequate for his object of study. Instead he opts for a kind of explanation that combines functional reasoning with a rational choice perspective:

> Functional explanations in social theory [including those developed by contractualism to account for international regimes] are generally *post hoc* in nature. We observe such institutions and then rationalize their existence. Rational-choice theory, as applied to social institutions, assumes that institutions can be accounted for by examining the incentives facing the actors who created and maintain them. *Institutions exist because they could have reasonably been expected to increase the welfare of their creators.* (Keohane 1984: 80 [emphasis added])

Understanding the functions of regimes, therefore, is also holding the key to explaining their very existence. Regimes, in short, are created by states as instruments to achieve certain (selfish) goals.[12]

Keohane applies this functional perspective to both regime formation and regime maintenance, developing two different, yet internally linked arguments. Regimes reduce transaction costs, i.e. costs associated with the negotiation, monitoring, and enforcement of agreements. Creating a regime, on the other hand, is not cost-free, either. After all, regimes, which usually result from multilateral negotiations, are not unlike agreements themselves. Consequently, creating and maintaining a regime involves transaction costs as well (Keohane 1988: 386f.). From a functional perspective, this means that actors will offset the costs of establishing a regime against the advantages to be expected from the regime. As the central advantage of a regime is that it enables actors to cooperate through agreements, states are more likely to create a regime if the set of potential mutually beneficial agreements in the issue-area is large or, in Keohane's (1984: 79, 90) words, the "policy space" is relatively dense. To put it differently, the more "efficient" (under given circumstances) a regime would be, the more likely it is to be created. This hypothesis can be used to explain why, with rising levels of interdependence between states and societies, the number of international regimes has grown as well (Keohane 1993a: 34–8).

Keohane is aware that this is only part of the story, though. For one thing, regimes do not emerge in a cognitive and institutional vacuum.

12 Keohane's functional approach must not be confused with sociological functionalism in the Parsonian tradition, which takes a holistic perspective on its object of study and rejects the methodological individualism inherent in Keohane's instrumentalism and consequentialism (Keohane 1993a: 36, n. 6).

Earlier experiences with regimes (and with one's prospective partners) affect the willingness of actors to create new ones. Even more important, however, the above argument considers only the demand-side of the matter. As theories of collective action show, the fact that a group of states "demand" a regime in a given situation (i.e. would benefit from a regime) does not guarantee that they will be able to "supply" it as well. In this connection, Keohane (1984: 78f.) gives some credit to the theory of hegemonic stability (see sect. 4.1 below) without, however, accepting its "crude" version which argues that a unipolar distribution of power is both *necessary* and *sufficient* for a regime to emerge and persist in any given issue-area. Neither of these claims, according to Keohane (1984: ch. 3), is ultimately tenable.

Arguments stressing the difficulties of creating institutions at the international level also have a central part in Keohane's theory of regime persistence. Regimes are created against the backdrop of a particular constellation of interests and power, which they reflect in the content of their principles, norms, and rules (Keohane 1984: 70–3; 1988: 387). Regime content is a matter of interest for states, since, according to the contractualist argument, regimes do not reduce transaction costs across the board. Rather, they facilitate legitimate bargains, while they raise the transaction costs associated with illegitimate ones (Keohane 1984: 90). What is legitimate and what is not, however, is determined by the content of the regime. Quite commonly, those initial conditions under which a regime has been formed and which are reflected by its structure change over time, often making the regime increasingly less attractive for some or even all of its members.[13] Such external change might therefore be expected to lead to a collapse of the regime (or, at least, to a far-reaching revision of its principles and norms). In fact, this is precisely what the crude version of the theory of hegemonic stability would predict. In contrast, contractualism offers the hypothesis that regimes will frequently persist even after the conditions that have shaped and facilitated their creation have disappeared, i.e. regimes will often prove *robust*. Part of the theoretical justification of this hypothesis once more makes reference to reputational concerns. Another argument, however, is even more peculiar to Keohane's approach: regimes

[13] Keohane usually emphasizes material conditions such as the distribution of power and (concomitant) interests. Yet, he acknowledges that regimes have "intellectual underpinnings" (Young 1992) as well (see, for example, Keohane 1993a: 43f. as well as sect. 5.1 below). It should be noted, therefore, that the following argument concerning regime persistence *mutatis mutandis* applies to this kind of initial condition as well.

persist despite the declining satisfaction of their members, precisely because *creating* a regime in the first place is so difficult. Thus, in many situations, the expected utility of maintaining the present suboptimal (albeit still beneficial) regime will be greater than that of "letting it die" (e.g. by returning to unfettered self-help behavior) in order to rebuild it, which is likely to result in a situation where no regime exists at all (or only a very weak one, i.e. one with a low degree of effectiveness).

> Ironically, if regimes were costless to build, there would be little point in constructing them. In this case, agreements would also be costless. Under these circumstances, governments could wait until specific problems arose, then make agreements to deal with them; they would have no need to construct international regimes to facilitate agreements. It is precisely the costliness of agreements, and of regimes themselves, that make them important. The high costs of regime-building help existing regimes to persist (Keohane 1984: 103).

Some open questions

In *After Hegemony*, as well as in various articles (Keohane 1983; 1989b; 1993a), Keohane has set forth a very impressive argument about the origins, functions, and effects of international regimes that combines parsimony and sophistication. He has shown how we can attribute causal significance to regimes without resorting to assumptions about the motivation of states which are highly dubious in the eyes of most contemporary scholars. Although his theory is deliberately systemic, by stressing the importance of (man-made) institutions it opens up perspectives for conscious activity towards improving the operation of the "international polity." To the extent that international cooperation is essential for mitigating global crises, contractualism, therefore, is also a source of hope, in particular as it suggests that purely instrumental learning (as opposed to moral improvement) can broaden the basis for peaceful cooperation among states insisting as before on their sovereignty.[14]

All these virtues, of course, do not make a critical examination of the

[14] Keohane (1984: 79; 1988: 380f.) is utterly clear that international cooperation is not *necessarily* desirable by the standard of overall welfare improvement and that the common interests that underlie it can be interests in the exploitation of third parties. He also thinks, however, that "without international cooperation . . . the prospects for our species would be very poor indeed" (Keohane 1988: 393). Keohane has discussed the ethical issues associated with international regimes in some detail in chapter 11 of *After Hegemony* as well as in a separate article (Keohane 1989a).

theory superfluous. As Keohane himself has observed, the task of subjecting contractualism to extensive empirical testing is still pending. Moreover, to the extent that contractualist conjectures have entered into empirical research, the results have been mixed (Keohane 1993a: 37). Although empirical ambiguity may well be resolved by further testing, such a situation also warrants directing attention once more to the deductive argument underlying the theory. Therefore, we close this outline of functional regime theory by raising a few questions concerning the argumentative structure of contractualism, which, at the same time, point to some difficulties facing any attempt to test Keohane's theory empirically.[15]

(1) To begin with, the *nature of the functional explanation* that Keohane relies on requires further clarification. The central questions here are twofold. First, what are the criteria a (complex) statement has to meet in order to count as an acceptable functional explanation? And second, what is the meta-theoretical foundation of these criteria? As we have seen, contractualism is a kind of theory in which "effect explains cause," without, at the same time, following the logic of evolutionary theory. He also points out that "functional arguments . . . are generally *post hoc* in nature" (Keohane 1984: 80) and that, consequently, "the most important danger lurking behind functional explanations is the *post hoc ergo propter hoc* fallacy: institutions may be interpreted as having arisen because of the functions they must have served, when they in fact appeared for purely adventitious reasons."

Apart from the Darwinian approach, he then goes on to argue, the only "way of avoiding this fallacy is to show that the actors being investigated are rational, and that the institutions and the social practices to be explained were designed to fulfill anticipated functions" (Keohane 1984: 81). However, this is precisely how Keohane does *not* proceed in *After Hegemony*; in particular, he does not show that actors are rational, but assumes it. Another meta-theoretical statement of his, therefore, appears much more adequate to characterize his approach: "[The] functional argument as applied to our subject-matter must rest on the *premise* of rational anticipation. Unless actors can be assumed to anticipate the effects of their behavior, effects cannot possibly explain causes, and understanding the functions of international regimes will

[15] Keohane (1993a: 30) seems quite optimistic about the possibility of empirically testing his as well as other theories of regimes. He also admits, however, that many theorists of regimes have failed so far to derive testable hypotheses from their theories.

not help to explain their occurrence." (Keohane 1984: 82 [emphasis added])

But if this is how things are in the functional theory of regimes, then how *do* we guard against the *post hoc ergo propter hoc* fallacy? Or is this asking the wrong question? Could it be that falling prey to this fallacy is the epistemological risk, as it were, that is inherent in functional explanations? If so, Keohane is mistaken to demand that a functional theory avoid this "fallacy" somehow. What one must demand of a functional theory of regimes then is only that it adequately describe the effects of regimes on the welfare (or security) of states and show that they are indeed beneficial for them. Rational actors can then be "trusted" to create and uphold them. If, however, we believe that this fallacy *has* to be avoided for the explanation to be acceptable, we are led to ask very different questions. We should be concerned not with the effects of regimes, but with the *beliefs* that actors hold about these effects (see also King, Keohane, and Verba 1994: 227). Or are we engaged in a two-step process, first building a theory about regime effects and then using this theory as a working hypothesis in our effort to build a theory about the implicit theory held by the actors? We feel that, as yet, Keohane has not been clear enough on this point. Without a sufficiently clear exposition of the logic of the explanations provided by contractualism, adequate testing of the theory is extremely difficult, if not impossible. To be sure, this problem is of a rather general nature, touching, as it does, upon complex arguments about as-if explanations etc. But this does not relieve contractualism (and closely related theories of regimes such as situation-structuralism [see sect. 3.2 below]) from the need to come to terms with it somehow.

(2) The next point we wish to raise is a conceptual one. While hardly any student of regimes would reject the proposition that there is a close connection between regimes and cooperation and while many would also agree with the more specific proposition that regimes *further* cooperation, few have given so much thought to this issue and have shown so much sensitivity for its logical implications as Keohane. As we have seen, he separates regimes from cooperation conceptually, which is a logical necessity given his theoretical purposes. So there is nothing to criticize about that. It is quite another issue, however, whether the specific conceptual decision he has taken is empirically adequate or fruitful. As we have noted, Keohane (1983: 153) operationalizes the concept of international cooperation in terms of "*ad hoc* substantive agreements."

As such it may not be too strong an objection to notice that few students of regimes seem to have followed this conceptual move, which thus has added to the conceptual muddle we have discussed in chapter 2. But this reservation on the part of other scholars may also indicate that, with regard to many empirical cases, the distinction between a regime, on the one hand, and various *ad hoc* agreements, on the other, simply does not stand or appears artificial.[16]

What is more, distinguishing between regimes and agreements in this way makes the issue of regime *compliance* a highly complicated and ambiguous one. Indeed, it seems that compliance would need to be studied at several levels. On the one hand, there are various *ad hoc* agreements (presumably concluded among non-identical groups of actors), which may or may not be complied with. On the other hand, there is the regime itself, the norms and rules of which also may or may not be complied with. Both levels may exhibit their own compliance patterns, which presumably need not correlate. This is not yet the end of the story, though, because compliance at the level of the regime, according to this conceptualization, is a complicated matter in itself. Non-compliance with a regime can mean violating a norm or rule by oneself: for example, state A fails to lower some sort of non-tariff barriers to trade, although it has promised to. (This is what most students of regimes think of, when they talk of non-compliance in a regime context.) From the point of view of contractualism, however, non-compliance also, and perhaps foremost, means striking an illegitimate *bargain*, which is not an individual, but a collective act: for example, states A and B grant each other trading privileges which they do not extend to third parties (although the regime in question contains the most-favored-nation clause as a norm). As a result, students of regimes are confronted with three different (sub)-types of compliance (or non-compliance): (1) compliance with the *ad hoc* agreements that have been concluded by members of the regime and (2) compliance with the regime which, in turn, can mean that members (2a) individually abstain from certain proscribed actions, or (2b) collectively abstain from certain delegitimized interactions (viz. concluding among one another agreements which are inconsistent with the provisions of the regime).

Given this complexity (which is seldom if ever reflected in empirical

[16] Note that Keohane's *ad hoc* agreements are *not* identical with the rules of the regime: they must not be, since otherwise they would be part of the regime. This is unambiguously implied in the passage from Keohane (1983: 153) that we have quoted above (p. 33).

studies of regime compliance) the question arises why Keohane has opted for a conceptualization which distinguishes between regimes and agreements in the first place. Operationalizing international cooperation in terms of agreements allows him to make use of a theoretical resource which helps him refine and specify his argument: the economic literature on market failure. "Market failure refers to situations in which the outcomes of market-mediated interactions are suboptimal, given the utility functions of actors and the resources at their disposal. That is *agreements* that would be beneficial to all parties are not made." (Keohane 1984: 82 [emphasis added]) The critical question then is whether the advantage of having access to this resource outweighs the associated costs on the part of concept operationalization, which might somewhat pointedly be described as empirical marginality, on the one hand, and conceptual complexity and ambiguity, on the other.

As our outline of contractualism, in which market failure is hardly mentioned, indicates, Keohane's main arguments do not seem to depend on having access to this specific theoretical resource. If so, he might be able to do without the distinction between regimes and more specific agreements. Dropping this distinction, however, would recreate the problem of operationalizing cooperation in such a way as to avoid tautological explanations (of cooperation in terms of regimes), and an alternative solution would be required. One alternative that might be considered in this case is operationalizing cooperation in terms of rule-consistent behavior. Opting for this possibility (which has difficulties of its own) would require adopting a formal definition of "regime" or one that has at most "thin substantive content" in the sense discussed above (ch. 2).

(3) Finally, there is a further problem that deserves scrutiny and that is highlighted by the conceptual decision we have just discussed. It may well be doubted that any sharp distinction between regimes and agreements is tenable. At the end of the day, it seems, regimes are but a particular *species* of agreements. In fact, this is precisely what Keohane's (1993a: 28) modified definition of the term "international regime" puts into words (see ch. 2 above). The problem for contractualism resulting from this observation is the following (Milner 1992: 477). Functional theory argues that states create (and maintain) regimes to enable themselves to conclude agreements. If, however, regimes must be regarded as agreements themselves, this argument appears to suffer from a fundamental circularity (Oye 1986b: 20f.; Müller 1994: 17, 18): the

success of the strategy that states are supposed to adopt in order to solve their "cooperation problem" (i.e. the strategy of regime-building) appears to depend on the absence, or *prior* solution, of this very problem! Consequently, there cannot seem to be such a strategy (for rational actors). To be sure, Keohane points out that regimes may be supplied by hegemons, thus relying in part on a power-based theory of regimes (see sect. 4.1 below). Hegemonic regime provision means that the collective action problems that make cooperation so difficult to achieve for states do not arise. To this extent, the explanatory circle is broken. However, Keohane (1983: 141; 1984: 83; 1993a: 36, n. 7) makes it quite plain that his functional argument in principle applies to regime formation as much as to regime maintenance.

The situation is a little more complicated than that, though. Surely, it would be incorrect to imply that this "circle" has escaped Keohane's notice, when he actually *uses* it in his theory. For, as we have seen, he argues that a main cause for the relative persistence of regimes is actors' awareness of the fact that regimes are difficult and "costly" to create in the first place. But, obviously, making use of an (alleged) circle does not mean having broken it. The question therefore is still open of how a functional explanation of *ad hoc* agreements in terms of regimes avoids a *regressus ad infinitum*. What essential difference between regimes and *ad hoc* agreements justifies the assumption that regime-building is a viable strategy for facilitating the conclusion of agreements and why? Contractualist theory so far seems to have failed to provide a convincing answer to this question.

3.2 A game-theoretic extension of functional regime theory: the situation-structural approach

The set of contributions to regime analysis which we refer to as the "situation-structural approach" shares many features with functional theory. In fact, situation-structuralism is best understood as an attempt at extending and further developing the kind of interest-based argument regarding regimes that Keohane has put forth. In doing so, its point of departure is Keohane's game-theoretic interpretation of the nature of the collective action problem which, according to functional theory, regimes help to overcome. As we have seen, Keohane assumes that the Prisoner's Dilemma (PD) captures central aspects of a wide range of issues in international politics and develops his deductive argument in view of this specific constellation of interests. The proponents of a situation-structural approach to international regimes – such as, *inter alia*, Arthur Stein (1983), Duncan Snidal (1985a; 1986), Kenneth Oye (1986b), Michael Zürn (1992; 1993b), and Lisa Martin (1993) – do not take issue on this, but they stress that the PD, both in (game) theory and in (international) reality, represents only one type of collective action problem among several. While regimes can be relevant to each of these kinds of cooperation problems, there are fundamental differences among them which, according to situation-structuralists, require differential treatment and circumscribe the validity of specific theoretical claims. By interpreting different kinds of regimes as collective responses to the functional requirements of *different kinds of collective action problems*, these scholars have sought to extend the explanatory scope of contractualism to the *form* of institutional arrangements. In addition, some have used the typologies of strategic situations (or "situation structures") which are characteristic of this approach to derive further propositions about the varying *likelihood* of regime formation across issue-areas.[17]

Explaining regime form on the basis of situational attributes

A collective action (or cooperation) problem exists when following the imperatives of individual rationality may lead, paradoxically, to collectively suboptimal (Pareto-inefficient)[18] outcomes. This is well illustrated by the (single-play) Prisoner's Dilemma. Here, each actor has the dominant strategy of not cooperating, i.e. of not choosing the course of action which puts his partner in a position to achieve his goal with regard to the issue at hand. Defection is the dominant strategy and thus would seem to be perfectly rational from the individual's point of view, because it secures the player a higher pay-off (as compared to acting cooperatively), no matter what the other decides. Nevertheless, ironically, both

[17] The term "situation structure" has been introduced by Zürn (1992: 151) to denote those elements of a choice situation which can be represented by a game-theoretic pay-off structure (including the actors, their behavioral options, and their preferences). In a similar fashion, Snidal (1985a: 924) talks of "the strategic structure" of a situation. Other authors use other terms in a similar sense. Hence, what all these scholars have in common is not nuances of terminology, but the conviction that, in any attempt to come to grips with regimes theoretically, the strategic nature of the situation in which states make choices about cooperation and institutions should be regarded as a central variable.

[18] An outcome is Pareto-efficient if and only if there exists no other outcome that (1) leaves any actor better off and (2) leaves no actor worse off.

actors would do better if they both *forwent* their individual-rational strategy. Moreover, for the dilemma to be resolved, it is not enough that the actors become aware of their situation and agree that they both should play "C." Since each actor continues to prefer his own exploitation of his partner's cooperative behavior (DC) to mutual cooperation (CC), (mutually known) incentives to renege on one's promise prevent cooperation from getting off the ground. Only when the players expect to meet again in the future does stable cooperation become possible. Part of the role of regimes, then, is to create and foster such expectations (see sect. 3.1 above).

The description of the PD we have just given implicitly assumes that there are only two players with two options each. It should be noted, therefore, that the 2 × 2 constellation is by no means an essential attribute of PD or any of the other games we are going to discuss. Introducing a situation structure in this way, however, is not only a matter of convenience, but accords with the practice of situation-structuralist argument as well. Most situation-structuralists base their hypotheses on these very simple models and then go on to analyze the qualifications that are necessary if a greater number of actors (and/or choices) are involved. Moreover, situation-structuralists usually have stated their hypotheses with respect not to individual games (such as PD) but to classes of games. Stein (1983: 120), for example, calls the theoretically relevant class of games, the best-known exemplar of which is PD, "dilemmas of common interest," which he defines as situations in which "independent decision making leads to equilibrium outcomes that are Pareto-deficient."[19]

Situation-structuralists agree with Keohane that collective action problems that resemble Prisoner's Dilemma are common in international politics. Both international trade issues and attempts at establishing collective security systems are often cited as real-world examples for this situation structure (Stein 1983: 123f.; Conybeare 1984: 10; Lipson 1984). They also point out, however, that by no means all situations of strategic interdependence in which individual and collective rationality can be at odds with one another – i.e. in Zürn's (1992: 153–61) terminology, all "problematic social situations" (Raub and Voss 1986) – correspond to PDs or PD-like games. For example, problems of standardization, such as of weaponry in NATO, or various issues in

[19] In the following, we use upper case to refer to particular payoff structures (e.g. "Assurance") and lower case to refer to classes of games (e.g. "assurance situations" for situations in which the underlying preference structure resembles an Assurance game).

		Actor B: B_1	Actor B: B_2
Actor A	A_1	$1,1_{P,N}$	0,0
	A_2	0,0	$1,1_{P,N}$

Fig. 2. A "pure" coordination situation.

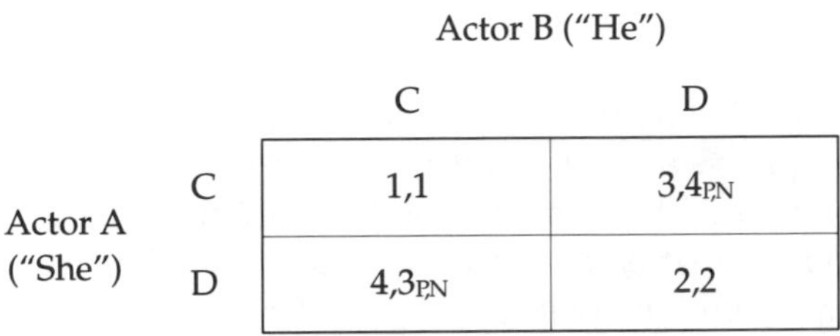

		Actor B ("He"): C	Actor B ("He"): D
Actor A ("She")	C	1,1	$3,4_{P,N}$
	D	$4,3_{P,N}$	2,2

P = Pareto-efficient; N = Nash equilibrium

Fig. 3. Battle of the Sexes.

global communications, such as the distribution of radio frequencies (Krasner 1991), should rather be classified and analyzed as *coordination games*. While in PD the only equilibrium outcome (mutual defection) is inefficient, in coordination situations several Pareto-efficient equilibria exist and actors face the problem of picking one of them collectively.[20] As long as actors are indifferent about where to coordinate, the problem is certainly not very serious, provided they can communicate effectively. However, a serious collective action problem may arise if, and to the extent that, they favor different coordination points, i.e. if the game that states are involved in is closer to Battle of the Sexes than to a "pure" coordination situation (figures 2 and 3).

The situation from which the name of the game is derived is that of a couple who would like to spend an evening together but have different preferences about what to do (e.g. watch a movie or go to the opera). To cooperate (from either individual's point of view) would mean to allow the other to make the choice of the venue. Thus, in Battle of the Sexes two Pareto-optimal outcomes exist (CD and DC) which are preferred by

[20] A (Nash) equilibrium is an outcome from which no actor can depart unilaterally without suffering a loss of utility.

both actors to a situation in which coordination does not take place (e.g. as a result of each going for his or her most favored outcome or seeking to avoid his or her most feared outcome irrespectively of what the other does). Moreover, both coordination points are equilibria such that coordination, if successful, can be expected to be stable. However, the actors disagree on where to settle on the "Pareto frontier" – "he" would be advantaged by CD, "she" by DC. (Both, of course, favor DD over CC, as CC amounts to both having made a pointless sacrifice.) It is this inherent distributional conflict which makes Battle a social situation no less problematic than PD, although for quite different reasons.

Situation-structuralists argue that in both PD-like and coordination situations international regimes can serve as facilitators of international cooperation (helping states to avoid Pareto-inefficient outcomes) and may therefore be created and maintained by rational actors. However, since the two types of situation structure pose very different problems, their institutional solutions will be rather different as well (Stein 1983: 127–32; Snidal 1985a: 936–9). Thus, PD-like situations require (relatively intense) collaboration, i.e. states must agree upon clear-cut injunctions that specify illegitimate behavior under the regime and they must devise procedures that assure actors that the others are not cheating. *Collaboration regimes* therefore can be expected to be comparatively formalized. Often they will involve international organizations, one of whose main tasks will be to collect and disseminate information which helps the parties to assess the extent to which their partners comply with the central provisions of the regime.

In contrast, *coordination regimes* can largely do without compliance mechanisms: the cooperative solution, once it is found (i.e. once states have settled upon a convention[21] specifying the coordination point), is self-enforcing. There is no problem of cheating. The (deliberate) noncompliance that occurs is to indicate dissatisfaction with the distributional consequences of the regime and is therefore *public*. Although coordination regimes in general are less formalized and less centralized than collaboration regimes, international organizations may be relevant

[21] On "convention" and "contract" as the solutions to problems of coordination and problems of collaboration, respectively, see Snidal (1985a: 937f.). Keohane (1989c: 4) regards conventions – informal and implicit rules and understandings of appropriate behavior that arise to solve coordination problems – as a separate type of institution apart from regimes. (Note that "convention" is used here in the sociological sense. In the language of international law the term has a quite different meaning, referring, as it does, to formal multilateral treaties.)

		Actor B	
		C	D
Actor A	C	4,4$_{P,N}$	1,3
	D	3,1	2,2$_{N,M}$

P = Pareto-efficient; N = Nash equilibrium;
M = maximin solution

Fig. 4. Assurance (Stag Hunt).

here as well. In the pre-regime stage they may provide important negotiation fora where states can resolve their disputes about the appropriate coordinating convention. Some formal institutional structure may also be functional in the regime stage. For example, in coordination regimes that operate on the basis of a first-come-first-served convention, international secretariats (such as the International Telecommunications Union within the regime for the allocation of the electromagnetic spectrum) may collect and distribute information about actors' intentions (as opposed to information about their current and prior behavior, which is what their partners want to know about when collaboration is at stake).

The distinction between coordination and collaboration regimes is a common tenet of all situation-structuralists. Adherents to this approach disagree, however, as to whether or not these two types of strategic situations exhaust the range of constellations of interest in which regimes may arise (i.e. the range of problematic social situations). While Stein (1983: 120) is quite clear that only in the face of a "dilemma of common interests" (a PD-like situation) or of a "dilemma of common aversions" (a coordination situation) states may find it in their interest to construct international regimes, Zürn (1992; 1993b) and Martin (1993) have argued for the inclusion of two further types of situation structure, which Martin calls assurance and suasion situations, respectively.

Assurance (or Stag Hunt) is akin to Battle of the Sexes in that the game contains two equilibrium outcomes (figure 4). The crucial difference is that only one of these equilibria (mutual cooperation) is Pareto-efficient and, consequently, is preferred by both actors. At first sight, there would not seem to be a cooperation problem at all. Nevertheless, failure to reach the Pareto frontier is possible if at least one of two conditions is met: (1) at least one actor fears (erroneously) that the other's preference ordering is not really Assurance (but PD, for example); (2) at least one actor doubts that the other can be trusted to act rationally on the given issue. In both situations, particularly when stakes are high and uncertainty is pronounced, it may not be unreasonable for actors to play safe and to opt for defection, which, in Assurance, is the only possibility actors have of making sure unilaterally that they will not end up with their worst-possible outcome (CD). Robert Jervis (1978) has analyzed the security dilemma in terms of an assurance situation. As Zürn (1992: 174–84) and Martin (1993: 106–9) argue, regimes can help to solve (or avoid) assurance problems by facilitating communication among states, even though, as is the case with other types of situation structure as well, (less costly) functional equivalents to regimes may exist in concrete situations. Thus, the mutual transparency that comes with democratic domestic institutions may often be sufficient for "assuring" states of the nature of the game at hand (and of the appreciation of this nature by their partners). Accordingly, Zürn (1992: 177) took his example for an assurance regime – the superpowers' regime for the prevention of inadvertent war – from Cold War East–West relations, where transparency was not a by-product of the normal operation of the political systems involved. By contrast, Stein (1983: 119f.) tends to reject the notion of assurance regimes altogether, since for him regimes are characterized by joint decisionmaking, which clearly goes beyond sharing information (this is, incidentally, an interesting example for how conceptual differences may affect theory).

In a nutshell, Assurance poses a cooperation problem, because, under specific circumstances, choosing the maximin strategy[22] may be individually rational, even though it is bound to lead to a collectively suboptimal outcome.

By contrast, the second class of situation structures that Zürn and Martin have added to the initial coordination – collaboration dichotomy are less readily subsumed under the concept of collective action problems. Indeed, Stein (1983: 120), once again, denies out of hand the relevance of this situation for regimes. Nevertheless, both authors argue that these situations are essential to a complete understanding of how and why international regimes are created. Martin (1993: 103–6) refers

[22] Maximin ("Maximize your minimum") is a decision rule that recommends choosing that option which would yield the highest pay-off in a situation where your partner (1) moves second (or knows how you will decide) and (2) pursues no other aim but to minimize your utility.

		Actor B	
		C	D
Actor A	C	$4,3_{P}$	$3,4_{P,N}$
	D	2,2	1,1

P = Pareto-efficient; N = Nash equilibrium

Fig. 5. A suasion (Rambo) game.

to this type of situation as *suasion games*, whereas Zürn (1992: 209–18) speaks of *Rambo games*. The characteristic feature of suasion games is that they have a single equilibrium outcome, which satisfies only one actor and leaves the other aggrieved (i.e. one actor receives her most preferred outcome, while the other does less well). In other words, an instance of unrequited cooperation (CD) is the only stable outcome of the game.

In a suasion game (figure 5) *either* one actor has a dominant strategy to cooperate, which the other can exploit, *or* one actor has a dominant strategy to defect, while the other must cooperate in order to avoid an even worse outcome. Our matrix depicts a situation belonging to the first variant.[23] Under such circumstances the privileged player has to be persuaded to cooperate. Within the confines of rationalist reasoning, this means that all the dissatisfied actor can do is to try to manipulate the other's preferences by making threats (decreasing for the other the utility of defection) or promises (increasing for the other the utility of cooperation). Such threats and promises are attempts at tactical issue-linkage (E. Haas 1980). If they are successful, the situation structure is no longer the same, but has been changed to one that is less hostile to cooperation than suasion. Both the status of Berlin and the intra-German trade issue-areas seem to exemplify situations in which two inverse suasion games have been deliberately linked in order to create a more regime-conducive PD-like situation, which, in both cases, eventually allowed for the formation of a regime (Rittberger and Zürn 1990: 41; Schwarzer 1990a: 209; Zürn 1990: 166–73).

Theoretically, in the situation represented by our matrix, the

23 Examples of the latter variant are Called Bluff (Snyder and Diesing 1977: 46) and Stein's (1983: 121) case of an "equilibrium outcome that leaves one actor aggrieved."

dissatisfied player (A) could also threaten to act irrationally, i.e. to opt (against his own immediate self-interest) for defection. For example, the rejected lover might threaten to commit suicide. To the extent that this threat were credible to his partner (B), the cooperative course of action would become rational from her point of view (as in her preference-ordering CC ranks higher than DD). The practical difficulty, though, is how to establish that credibility. Moreover, apart from all practical problems, this strategy is feasible only in some situations of the suasion type: in particular, it cannot work in those situations in which the privileged actor has a dominant strategy not to cooperate. Conybeare (1984: 16–18) provides an example from the politics of international trade. According to his analysis, a suasion game may result when a small country bargains with a large one, for the

> small country cannot improve its welfare with a tariff, but can only worsen the large country's welfare with a retaliatory tariff, even though retaliation would make the small country worse off than if it had not retaliated. Success for the small country would therefore depend on being able to convince the large country that the small country would be willing to act irrationally, hurting itself in order to punish the larger power. (Conybeare 1984: 16f.)

What role (if any) can regimes play in suasion situations? Regimes and international organizations may help states to arrange the side-payments necessary to secure the cooperation of the actors that are privileged by the situation. Likewise, through their principles and norms, they may foster and institutionalize the issue-linkage on which cooperation depends. Since incentives to defect continue to exist on the part of the "persuaded" actors, suasion regimes may display some features of collaboration regimes (especially, monitoring capacities). As Martin (1993: 103f.) suggests, suasion regimes are often sponsored by hegemons. Two reasons working together may account for this: (1) because of their ample power resources, dissatisfied hegemons, more frequently than others, will be able to elicit cooperation from their situationally privileged partners by means of threats or promises (see also Zürn 1992: 217); (2) the very asymmetry that defines hegemonic relationships often creates configurations of interests that can be interpreted as suasion games. When collective goods are at stake, hegemony may create a situation in which one actor (the hegemon) is willing and able to provide the good all by himself, which, in turn, gives the others the opportunity to free-ride. Martin points to the case of East – West trade in high-technology goods. Since (at least in some time-period) the distribution of production capacities among the Western allies was such that the overall success of the embargo depended more or less exclusively on US export policy, the smaller partners could safely abstain from self-restraint and enjoy the benefits of export in sensitive goods as well. The United States, in turn, sought to enhance its bargaining position *vis-à-vis* the other members of CoCom by trying to establish a credible link between export control and Marshall Plan aid.[24]

Accounting for success and failure in regime-building

Situation-structuralists focus on the question how regimes can help states to cooperate in different strategic situations and how these differences in situational context affect the nature of institutional solutions. However, regime form has not been the only dependent variable studied by proponents of this approach. Zürn (1992: 165–220), in particular, has used game-theoretic reasoning to derive hypotheses concerning the *likelihood of regime formation* in different types of strategic situations. His central hypothesis is that, assuming recurrent situations, the four types of situation structure discussed above can be ordered by their propensity to give rise to international regimes:

(1) assurance situations
(2) coordination situations
(3) collaboration situations
(4) suasion (Rambo) situations

where the probability of an institution emerging is highest in assurance and lowest in suasion situations. The rationale underlying this hypothesis is the assumption that the creation of a regime (or, more broadly, a normative institution) is more likely, the less demanding the cooperation problem. Unfortunately, Zürn does not explain what it is exactly that

[24] This argument, of course, sounds familiar. The theory of hegemonic stability which we have mentioned in connection with Keohane's contractualist theory and which we will discuss in some detail below (sect. 4.1) refers to precisely this kind of situation: a superior actor is needed to provide a group of states with an international public good. In contrast to the conventional analysis of public goods situations as *n*-personPDs (Hardin 1982: 27f.), though, Martin's suasion perspective highlights the strategic relationship between the hegemon and the group of (potential) free-riders. (The fact that the *weaker* actors are often in the position of Rambo – the movie character who gets his way without ever cooperating – suggests that Zürn's terminology can be misleading. This is why here we have adopted the language of "suasion" rather than "Rambo games.") For a recent book-length study of CoCom from a regime-analytical perspective, see Noehrenberg (1995).

determines the gravity of the cooperation problem at hand. It is rather obvious, however, that two, lexically ordered, principles have guided his intuition at this point: (1) cooperation is more difficult when incentives to defect remain even after actors have begun to cooperate (i.e. equilibrium outcomes are Pareto-inefficient); (2) all other things being equal, cooperation is more difficult, when actors disagree how (or even whether) to cooperate (i.e. prefer different Pareto-efficient outcomes).

Another, perhaps even more elegant, interpretation has been suggested by Bernhard Zangl (1994: 282–95), who proposes to explain Zürn's hierarchy of problematic social situations in terms of the variety and intensity of so-called *second-order problems* they give rise to. Second-order problems are defined as states of affairs which may prevent actors from cooperating with regard to some issue, even when opportunities for cooperation exist. Accordingly, suasion games are most adverse to cooperation, because they involve problems of monitoring, of sanctioning, and of distribution. PD-like situations are somewhat more conducive to cooperation, because they produce less intense problems of distribution than suasion games (although the other two second-order problems are still present). Coordination games pose fewer problems to cooperation than both suasion and PD: only the second-order problem of distribution (i.e. the problem of agreeing on a specific set of rules, where alternatives with different distributional consequences exist) has to be solved by the actors. Finally, in assurance games none of the three second-order problems that plague efforts at cooperation in PD-like and, even more so, in suasion situations is operative.[25]

Zürn goes on to argue that his regime formation hypothesis based on the four types of problematic social situations can (and should) be refined by taking into account a set of *secondary variables*. These include (1) the expected frequency of interaction through time (diachronic iteration), (2) the density of transactions (synchronic iteration), (3) the type of foreign policy (e.g. specific reciprocity) that is practised by the actors (see also Zürn 1993a), (4) the distribution of issue-specific resources, (5)

[25] Note that when Keohane talks of the "sanctioning problem" of decentralized cooperation (see sect. 3.1 above) he refers to both the monitoring and the sanctioning problem in Zangl's terminology. Critics have pointed out that Keohane has virtually ignored the third second-order problem mentioned by Zangl, the problem of distribution (seen by some as part of a more encompassing "supply problem"), and that this blind spot is a major flaw of his functional theory (see sect. 4.2 below) and indeed of the so-called new institutionalism in economics and political science of which it forms a part in general (Bates 1988; Ostrom 1990: 42–5).

the presence or absence of salient solutions, (6) the number of actors in the issue-area, and (7) the state of the overall relationship of the actors (i.e. the extent to which it is competitive or hostile). Each of these variables makes reference to specific arguments discussed in various strands of regime theory. Zürn stresses that (and shows how) both the relevance and the precise effect of individual secondary variables with regard to the prospects of regime formation vary across types of situation structure. Thus, for example, he argues that the distribution of resources among actors makes a difference for coordination, collaboration, and suasion situations, but hardly so for assurance situations. By contrast, he expects competition to have a negative effect on regime formation in assurance and coordination situations, yet to be inconsequential if the problems at hand are of the collaboration or suasion types (but see Snidal 1991b: 704–14). The promise of this approach is twofold. First, it may help to solve theoretical disputes by putting deductive arguments and empirical observations into perspective; in particular, it suggests that some of the ambiguity dimming the empirical record of certain hypotheses regarding regime formation (e.g. the hegemonic stability hypothesis) may have to be put down to failure to control for situation structure (see also sect. 4.1 below). (Here Zürn takes up a line of reasoning that, within the study of regimes, Snidal [1985a; 1985b] has pioneered with great subtlety.) Second, relating situation-structural and other theoretical variables in this way may turn out to be a viable strategy to overcome a present deficiency of regime analysis which has repeatedly been pointed to by students of regimes – the lack of integration of different theoretical approaches (Efinger, Mayer, and Schwarzer 1993: 272–8; Levy, Young, and Zürn 1995: 286f.).

Regime demand and the difficulties of cooperation – an unresolved tension in the situation-structural argument?

Overall, situation-structuralists have contributed significantly to the neoliberal research agenda. Their approach appears to be fully compatible with the contractualist theory of regimes and further develops and refines Keohane's argument that states create and maintain regimes in pursuing their individual self-interests. Not too surprisingly, therefore, Keohane (1993a: 39–41), inquiring into the functional origins of varying arrangements for institutional membership, has recently employed situation-structural arguments as well (see also Keohane and Martin 1995: 45). The most obvious advance of situation-structuralism *vis-à-vis* contractualism is the inclusion in the explanandum of institutional form.[26] Taking quite simple game models as their point of departure, situation-structuralists, furthermore, achieve a considerable measure of contextual richness in their analyses by taking into account secondary variables such as the number of actors, the distribution of power, and expectations of continuity of interactions. Game theory provides a language that allows rationalist sense to be made of a wide range of factors discussed in different strands of the regime literature. Relying on this language, the situation-structural approach has a significant integrative potential, although, as critics of the rationalist paradigm have argued, this basic meta-theoretical orientation imposes limits as well (see sect. 5.2 below). Up to this point, however, game theory has proven to be an amazingly flexible tool and has shown a great capacity for development. Therefore, defining its inherent limits and thus those of the situation-structural approach to analyzing international regimes is surely a risky undertaking (Snidal 1986; Kydd and Snidal 1993).

On the other hand, given its close connection with contractualism, it is not surprising that the situation-structural approach should share some of the problems of that theory as well. Like functional theory, the situation-structural approach seems to have more to say about the demand-side than about the supply-side of international regimes. It tells us quite convincingly when (and why) regimes are desirable from the point of view of the actors in an issue-area. It is less explicit, however, as to when and how the demand is actually met (Müller 1994).

Among situation-structuralists, Zürn has tackled the problem of accounting for both the events and the "non-events" of regime formation (i.e. the failure of regimes to emerge in problematic social situations) most vigorously. His solution raises questions as well, though. As we have seen, his general idea is that regimes are more likely to be created, the less difficult (due to situation structure) cooperation is in the issue-area at hand. Assuming (with neoliberalism) that the one purpose and *raison d'être* of regimes is to facilitate cooperation, this amounts to arguing that regimes are the more likely the *less* they are needed. This relationship, if normatively undesirable, may have considerable analytical plausibility. The point is, though, that it implies that *demand* can only be part of the story of regime formation. For, otherwise, we would be led to expect that, *ceteris paribus*, regimes are the more likely to be created the *more* they are needed to foster cooperation – a statement

[26] Hence, Ruggie (1993b: 35) is not correct when he criticizes the regime literature for ignoring this question.

which is in open contradiction with Zürn's heuristic assumption. The question then is: what is the rest of the story?[27]

One way out of this uncomfortable situation is to resolve the tension by relying solely on Zürn's assumption: regimes are the more likely to emerge, the less serious the cooperation problem. This solution, however, comes at a cost, having the unintended consequence of obscuring the causal role of regimes with respect to cooperation. Regimes and (durable) cooperation tend to become theoretically indistinguishable phenomena (whatever conceptual differences may remain between them): what explains regimes (viz. a favorable situation structure) also explains (durable) cooperation, and vice versa. Under these circumstances, it is difficult (if not impossible) to confirm empirically functional regime theory's central tenet that regimes matter for states' ability to cooperate, when, in fact, it seems that states' ability to cooperate matters for regimes.

To put it differently, a critic of regime analysis such as Andrew Moravcsik (1992), who has *questioned* the existence of an independent impact of regimes on the prospects of cooperation among states, should be perfectly comfortable with Zürn's rationale. Moravcsik argues that, from what he claims to be the genuine liberal point of view, cooperation is simply a function of the degree of convergence of (largely domestically determined) state interests, while uncertainty and transaction costs are of minor importance for the spatial, temporal, and sectoral distribution of instances of inter-state cooperation. (Of course, there are regimes, but they are the *form* that much of international cooperation takes today rather than a major source of it.) Confronted with Zürn's hypothesis, he might then go on to argue – not implausibly – that situation structure is nothing but a measure for the convergence of state interests. In other words, adopting a rationale such as Zürn's (which shines through the contributions of other situation-structuralists as well) may not be incompatible with positing an independent impact of international regimes on cooperation; yet, what makes it problematic from the perspective of a functional approach to regimes is that it may serve to veil this impact (assuming there is one) rather than to unpack it.

[27] The unresolved relationship between demand for regimes, on the one hand, and the difficulty of cooperation, on the other, is reflected in situation-structuralists' divergent views about the range of regime-relevant situations. Thus, while for Zürn regimes (in the broadest sense) are most likely to arise in assurance situations, for Stein assurance regimes are (at least, for the most part) superfluous and therefore will not be created by rational actors. Note, in this connection, Keohane's (1988: 386) insightful, but empirically vague remark about the curvilinear relationship between regimes and transaction costs: regimes, he argues, will not be created if transaction costs are either too high or too low.

Note that none of this implies that the heuristic assumption on which Zürn's theory of regime formation is based is unreasonable as such. Indeed, empirical research suggests that this approach has considerable potential when it comes to accounting for *rule-based cooperation* among states, i.e. for regimes in the language of those who favor a "behavioral" definition of this term (see ch. 2 above). A Tübingen-based research team has made in-depth studies of thirteen issue-areas, most (but not all) of which belong to the broader context of (pre-1989) East–West relations and, sooner or later, saw the emergence of an international regime. The cases under scrutiny covered a great variety of issue-areas including security (e.g. conventional forces in Europe), economic (e.g. intra-German trade), environmental (e.g. protection of the Baltic Sea), as well as human rights (e.g. constitutionalism in Western Europe) affairs.[28] These cases were used, *inter alia*, to probe various hypotheses regarding the determinants of regime formation – including realist (power-structural), liberal (transactionist), and problem-structural propositions. What is most remarkable in this connection is that the hypothesis linking the prospects of regime formation to the type of situation structure at hand as well as to various secondary factors (as outlined above) did extraordinarily well in the test, both in absolute terms and in comparison with the rival hypotheses (Efinger, Mayer, and Schwarzer 1993: 260–6, 269). While it should not be claimed that this result comes anywhere near a conclusive vindication of situation-structuralism or this particular hypothesis about regime formation,[29] it does justify and

[28] For a brief description of the cases see Efinger, Mayer, and Schwarzer (1993: 255–60). The (published) case studies are to be found in Rittberger (1990b: part II), Schrogl (1990), Schwarzer (1990b; 1994), List (1991; 1992), and Zürn (1992: ch. 3).

[29] As perhaps in most empirical studies on this subject the conditions under which the test was carried out were less than optimal. Thus, the number of cases (although greater than in most other empirical studies of regimes) was still far too small to allow for a statistical analysis of the data. Moreover, the authors of the case studies repeatedly faced difficulties attributing their issue-area unequivocally to a type of situation structure, which might have distorted the results (as well as indicate a more general problem with this approach). The selection of cases was not randomized, although the criteria of selection (macropolitical context, problem structure) were unrelated to situation structure. Controls for perturbing variables may have been insufficient, although this problem is reduced by the fact that Zürn's approach as such integrates and, thus, takes into account several further variables as so-called "secondary variables." Finally, it should be noted that (for a number of reasons) members of the research team could test only a simplified version of Zürn's hypothesis. It remains to be seen, therefore, whether the complete version does an even better job or whether Zürn has in fact "sacrificed" parsimony when constructing his theory.

encourage continuing efforts to explore empirically and, in the process, refine the situation-structural approach to international regimes.

3.3 The problem-structural approach

By definition, international regimes are partial orders: they pertain to specific *issue-areas* (trade, money, arms control, etc.) rather than to the totality of the political relationships of their members (see ch. 2 above). Moreover, the same set of actors may cooperate through regimes in some issue-areas, while relying on self-help strategies (independent decisionmaking) in others. For example, in the mid-eighties, the Eastern and Western blocs had established a regime regarding the peace-time movements of troops in certain areas (known as the regime defining "confidence- and security-building measures in Europe"), but not (yet) one specifying admissible levels of conventional forces in Europe or one regulating the working conditions of foreign journalists (in particular Western journalists in the Warsaw Pact countries, but also vice versa), *even though* negotiations about these issues had been going on for many years. Similarly, in the mid-nineties, a global regime for the protection of the stratospheric ozone layer has been in place for almost a decade, whereas repeated attempts to create a (regulatory) regime for the management of climate change have not met with success so far.

This observation suggests that neither unit-level nor (global) system-level theories of cooperation are perfectly satisfactory. Hence, Michael Zürn, Klaus-Dieter Wolf, and Manfred Efinger (1990) have argued that students of international relations are well advised to explore a set of approaches which are best located at a medium level or "third pole" between those two extremes. For these authors, the situation-structural approach occupies such an intermediate position between the two traditional levels of analysis. They also point out, however, that it is not unique in this regard, but shares this particular position in the topography of explanations in international relations with another: the so-called *problem-structural approach.*

The core argument: issue properties and conflict management

The basic idea underpinning the problem-structural approach is straightforward: if neither the attributes of the actors nor the characteristics of the international system as a whole can account for all variation of behavioral patterns across issue-areas, the nature of the issue-areas themselves (or of the issues they are composed of) may well be responsible for at least part of the observable differences. Proponents of a problem-structural approach in the study of regimes (and, in particular, regime formation) have elaborated on this basic idea in three steps. First, they sought to clarify the concept of issue-area; they then gave a (partial) re-conceptualization of "international regime" which builds directly upon this clarification; and finally, they came up with various issue (or issue-area) typologies in order to categorize their independent variable and to generate hypotheses linking these typologies to the likelihood of regime formation (Efinger, Rittberger, and Zürn 1988: chs. 3–5).[30]

As we have seen (ch. 2 above), students of international regimes have discussed their key concept quite extensively. However, they have paid surprisingly little attention to the concept of issue-area, which forms part of the early consensus definition of "regime" (Krasner 1983c: 2f.) as well as of most of the alternatives that have been proposed since (Keohane 1989c: 4; 1993a: 28f.; Young 1989a: 13; Rittberger and Zürn 1990: 11f.; 1991: 166). Yet, if issue-area specificity is an essential attribute of regimes, the concept of regime can only be as clear as the concept of issue-area has been made.[31]

This relative lack of interest in the concept is most uncomfortably felt in empirical research, particularly if analysts are not content with equating regimes with specific treaties and, when studying regime formation, recognize the need to look into "non-regime" cases as well (i.e. issue-areas in which actors failed to establish such an institution): if there is no regime its scope cannot help define the issue-area to be analyzed. Also, because of their preferred independent variable, the nature of the issue (or issue-area), proponents of a problem-structural approach can be expected to be more sensitive than others to the need to operationalize terms such as "issue" and "issue-area." Consequently, various attempts towards this end have been made by scholars contributing to this research agenda.

Building on an earlier formulation by Keohane and Joseph Nye (1977: 64f.), German students of regimes, who have exhibited a particular affinity to problem-structuralism (Rittberger 1993b: 13–16), have proposed the following definition: "Issue-areas . . . consist of one or more, in

30 For a survey and discussion of issue typologies in the study of international relations, see Mansbach and Vasquez (1981: ch. 2).

31 For a critique of the use of the concept of issue-area in much of contemporary regime analysis, see Kratochwil (1993a: 75–83).

the perception of the actors inseparably connected objects of contention and of the behavior directed to them. The boundaries of issue-areas are determined by the perception of the participating actors." (Efinger and Zürn 1990: 68; see also Efinger, Rittberger, and Zürn 1988: 68; Zürn, Wolf, and Efinger 1990: 153) The perception-dependency of issue-areas deserves to be stressed: it has the important implication that issue-areas can change without any corresponding change taking place in the objective facts to which policymakers are responding. Moreover, analysis is complicated by the fact that perceptions of actors as to which issues are indeed "inseparably connected" can diverge: typically, the formation of an issue-area is itself a highly political process.

Another term to be highlighted in this definition is "objects of contention," which emphasizes the *conflictual* character of issues. As regimes are internally related to issue-areas, adopting this perspective has implications for our understanding of that concept as well. Problem-structuralists have sought to bring this to the fore by explicitly conceptualizing international regimes as a particular mode of (regulated) *conflict management* thus anchoring regime analysis in peace and conflict studies (Rittberger 1993b: 11–13). The distinction between conflict and conflict management is crucial for this approach. "Conflict" as used by these authors is not defined in terms of behavior (e.g. violence) or attitudes (e.g. hostility), but in terms of incompatible preferences or "differences in issue position" (*Positionsdifferenzen*) (Czempiel 1981: 198–203; see also Boulding 1962: 5). Whatever actors do in handling such differences (henceforth abbreviated as "positional differences") comes under "conflict management," which, therefore, spans a broad spectrum of individual and collective behavior – literally ranging from total war to stable peace. For all practical purposes, cooperation – whether sustained by agreed-upon rules or merely of an *ad hoc* nature – is also best understood as a form of conflict management (Efinger and Zürn 1990: 67; Rittberger and Zürn 1990: 13–19; 1991: 166). This conception of the relationship between cooperation and conflict clashes with a large body of international relations literature where cooperation and conflict are treated as opposites on a single dimension (e.g. Vasquez and Mansbach 1984: 413). It is compatible, though, with Keohane's conceptualization of cooperation as a form of collective behavior which does *not* take place under conditions of harmony (see sect. 3.1 above). What (if anything) distinguishes the contractualist approach from the problem-structural one in this regard is a difference in emphasis: while Keohane stresses common interests as a basis for cooperation and regimes, problem-structuralists highlight the conflictual background of regime-based cooperation.

Insisting on a conceptual separation of conflict and conflict management is not denying an empirical relationship between characteristics of conflicts (or issue-areas) and the forms of behavior they give rise to. On the contrary, it is a prerequisite for any investigation into this relationship, which is the core of the problem-structural research agenda. To further this agenda, problem-structuralists have designed and explored various issue-area and conflict typologies. We briefly discuss an example for each of these two basic kinds of problem-structural variables and associated hypotheses.

"Policy domains" and "conflict types": two problem-structural hypotheses

Issue-area typologies are constructed because it is presumed that "the characteristics of the issue-area, in which a conflict occurs, as such predict, to a large extent, whether the conflict is dealt with cooperatively or by using unilateral self-help strategies" (Efinger and Zürn 1990: 67). Ernst-Otto Czempiel has provided a simple typology which classifies issue-areas of international politics into the three broad *policy domains* (*Sachbereiche der Politik*) of security, economic well-being, and (system of) rule (*Herrschaft*). He explains these categories as follows:

> The value of *security* comprises the protection of physical existence against internal and external threats. In its internal dimension it borders on the domain of *rule* in which opportunities for exercising freedom and for political participation are allocated among individuals. [These two domains] secure the preservation of the physical existence of the individual and serve its advancement [, respectively]. With regard to material needs, the latter is provided for in the domain of *economic well-being,* by means of the allocation of economic gains as well as opportunities for achieving such gains. (Czempiel 1981: 198 [our translation, emphasis added])

Problem-structuralists have hypothesized that the propensity of issue-areas to give rise to a cooperative and, in particular, a regulated mode of conflict management (i.e. the formation of an international regime) varies systematically with the policy domain they come under. Czempiel (1981: 196, 213) himself has suggested that economic issues – in which divisible "gain" rather than indivisible "power" is at stake – display a greater propensity to cooperative management than the other two domains. He has failed, though, to specify possible systematic differences between security and rule in this respect. Consciously resorting, at this point, to realist thinking, which recognizes the possibility of security cooperation through alliances, but tends to deny human rights and ideology in general a place on the agenda of international politics, Efinger and Zürn (1990: 75) have sought to fill the gap Czempiel has left open. Hence, they were led to hypothesize the following hierarchy: issue-areas in which the allocation of *economic* values is contested are most regime-conducive, while issue-areas belonging to the domain of *rule* (perhaps best exemplified by human rights issues) are least amenable to cooperative treatment. *Security* issues, by implication, occupy a middle position.

Conflict typologies are classifications of either conflicts (positional differences) or objects of contention rather than issue-areas. The distinction between conflict and object of contention is fairly subtle, but has proven useful for analytical purposes. As we have noted, for problem-structuralists *conflict* refers to an abstract entity, namely an incompatible difference in positions taken by actors. All conflicts, in turn, involve an *object of contention* which can be material or immaterial and with respect to which actors take those incompatible positions, disagreeing on whether, or how, to create it, to keep it in existence, or to distribute it among themselves (Rittberger and Zürn 1990: 15). As Efinger and Zürn (1990: 68) have put it, in comparison to issue-area typologies, conflict typologies "go even a step further in the disaggregation of a relationship between actors." Again, it is presumed that inherent properties of conflicts (or of objects of contention) account for (at least part of) the observable conflict management. Problem-structuralists have paid special attention to a classification which distinguishes four types of conflict: conflicts about values, conflicts about means, and two types of conflict of interest (Rittberger and Zürn 1990: 31f.; 1991: 168).[32]

In a *conflict about means* actors share a common goal, but disagree on how best to pursue it. In a *conflict about values* actors hold incompatible principled beliefs regarding the legitimacy of a given action or practice. Both conflicts about values and conflicts about means are *dissensual* in that actors disagree on what is desirable, not just for each of them individually but for all of them collectively. By contrast and seemingly paradoxically, *conflicts of interest* presuppose a specific *consensus*: the actors value the same – scarce – good, and this is precisely what makes

[32] The typology makes use of distinctions that were introduced by Aubert (1963) and Kriesberg (1982: 30–42).

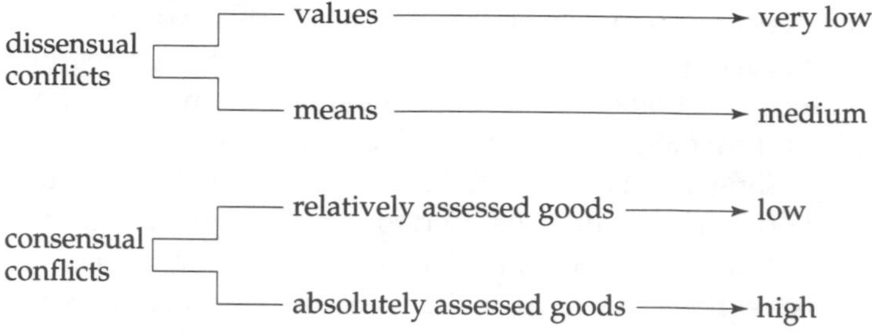

Fig. 6. Types of conflict and regime-conduciveness.

them parties to a conflict in the first place, which, in this case, takes the form of a competition. The class of conflicts of interest can be further subdivided in terms of the nature of the good that is sought by the actors. There are some goods (such as "guns") which tend to be assessed *relatively* such that an actor's valuation of (or satisfaction gained from) a *given* amount of the good is not independent of the amount that accrues to his competitors. By contrast, other goods (such as "butter") tend to be assessed *absolutely* such that an actor's enjoyment of his share neither increases nor decreases considerably *just* because the quantity of the good held by others changes. A counterfactual can help clarify this distinction: we may say that the parties to a conflict of interest value their object of contention in absolute rather than relative terms if the destruction (as opposed to the redistribution) of an actor's share would *not* affect the level of satisfaction on the part of the other actors.[33] Figure 6 depicts the hypothesis regarding the relative regime-conduciveness of the four types of conflict that problem-structuralists have advanced.

Along with several others the two examples of problem-structural hypotheses we have introduced – the one based on Czempiel's three-part issue-area typology ("policy domains") and the one based on the four-part conflict typology – have been subjected to a quantitative empirical test using data about conflicts and conflict management in postwar East–West relations. For this purpose a database ("The Tübingen Data Bank of Conflicts in East–West Relations") was constructed and evaluated (Beller *et al.* 1990; Efinger and Zürn 1990: 68–70). Owing to resource limitations the variable "conflict management" could not be coded in terms of (behaviorally defined) international

[33] The distinction between absolutely and relatively assessed goods is related to Hirsch's (1976: ch. 3) dichotomy of material and positional goods (Efinger and Zürn 1990: 82).

regimes, but only in terms of less stringently defined "agreements." With this restriction in mind, a striking result of this test is that both hypotheses turned out capable of accounting "for a great deal of variance in conflict management in East–West relations" (Efinger and Zürn 1990: 83). In addition, the hypothesis referring to the four types of conflicts was evaluated within the case-study based module of the Tübingen-based project on East–West regimes (see sect. 3.2 above). In this context, too, the hypothesis did rather well, surpassing most of the other hypotheses included in the test (Efinger, Mayer, and Schwarzer 1993: 269).[34]

Some problems of the problem-structural approach

While definitely encouraging for problem-structuralists, these results should not detract attention from continuing weaknesses of this approach in its present form (see also Underdal 1995: 115f.). In particular, these weaknesses concern, first, the as yet unspecified theoretical foundations of the approach in general as well as of some hypotheses in particular and, second, unresolved difficulties that arise when it comes to applying problem-structural typologies to actual cases.

Empirical studies have lent a considerable measure of support to the problem-structural hypothesis relating cooperative and self-help behavior to the variable "type of conflict" as measured by the four-part typology of "conflict about values," "conflict about means," "conflict of interest about absolutely assessed goods" and "conflict of interest about relatively assessed goods." Thus far, however, contributors to the problem-structural agenda have failed to come up with a theoretically grounded explanation for this empirical relationship, and a coherent theoretical argument to motivate this particular "hierarchy of probabilities" is still pending. Rationalizations that have been provided are both incomplete and *ad hoc*. For example, why is it that conflicts about means are less regime-conducive than conflicts about absolutely assessed goods? Is it because they are dissensual whereas the latter are consensual in character? But then again, dissensual conflicts are not generally

[34] The latter result should be assessed with particular caution, though, since cases were selected with an eye to the prevailing "type of conflict," e.g. by deliberately picking a small number of deviant cases for in-depth study (Rittberger and Zürn 1991). Caveats such as these suggest the potential value for students of regimes interested in empirical research of an international regimes database which has been developed as part of the International Environmental Commitments project of the International Institute for Applied Systems Analysis (IIASA) at Laxenburg (see Breitmeier *et al.* 1996a; 1996b).

less amenable to cooperation than consensual ones: compare conflicts about means and conflicts of interest about relatively assessed goods. Efinger and Zürn (1990: 83) make it clear that they regard the correlational success of this hypothesis as quite extraordinary. But if this is true, students of cooperation and regimes would all the more like to understand the mechanisms that are at work in producing this relationship.

While situation-structuralism is firmly rooted in the interest-based view of international politics in general and international cooperation in particular, proponents of a problem-structural approach to international regimes have taken less care in explicating the theoretical background of their preferred approach. Problem-structuralists have pointed out, however, that their focus on the autonomy of issue-areas implies a rejection of the *realist* assumption of a hierarchy of issue-areas in which security and the (military) means to protect one's security are always trump (Keohane and Nye 1977; Mansbach and Vasquez 1981; Zürn, Wolf, and Efinger 1990: 152). Moreover, they have stressed the "objectivist" character of their approach (Zürn, Wolf, and Efinger 1990: 156), which sets it apart from *cognitivist* theories of regimes (see ch. 5 below). It is the properties of issues as such, not actors' interpretations of them that predispose the parties to a certain kind of collective behavior.[35] Conversely, the similarities of the problem-structural approach and Zürn's account of regime formation in terms of situation structure are obvious, suggesting that both approaches belong to the same school of thought in regime analysis, i.e. *neoliberalism*. Thus, it might be argued that situation structure (assurance games, coordination games, etc.) is just another way of classifying issue-areas and/or the conflicts that dominate them, and is distinguished from problem-structural typologies only by virtue of the specific toolkit (game theory) that it uses. This kinship is also reflected in the view expressed by Zürn, Wolf, and Efinger (1990), and mentioned earlier in this section, that situation-structuralism and problem-structuralism together represent some-

[35] Problem-structuralists' major concession to cognitivism is their acknowledgement that the boundaries of issue-areas are subjective in nature. Objectivism is not the view that actors' perceptions are irrelevant. What it means is that variations in characteristics of the objects of contention (such as the differences between butter and guns) account for a far greater amount of the variation in outcomes (collective behavior) than does variation in the subjective elements of perception (i.e. perspectivity). This said, problem-structuralists themselves have voiced dissatisfaction with the way perception is handled in their approach (Zürn, Wolf, and Efinger 1990: 159).

thing like a "third pole" (beside or between actor- and system-centric accounts) within the study of international relations.

Still, problem-structuralism's compatibility with neoliberalism is not perfect. Neoliberals portray states as rational *egoists* who are indifferent as to how well others do. Realists have criticized this characterization as inadequate, pointing out that states are *positionalists* (i.e. concerned with their relative power position) and therefore highly sensitive to relative performance (see sect. 4.3 below). By this criterion, however, problem-structuralism is *not* easily subsumed under interest-based (neoliberal) theorizing. For, as we have seen, one of its most important propositions refers to a classification of international conflicts which, *inter alia*, distinguishes between conflicts of interest about absolutely assessed goods and conflicts of interest about relatively assessed goods. Consequently, contrary to neoliberalism, it is assumed by problem-structuralists that, under certain conditions, states *are* concerned with relative gains. Meanwhile, failure to come down neatly on one side of the realist – liberal divide as such says nothing about the substantive adequacy or inadequacy of an approach. Indeed, allowing for both absolute-gains and relative-gains oriented behavior and specifying the *constraints* (here: the nature of the object of contention) that determine what kind of behavior (or motivation) prevails in a given situation may be a more promising approach to theory-building than placing one's bets dogmatically on one or the other (Powell 1991; 1994: 334–8).

The second set of difficulties tend to crop up in the application of problem-structural typologies and hypotheses to concrete cases. As with the types of problematic social situations focused on by situation-structuralists, students of regimes have often found it difficult to attribute concrete issue-areas to a particular type of conflict. This is hardly surprising given that issue-areas will often comprise more than one object of contention and there is no *a priori* reason why actors should link only conflicts of the same type. Louis Kriesberg (1982: 42) goes so far as to claim that "[i]n any specific dispute, the contending parties have both consensual and dissensual bases for conflict." The possibility (and reality) of mixed conflicts poses problems to problem-structural analyses with which proponents of this approach so far have not really engaged.[36] How do the "effects" of different types of conflict on the

[36] For an effort to shed some new light on the past and the future of East–West relations by drawing attention to changes in the "conflict mix" within this segment of the international system and their likely consequences from a problem-structural point of view, see Rittberger and Zürn (1992).

regime-conduciveness of issue-areas add up? Is the likelihood of regime formation simply a function of the most problematic type of conflict represented in the issue-area or can we observe "interaction effects" (e.g. in terms of "benign" issues to some extent neutralizing "malign" ones)?[37] How do actors handle different types of conflict, whether occurring in a mixed way or separately? For example, can regime formation be described as a sequence of stages in which actors first tackle benign conflicts and then move on to more malign ones? That problem-structuralists have not yet come up with answers to this long list of questions indicates that much remains to be done for proponents of this approach, particularly if they aspire to theory. Yet, at the same time, the very existence of this list shows that a problem-structural perspective is capable of generating some interesting questions for empirical research and thus might have progressive potential as a particular, though hardly a self-sufficient,[38] line of research within the study of regimes.

3.4 Institutional bargaining: Young's model of regime formation

Oran Young (1977; 1980; 1982) is one of the pioneers of regime analysis and, during the last two decades, has always been one of the most innovative and productive scholars in this field. While his work spans all aspects of regime analysis including the study of regime consequences (Young 1992; 1994: ch. 6; Levy, Young, and Zürn 1995: 287–312), perhaps the most original and most ambitious among his many contributions so far is a *model of regime formation* which he refers to as "institutional bargaining" (Young 1989b; 1991: 282– 5; 1994: ch. 4). This model is interest-based in that it assumes selfish actors who are confronted with both the

[37] The language of "benign" and "malign" issues is borrowed from Wettestad and Andresen's (1991) work on sources of regime *effectiveness*. While their dichotomous typology is comparatively simple, they do go beyond the kind of problem-structural work reviewed in this section by introducing the additional variable "problem-solving capacity."

[38] The authors whom, for convenience, we have referred to here as "problem-structuralists" are far from regarding this approach as a panacea and readily concede that other variables need to be taken into account as well when it comes to explaining particular instances of institution-building (Efinger and Zürn 1990: 84). For an attempt to integrate several hypotheses regarding the determinants of regime formation which uses problem structure as a "context variable" setting the stage, as it were, for the operation of other factors, see Rittberger and Zürn (1991: 171–7).

possibility of achieving joint gains from effectively coordinating their behavior and the *difficulty* of settling upon a specific set of norms and rules for that purpose. At the same time, Young is critical of neoliberal (in particular, situation-structural) accounts of regime formation whose utility as a means of explaining "the actual record of success and failure in efforts to form international regimes" (Young 1989b: 352) he regards as rather limited (Young 1989b: 359; Young and Osherenko 1993a: 11–13). Indeed, he develops his alternative model, in large part, through a critique of the "principal models or streams of analysis embedded in the existing literature on regime formation" (Young 1989b: 349). Young identifies two such streams, one of which he refers to as "utilitarian models." Utilitarian (or rationalist) models include situation-structural hypotheses, but, to him, are best represented by various formal theories of bargaining. (The other stream of analysis Young takes into consideration is power-based accounts of regime formation, mainly represented by the theory of hegemonic stability [see sect. 4.1 below].) As a consequence, Young, although his approach to regime formation is self-consciously interest-based, cannot be called a rationalist and, to that extent, his neoliberalism has to be qualified.[39]

A critique of mainstream rationalist models of bargaining

Young's model of regime formation centers on the bargaining process that is meant to result in a "constitutional contract" specifying the content of a regime for the issue-area in question (Young 1991: 282), i.e. it focuses on what he had earlier called "negotiated regimes" and juxtaposed with "spontaneous" and "imposed regimes" (Young 1983: 98–101). (In the meantime, Young has come to believe that regimes normally emerge from negotiations. He continues to regard his typology of regime formation processes as useful, but stresses its analytical character [Young and Osherenko 1993b: 225–7]). Young's neologism for that process, "institutional bargaining," is simply a shorthand for "bargaining with the objective of creating an institution." The term is not intended to highlight the institutional setting in which international

[39] This imperfect fit is even more pronounced with other aspects of his thinking about international regimes. In particular, his views about the significance (and pervasiveness) of international institutions are closer to those of the cognitivists than to those usually held by neoliberals. Accordingly, he sees considerable merit in a behavioral model which portrays states as role-players rather than pure utility-maximizers (see Young 1989a: chs. 3 and 8).

negotiations take place. Both functional and situation-structural analyses of regime formation also deal more or less exclusively with regimes that are created through explicit agreement by states (see, for example, Keohane 1989c: 17, n. 5). Nevertheless, they have paid little (if any) attention to the concrete bargaining processes that regularly precede such agreements. There is, however, an extensive rationalist literature, rooted in game theory and economics, that is directly concerned with explaining and predicting the results of negotiations. It is this literature which is the immediate object of Young's critique and the contrast foil which helps him clarify the features of his own model.

Young (1989b: 356–9) perceives two major flaws in the mainstream rationalist (or utilitarian) literature about bargaining. On the one hand, it is overly optimistic as regards the ability of rational actors to cooperate. More specifically, it fails to take into account a number of "severe obstacles" often standing in the way of reaching mutual agreement, even when the presence and locus of a zone of agreement (i.e. a set of possible exchanges which are Pareto-superior to the initial situation) are not under dispute among the participants. Here, Young points to problems arising from strategic behavior, intra-party bargaining (two-level games), linkages and considerations of precedent, and lack of trust among the parties (i.e. fear of cheating).

In this connection, it is striking that, although Young's (1989b: 350) discussion of the "streams of analysis" that "dominate the study of regime formation in international society" contains a couple of passing references to the situation-structural approach, he does not mention Keohane's contractualism (functional theory). As a matter of fact, while contractualism is a self-consciously rationalist theory of regimes, it would be difficult to find evidence in *After Hegemony* for the kind of naïvety of which Young accuses "mainstream utilitarians". Certainly, the problems for international cooperation that arise from concerns with the possibility of being double-crossed by one's partners *are* acknowledged by functional theory. What is more, the assumption (or insight) that common interests do not automatically lead to cooperation is one of the building blocks of this theory. Indeed, Keohane and Young basically start from the same premise: the presence of a zone of agreement is a necessary, but not sufficient, condition for cooperation (Keohane 1984: 6; Young and Osherenko 1993a: 11f.). How the two authors proceed from this common point of departure is very different, though. And these differences run deep, insofar as they reflect incompatible basic conceptualizations of the subject matter as well as fundamentally different explanatory strategies. In Keohane, regimes are functionally explained in terms of the agreements (i.e. the cooperation) they facilitate; in Young, regimes *are* (or are constituted of) agreements, and, therefore, explaining regimes is simply explaining a kind of agreement (for which Young uses the term "constitutional contract"). Consequently, there is little (if any) room in his account for a functional argument linking the cooperation-value of regimes (i.e. the way in which they influence the feasibility of agreements) with their existence.[40]

At any rate, the implication of Young's *first* critical argument – whether or not it does justice to the rationalist mainstream in the study of regime formation – is that the real-world prospects for "getting to yes" in negotiations among self-interested actors are considerably *worse* than theory would want us to believe. However, the picture changes once again on the introduction of his *second* critical argument. Ironically, this second set of inadequacies inherent in the prevailing rationalist models of bargaining works against the apparent implication of the first one (which, for a moment, has made regime formation appear extremely difficult) such that, *once those inadequacies are recognized and rectified*, we can understand why attempts to form international regimes so often (though by no means always) *are* successful.

The inadequacy Young points to is the following. A central feature of standard utilitarian models – Young (1989b: 357f.) has in mind "work [which] takes as its point of departure either an Edgeworth box diagram with its depiction of a well-defined contract curve... or a game-theoretic formulation with its identification of a well-defined negotiation set" – is that they are highly formalized and therefore (in a sense) highly developed.[41] At the same time, according to Young, they rest upon a number of very problematic assumptions such that they "abstract away a great many considerations that are major preoccupations of negotiators under real-world circumstances" (Young 1989b: 358). Thus, rather heroic assumptions are made as to the knowledge participants have regarding the identity of the parties, the strategies that are available to

[40] As we have seen (ch. 2), Keohane now prefers a definition of "regime" according to which regimes are a kind of agreement. Therefore, it is important to stress that this – in the overall context of Keohane's theory – problematic terminological move (see note 9 above) does *not* affect the conceptual-theoretical difference between contractualism and the model of institutional bargaining that is at issue here.

[41] As editor of a collection of seminal papers contributing to these two lines of analysis Young (1985) is intimately familiar with these models.

them, and the pay-offs that would result from the numerous possible combinations of these strategies. Moreover, it is usually assumed that none of these parameters changes in the course of the negotiation. However, each of these assumptions, Young argues, is highly doubtful as a description of actual bargaining. Yet, only if all these assumptions can be made can we infer the proposition which we have just treated as a seemingly self-evident and insignificant premise, namely that the participants to an international negotiation are fully aware of what their interests are and where they overlap and clash with those of the other parties. As it turns out, this premise is not at all self-evident or insignificant: neither is it empirically unproblematic nor is it true that nothing much follows from it for the likelihood of cooperation. On the contrary, it is precisely the (at least initial) *absence* of a specified and commonly known zone of agreement that, in the real world, encourages the kind of behavior that in many cases allows the parties to come to a final agreement. Hence, for Young, uncertainty can be productive.

"Institutional bargaining" as a more realistic model of regime formation

On the basis of these critical observations Young (1989b: 352, 374) develops a model which he claims to be "more realistic" than those prevailing in the literature (i.e. conventional utilitarian and power-based models). Among the defining features of this model, at least two are directly related to a form of uncertainty. As we have seen, Young points out that in real-world situations actors are usually uncertain as to what exactly the strategies are that are available to themselves and to their partners. Similarly, they are often only vaguely aware of the outcomes that might result from any possible combination of strategies. And finally, they are not always sure how these outcomes relate to their core interests. One of Young's key arguments is that these conditions produce a disposition in the actors to engage in *integrative* (rather than *distributive) bargaining*, i.e. willy-nilly, the first and foremost concern of the parties shifts from "the distribution of fixed payoffs" (which do not exist under the circumstances) to the cooperative "production of expanded benefits" (Young 1994: 126f.). Young is aware that elements of distributive bargaining are always present in attempts at international institution-building. However, he stresses "that regime formation in international society typically centers on integrative (or productive) bargaining" (Young 1989b: 361).

Uncertainty comes in in yet another (though closely related) way.

Here, the emphasis is on time and the unforeseeability of the future as key factors facilitating agreement among self-interested actors. Using a concept introduced by Geoffrey Brennan and James Buchanan (1985: 28–31) in the context of constitutional political economy, Young points out that the parties to institutional bargaining regularly act under a *"veil of uncertainty"* regarding their own future positions and interests. Since, however, institutions once they are put in place are never easily changed (even when most of those affected by them are no longer happy with them) (Young 1989a: ch. 3), this "veil" creates incentives for the parties to opt for institutional arrangements that produce acceptable results for states in quite different positions (as far as their resources, interests, etc. are concerned) – a fact that, *ipso facto*, makes agreement among differently situated states easier to reach.[42]

Note that, although uncertainty is central to both Young's and Keohane's theories of regime formation, its precise meaning and role in the two formulations are quite different. While Keohane refers to the actors' uncertainty about what their partners will do (will they keep their promises?), Young stresses a kind of uncertainty that is much more fundamental (what can we and what can they do? what may result? how should we think about what may result?). In both theories uncertainty is productive, but in different ways. In Keohane's account uncertainty (together with the possibility of joint gains) *motivates* states to create regimes which serve to *reduce* uncertainty (asymmetical information). In Young's model uncertainty is a condition which *enables* actors to form regimes. The veil of uncertainty may diminish during the operation of the regime, but this is neither one of the regime's purposes nor likely to stabilize the regime.

This beneficial effect of the veil of uncertainty is all the more important, because, according to Young, regime formation in international society is generally subject to a *unanimity rule*. The identity of the negotiating parties may often be unclear initially and may itself be a matter of dispute, but once this issue is settled, each of the remaining actors

[42] The "veil of uncertainty" is related to, but not identical with Rawls's (1971) more famous "veil of ignorance." One important difference that Brennan and Buchanan (1985: 30f.) themselves have pointed to is that the first is not a purely hypothetical construction, but "may be approached, if never fully realized." Other than in Rawls's highly abstract thought experiment the persons who choose a constitution under a veil of uncertainty "are modeled as they are." The veil of uncertainty is less a philosopher's trick to model the idea of impartiality than a state of mind which forms naturally whenever choices about rules which are both very general in application and quasi-permanent have to be made.

enjoys a *de facto* veto power in the subsequent negotiation process. Moreover, institutional bargaining is complicated by the fact that multiple autonomous actors have to reach agreement. This is in sharp contrast to the comparatively simple two–actor models from which situation-structuralists take most of their cues (Young 1989b: 360).

These three features – integrative bargaining (as engendered by the parties' ignorance of the contract curve), the existence of a veil of uncertainty, and the requirement of unanimity – are not the only defining characteristics of the model of institutional bargaining, but they are of central importance in the derivation of the more specific hypotheses Young puts forward to explain processes of regime formation. The other characteristic properties of institutional bargaining that Young highlights are (1) the problem-oriented approach that actors tend to adopt (i.e. their tendency to focus on a limited number of key problems rather than seeking to "perfect their information regarding the full range of outcomes and the dimensions of the contract zones before getting down to serious bargaining" [Young 1989b: 362]), (2) the existence of intrastate divisions, which create scope for the formation of transnational alliances supportive of international cooperation, and (3) the embeddedness of the negotiation process in a broader political and socioeconomic context, which generates opportunities for linkages which may either further or undermine the efforts of the negotiators.

Hypotheses to account for success and failure in institutional bargaining

The model of institutional bargaining has both a descriptive and an analytical aspect. Descriptively, it seeks to outline the essential circumstances under which collective efforts to form regimes *regularly* take place. Analytically, it points to a number of factors that are critical for the *success* of such efforts. In rough correspondence to these two aspects of the model, the more specific hypotheses that Young subsequently develops may be seen as falling within two categories.

The *first set of hypotheses* corresponds to the analytical aspect of the model and refers to conditions external or prior to the negotiations which permit or improve the operation of the factors that the model specifies as regime-conducive. Thus, Young (1989b: 366) hypothesizes that "[i]nstitutional bargaining can succeed only when the issues at stake lend themselves to contractarian interactions." In other words, the *contractual environment* must be such that "the absence of a fully specified zone of agreement encourages integrative bargaining and the pres-

Table 2. *Factors contributing to success in institutional bargaining*

I. Factors encouraging integrative bargaining
(1) Contractual environment blurring the zone of agreement and veiling the future distribution of benefits
(2) Exogenous shock of crisis
II. Factors promoting the success of integrative bargaining
(1) Availability of equitable solution
(2) Availability of salient solution
(3) Availability of clear-cut and effective compliance mechanisms
(4) (Mixture of entrepreneurial, structural, and intellectual) leadership

ence of imperfect information ensures that a veil of uncertainty prevails" (Young 1989b: 366f.). While this hypothesis refers to more or less stable traits of the situation at hand (and seems to amount to little more than a restatement of the core idea that underlies Young's model),[43] a second one, which also falls under this category, emphasizes the significance of certain chance events within the broader context of the negotiations. To be specific, Young (1989b: 371) expects *exogenous shocks or crises* to "increase the probability of success in efforts to negotiate the terms of international regimes." Such events – the discovery of the "ozone hole" over Antarctica in 1985 provides a good example – can help the negotiating parties to refocus on their common interest (i.e. to return to integrative bargaining) and to overcome stalemates that commonly occur in institutional bargaining.

Rather than treating particular features of the model as variables, the *second group of hypotheses* take the operation of these factors for granted and specify further variables which may tip the balance against or in favor of agreement in institutional bargaining. Thus, from the unanimity rule it can be inferred that the "availability of arrangements that all participants can accept as equitable (rather than efficient) is necessary for institutional bargaining to succeed" (Young 1989b: 368). (Young does not present the need to find an *equitable solution* as a product of the veil of uncertainty, although he might have. The least that can be said is that the veil of uncertainty which, according to Young, is characteristic

[43] In a subsequent empirical test of the institutional bargaining model (Young and Osherenko 1993c) this hypothesis is disregarded. In its place, a hypothesis referring directly to integrative bargaining and uncertainty is examined.

of institutional bargaining *helps* the participants to settle upon terms of a constitutional contract that are regarded as equitable by all [see also Brennan and Buchanan 1985: 30].)

The next two hypotheses point to conditions the presence of which is not presumed to be necessary for regime formation to take place, but to increase the probability that a bargain is struck eventually. The first of these conditions is met, when a *salient solution* to the problem at hand exists. Salience, in turn, derives from simplicity and clarity, or familiarity (Young 1989b: 369; Young and Osherenko 1993a: 14). Young is aware that this hypothesis may appear as incompatible with the reasoning that had led him to consider the presence of a veil of uncertainty an important *facilitating* condition in the process of international regime formation. He believes, however, that it is not impossible for the two ideas to be valid simultaneously: "While a salient solution must be formulated in a simple manner that is easy for everyone to grasp and remember, its very simplicity may also cause it to be ambiguous and uncertain, leaving much to be resolved after the regime is in place." (Young and Osherenko 1993a: 15)

The other condition making success in negotiations among self-interested, autonomous actors more likely is the availability of "clear-cut and effective" *compliance mechanisms* (Young 1989b: 370). Here, Young resumes a theme he had touched upon in the first part of his critique of mainstream utilitarian models of regime formation: the fear of states that their partners in a projected regime may attempt to cheat on them, which may keep them from concluding an agreement in the first place. The more easily, therefore, this fear can be removed or diminished, the more likely a collective attempt is made to coordinate state behavior in the issue-area for mutual benefit.

The final hypothesis recasts an argument which has played a central role in power-based accounts of regimes (see sect. 4.1 below): "Institutional bargaining is likely to succeed when effective leadership emerges; it will fail in the absence of such leadership." (Young 1989b: 373) *Leadership*, in this sense, may be provided by one actor or by several. In the original formulation of his model, Young (1989b: 373f.) characterizes leaders as "entrepreneurs" or "brokers" who use negotiation skill and ingenuity (rather than power) to present issues in such a way as to facilitate agreement and to come up with new institutional options when negotiations are in danger of becoming stuck. This catalytic role may be played by states, international organizations, NGOs, or even individuals.

In the course of subsequent research, Young (1991) subjected this hypothesis to a couple of significant modifications, which include both revisions and refinements (see also Young and Osherenko 1993a: 18f.). First, he no longer maintains that leadership is a sufficient condition for success in institutional bargaining (Young 1991: 285; 1994: 114). Second, in the revised version of the hypothesis, only individuals are leaders in the relevant sense. Certainly, this is an important modification and one which contrasts sharply with the mainstream of contemporary international relations theory (including the study of regimes), where third-image (i.e. system-level) and second-image (i.e. state-level) explanations prevail. (Note that this specification does not imply that leaders in processes of regime formation cannot be representatives of states or other organizations. Much more often than not, they are.) Third, entrepreneurial leadership is only one way in which the activities of individuals may be crucial for success in institutional bargaining. Two other types of leaders are equally significant: (1) structural leaders, who, usually acting as representatives of a major state, skillfully convert power based on the possession of material resources into bargaining leverage, employing carefully timed and directed threats and promises to further the process of institution-building; and (2) intellectual leaders, who use "the power of ideas to shape the way in which participants in institutional bargaining understand the issues at stake and to orient their thinking about options available to come to terms with these issues" (Young 1991: 288). Finally, this differentiation of the leadership concept forms the basis of another specification of the hypothesis: Young (1991: 303–5) expects attempts at regime formation to fail unless at least two forms of leadership interact.

Evaluating the model empirically

Young did not content himself with enriching the theoretical discussion about international regimes with a new model of regime formation. Together with Gail Osherenko he initiated and directed a multinational collaborative research project in which various hypotheses designed to account for the formation of regimes were tested empirically (Young and Osherenko 1993c). The hypotheses under scrutiny include the interest-based ones associated with the model of institutional bargaining as well as various power-based and knowledge-based propositions (Young and Osherenko 1993c: 263–6). Methodologically, the project relies on "structured or focused case studies" (Young and Osherenko 1993c: ix). Among the six cases examined there is only one non-regime case, i.e. only one case study deals with an issue-area in which no regime was instituted during the period of inquiry (Arctic haze). Geographically, the project concentrates on issue-areas which are related to the Arctic region. Finally, all cases under consideration belong to the policy arena of environmental and resources issues (although one, the Svalbard regime, has a security dimension as well).[44]

The overall result of the test for the hypotheses derived from the model of institutional bargaining is quite encouraging. Only for two of these hypotheses do the authors of the case studies report evidence "that tends to disconfirm [the] hypothesis" (Young and Osherenko 1993b: 232f.). Moreover, with both hypotheses, this disconfirming evidence is not found across the board, but only in one of the six case studies. Young and Osherenko, therefore, are not prepared at this stage to scrap either of these hypotheses. In fact, as far as the degree of confirmation is concerned, they find it necessary to distinguish between only two sets of interest-based hypotheses. "With regard to the specific hypotheses tested, the role of individual leaders received such strong support that we now believe it may constitute a necessary condition for regime formation. A second group of hypotheses received enough support to suggest that they tap important (though not strictly necessary) conditions for the formation of regimes." (Young and Osherenko 1993b: 232) This second group comprises the hypotheses emphasizing the importance of equity, salience, compliance mechanisms, exogenous shocks, integrative bargaining, and a veil of uncertainty. In other words, none of the hypotheses implicit in the model of institutional bargaining has failed the test. This is certainly good news for Young's approach as well as for anyone seeking a better understanding of the factors driving the emergence of international regimes.

At the same time, the very success of the model makes it important not to overlook the limitations of this test. Young and Osherenko (1993c: vii) themselves point to some such restrictions and refer to their project as a beginning rather than a conclusion. Thus, the number of cases (even though larger than in many comparable studies) is still quite small, and selection bias cannot be ruled out. Consequently, Young and Osherenko (1993b: 252) do not regard their results as in any way definitive, but encourage further empirical studies, which may either lend

44 Except for those already mentioned, the cases studied in the project are the regime for the management of the North Pacific fur seals, the regime for the conservation of the polar bear, the ozone protection regime, and the regime for the reduction of long-range transboundary air pollution (introduced as a contrast case to Arctic haze).

additional support to their findings or raise questions as to their generalizability.

In our view, it is particularly important that future tests aim at a better overall balance between regime and non-regime cases. As long as the cases studied display little (or no) variation on the dependent variable, causal hypotheses seeking to explain outcome variation with regard to this variable cannot be evaluated (King, Keohane, and Verba 1994: 129; Collier 1995: 464).[45] To be sure, some of the hypotheses that Young, Osherenko, and their collaborators have examined state necessary conditions for the emergence of regimes and thus can be falsified (or disconfirmed) within the confines of a research design that does not include non-regime cases. But even so, we would need to look at non-regime cases as well, not in order to test the truth of these hypotheses (a purpose for which non-regime cases would not be appropriate), but to make sure that we really gain explanatory leverage from them. The following consideration may explain why this is the case.

At first sight, any corroborated hypothesis that pinpoints a necessary condition of regime formation would seem to be a highly useful instrument for explaining failure (though not success) in institutional bargaining. But on reflection it turns out that this is not so. The reason is that the fact that all regimes emerge in the presence of some phenomenon does not imply that this phenomenon is likely to be ever absent in the universe of cases (i.e. the set of institutional bargaining events). On the contrary, the presence of this phenomenon may be systematically associated with the occurrence of institutional bargaining. Thus, the fact that leadership is observable in any regime formation process (assuming it is a fact) is perfectly compatible with the possibility that leadership activities are a regular concomitant of institutional bargaining as such. If this possibility were reality, however, *which we cannot rule out without taking non-regime cases into account*, knowing that leadership is a necessary condition for regime formation would be of no help in "accounting for the actual record of success and failure in efforts to form

45 As noted earlier, the sample of issue-areas studied by Young, Osherenko, and their collaborators includes only one in which no regime has been created during the period of inquiry. Moreover, the relevance of this one non-regime case (Arctic haze) may be doubted, because it does not seem to meet the precondition under which we would expect interest-based hypotheses to operate, viz. the existence of a zone of agreement (Soroos 1993: 197). It is not strictly true, though, that no non-regime cases whatsoever are included in the study. On some occasions, researchers, in their evaluation of a given hypothesis, take into account earlier periods in which the value of the relevant variable was different (e.g. no effective leader existed).

international regimes" (Young 1989b: 352) – just as knowing that regime formation requires a process of institutional bargaining cannot help us explain successful instances of institutional bargaining.

The task may also be put this way: we need to determine how constraining or selective with respect to the universe of cases the conditions hypothesized as necessary or facilitating really are. Also, we believe that this task cannot be fulfilled unless additional efforts are made to operationalize some of the independent variables included in the model of institutional bargaining. For example, exactly what does it mean for an *equitable solution* to be available in a given instance of institutional bargaining? To apply the equity hypothesis meaningfully, we need to have answers to at least two questions: (1) What is a possible *solution* to an international issue? (2) What marks a solution that is likely to be regarded as *equitable* by participants in a process of institutional bargaining? As to the first question, a conceivable specification of the range of possible solutions to an international problem is the set of institutional arrangements that would be Pareto-efficient (or, alternatively, Pareto-superior) in this situation. To answer the second question, we would have to identify (independently of the outcome) the relevant "community standards regarding equity" (Young 1989b: 369). Knowing these standards we can then ask whether the contract curve (or, if we choose the alternative option for specifying possible solutions, the contract zone) in the situation at hand includes a point (i.e. a possible arrangement) that satisfies these standards. If it does not, we would expect no regime to be formed, and, accordingly, if (or to the extent that) this expectation is proven wrong the hypothesis is disconfirmed. But no matter if these answers are helpful or misleading, the point remains that the questions must be asked, when it comes to probing the empirical validity of the equity hypothesis as well as the explanatory leverage we achieve as a result of its corroboration.[46]

[46] In the empirical test, Young's research team encountered difficulties in applying this hypothesis. Occasionally, equity and efficiency (which had been opposed to one another in the original version of the hypothesis) were found to coincide. It was then agreed to regard the hypothesis as confirmed as long as no proposed arrangement (whether efficient or not) is adopted that the parties cannot accept as equitable (Young and Osherenko 1993b: 255). But note that this clarification at best solves only part of the problem of operationalization. We still do not know what characterizes situations in which equitable solutions are available. Moreover, if our suggestion of identifying the set of possible solutions with the contract curve makes sense, the reformulation of the hypothesis may even be misleading: it is not only that equitable solutions *can* also be efficient – any equitable *solution* there is *must* be. (It may be argued that our suggestion

What if it should turn out that the explanatory leverage of some of the hypotheses derived by Young so far is indeed not very great, because the values of the corresponding variables hardly change across the universe of cases, or because, in other words, the availability of equitable solutions (or salient solutions or effective compliance mechanisms, etc.) is the rule in institutional bargaining, while success in such efforts is not? This may be unlikely, but as long as additional cases have not been examined and clear-cut operationalizations have not been provided, the question is an open one. We believe that even in that case the hypothesis concerned would not necessarily become useless. However, it would have to be recast as a descriptive hypothesis regarding some generic feature of regimes (e.g. regimes tend to incorporate equitable solutions or salient solutions, etc.) rather than a causal hypothesis about some determinant of the success or failure of institutional bargaining.[47]

The final issue we would like to raise has to do with the logical structure of Young's approach. As we have seen, in his original formulation, Young (1989b: 349) made a distinction between the *model* of institutional bargaining (in which integrative bargaining and a veil of uncertainty occupied key roles) and various *hypotheses* "about the determinants of success in institutional bargaining," which, in his view, can be derived from this model. It is, therefore, somewhat surprising to discover that, in the context of the empirical test, integrative bargaining and the veil of uncertainty seem to have lost their special status as theoretical assumptions and are treated as just two interest-based variables among several. We think it is unfortunate to blur the distinction between the model (or theory) of institutional bargaining and the hypotheses derived from this model, because doing so tends to jeopardize much of the unusual coherence and deductive promise of this approach to regime formation. Without a separation of core assumptions, students of regimes have no way of knowing which hypotheses belong to this theory and which do not. They are in danger of ending up with a mere list of variables which provide them with no clue whatsoever as to how to construct theory

is beside the point, because it is incompatible with Young's overall approach, which stresses the absence of a well-specified contract curve. Perhaps this is true, but this must not detract attention from the fact that *some* plausible answer is needed to the question of what defines the set of possible solutions to an international issue.)

47 Indeed, most of the supportive evidence that Young, Osherenko, and their collaborators come up with in the case studies might as well be read to indicate that actors involved in institutional bargaining seek (or select) equitable solutions, salient solutions, etc. rather than respond to their "availability."

from them. Rather than dispensing with the model as a separate set of basic ideas,[48] therefore, it may be worthwhile elaborating on it by carefully rethinking these ideas and trying to tighten up the logical connection between the model, on the one hand, and the specific hypotheses, on the other. Presumably, looking more closely at the logical relationship between model assumptions and hypotheses would reveal that some of the hypotheses presently under consideration are closer to the core than others. This, in turn, would help us draw the appropriate theoretical conclusions from future empirical tests. Not least important, we would have a better idea of when to regard the theory as falsified.

[48] It is tempting to attribute at least part of the difficulties members of the research team had applying the integrative bargaining hypothesis (Young and Osherenko 1993b: 239) to the inadequacy of trying to test theoretical assumptions directly (Waltz 1979: ch. 1). Note also that mixing assumptions and hypotheses may lead to confusing and paradoxical results, something which seems to have happened here: the underlying theoretical propositions ("integrative bargaining," "veil of uncertainty") have done worse in the test than the derivative hypotheses (all except for "exogenous shocks or crises") (Young and Osherenko 1993b: 232f.)!

4 Power-based theories: hegemony, distributional conflict, and relative gains

Neoliberal theories of regimes may be characterized in terms of their "dialectical" relationship to realism. Neoliberals not eschewing Hegelian jargon could describe their approach as a "synthesis" of realism and its traditional antithesis, liberalism, which "preserves" elements of "truth" to be found in the two opposing perspectives on international relations. Thus, neoliberals can adhere to the *realist* tenet that states are the most important actors on the world scene which act out of self-interest in an anarchical environment, without needing to renounce the *liberal* insight that states are able to realize common interests through cooperation and use international institutions to this end. Such a description, of course, implies that neoliberalism as theory is superior to both realism and more traditional forms of liberalism.[1] Not surprisingly, realists (Mearsheimer 1995) as well as liberals (Moravcsik 1992) have taken up this challenge and defended their preferred theoretical perspectives against the pretensions of neoliberalism.

What is more important in this context, however, is that the realist contribution to the debate about international regimes can by no means be reduced to restatements of orthodox realist interpretations of international politics as a state of war which militates against any significant role for international institutions. In this chapter we examine three

[1] Keohane (1984: 14) himself has usually preferred to describe the claims of neoliberalism in more modest terms, referring to his approach as a supplement to, or modification of, realism. Occasionally, however, he has not shirked a more assertive language: "In comparing neoliberal institutionalism with neorealism, we must understand that neoliberal institutionalism is not simply an alternative to neorealism, but, in fact, claims to subsume it." (Keohane 1989c: 15) Keck (1991; 1993) has explicitly argued that neoliberalism (or, in his terms, "rational institutionalism") represents a (successful) *synthesis* of realism and liberalism (or, as Keck prefers to say, "functionalism").

formulations which are self-consciously realist and yet take international cooperation and regimes, both in the security realm and beyond, seriously as significant phenomena to be accounted for by international relations theory. Each in its own specific way, they offer outlines of alternative power-based explanations of international regimes which depart from neoliberalism in important respects.

Realist theories of regimes emphasize relative power capabilities as a central explanatory variable and stress states' sensitivity to distributional aspects of cooperation and regimes. They share neoliberalism's commitment to rationalism and parsimonious systemic theorizing, although they tend to specify states' utility functions differently. Unlike the persons in John Rawls's (1971) famous "original position" who are rational but feel no envy, states in the realist paradigm care for how well their competitors do. In this case, envy is born out of fear, i.e. concerns about one's survival and independence. As a consequence, rule-based cooperation is less easily established than neoliberal theories suggest, and more likely to unravel as a result of shifts in the distribution of power resources or of unforeseen distributional consequences of regimes.

A classical example of a power-based theory of international regimes is the *theory of hegemonic stability* which links the existence of effective international institutions to a unipolar configuration of power in the issue-area in question. We trace the argument underlying this account and discuss some of the problems it encounters in the following section (4.1). Looking into this theory is worthwhile not least because it has played a catalytic role in the articulation of the neoliberal and now mainstream argument about regimes. To some extent, the interest-based account of regimes, in particular contractualism, has emerged from a critical analysis of the limits of the hegemonic stability hypothesis (Keohane 1984). This productive pattern, although with reversed premises, has recurred in the case of the two realist accounts of international regimes under scrutiny in the remainder of this chapter: both Stephen Krasner's *power-oriented research program* (sect. 4.2) and Joseph Grieco's reconstruction *of modern realism's theory of cooperation among nations* (sect. 4.3) have grown out of thorough critiques of Keohane's functional (contractualist) theory of regimes.[2]

[2] Neither Krasner nor Grieco has come up with a handy tag for his approach. But occasionally they have used expressions to refer to their own perspectives which may be appropriated for this purpose, even though it is quite obvious that these somewhat unspecific terms were not meant to serve as quasi-official labels in the same way as

Not surprisingly, Krasner and Grieco also share numerous critical themes in their dealings with neoliberalism. Most important among these is their common emphasis on relative power capabilities and distributional issues which they regard as strongly (and fatally) undervalued in neoliberal arguments about regimes. As a consequence, they dismiss the standard 2 × 2 Prisoner's Dilemma representation of the cooperation problem faced by states: since PD exhibits a single cooperative solution (each player forgoes his dominant strategy), which appears to be equally valued by both actors (both receiving a pay-off of 3), the distributional conflicts that plague real-world cooperative ventures are obscured in this representation. Yet, as we have seen (sect. 3.1), neoliberalism, especially in its contractualist variant, relies heavily on precisely this game model when developing its argument about the role of regimes in furthering international cooperation.[3] Moreover, according to both accounts, regimes display less robustness and thus depend for their continuing effectiveness more strongly on favorable circumstances than is claimed by neoliberal formulations (let alone cognitivist ones).[4]

The most conspicuous *difference* between Krasner's and Grieco's

"contractualism" or "institutional bargaining." Thus, Krasner (1991: 362), after presenting his critique of neoliberalism and outlining his own approach, calls for a "power-oriented research program." Similarly, Grieco (1988a; 1990; 1993a; 1993b), in his central contributions to the most recent round of the realism – liberalism debate, tends to prefer the term "modern realism" to either "realism" or "neorealism" (although he also uses the latter terms now and then). Perhaps this preference reflects his view that, with regard to the issues he is interested in, realists and neorealists do not differ (Grieco 1988a: 485, n. 1).

[3] Other scholars engaged in developing power-based arguments about regimes and related objects of investigation (such as open trading systems) are similarly critical of using PD as a starting point for analysis. See Alt, Calvert, and Humes (1988: 460), Gowa (1989a), and Gowa and Mansfield (1993).

[4] Of the two authors, Grieco appears to be the more skeptical as regards the ability of international institutions to influence international politics and, in particular, patterns of cooperation and discord. Nevertheless, closer inspection of his argument reveals that he is far from denying regimes any impact in this connection (see sect. 4.3 below). The nature of Krasner's institutionalism is likewise difficult to pinpoint. In an earlier article, devoted to sovereignty (Krasner 1988), he even took an unambiguously cognitivist stance, attributing a high measure of robustness to this particular institution and arguing the inability of rationalist approaches (including both neoliberalism and realism) to cope adequately with this phenomenon (but then see also Krasner 1993b). In this chapter, however, we focus on Krasner's "power-oriented research program," which is most clearly articulated in two, more recent articles dealing with regimes in the issue-areas of global communications and human rights, respectively (Krasner 1991; 1993a).

approaches concerns the specific role that each author attributes to power within his account. As will become obvious in the course of our discussion, Krasner focuses on power as a *means* of statecraft, whereas Grieco emphasizes power as an *end* (though not the ultimate one) of foreign policy. This has important consequences for their predictions about regime content: whereas for Grieco, regimes tend to exhibit a balanced distribution of gains from cooperation or otherwise collapse, Krasner's analysis is consistent with pronounced distributional biases in favor of the most powerful actors in the issue-area.

4.1 Hegemonic stability theory

Hegemonic stability theory – a theory of regimes?

Historically, the relationship between the theory of hegemonic stability and the study of international regimes has been both close and complex (van Ham 1992). Given that hegemonic stability theory has been employed as a structural explanation of changes in international regimes (including their formation and demise) it would seem that it is best regarded as a specific theoretical account of regimes among others. Nevertheless, *regime theory* could be portrayed and indeed, to a considerable extent, has been developed as a conscious *alternative* to the theory of hegemonic stability and its implications for international cooperation.

This paradox can be solved by having recourse to the two aspects of regime impact, which, in the Introduction, we have labeled "effectiveness" and "resilience" (or "robustness") of international institutions. The theory of hegemonic stability, which links strong international regimes to the existence of a dominant state in the respective issue-area, seeks to explain when and why international regimes emerge and are *effective* in the sense that states follow cooperative policies which, in the absence of a regime, they would most likely not pursue. To that extent, the theory certainly *is* a theory of international regimes – a fact that, together with the extensive scholarly debate the theory has given rise to, justifies its inclusion in this overview. However, proponents of the hegemonic stability hypothesis are also characteristically skeptical as regards the *robustness* of international regimes: once the (unipolar) power structure that underlies a given regime dissolves, the regime itself, according to this view, is bound to collapse or turn into an ineffective cluster of norms and rules which are violated whenever states perceive this to be in their best interest. As a consequence, authors who emphasize the propensity of international regimes to "assume a life of their own, a life independent of the basic causal factors that lead to their creation in the first place" (Krasner 1983b: 357) tend to deny the theory of hegemonic stability – at least in its crudest, most uncompromising form – the status of a regime theory proper.

Thus, Keohane (1984: 31), referring to the hegemonic stability hypothesis and preluding a thorough critique of this hypothesis, remarks that "my emphasis on how international institutions such as regimes facilitate cooperation only makes sense if cooperation and discord are *not* determined simply by interests and power" (emphasis added). At the same time, it is in this author's writings and thought that the complex and sometimes ambiguous relationship between regime and hegemony theory is perhaps most pronounced. *After Hegemony*, arguably the most influential work on regimes so far, relies almost as much on the theory of hegemonic stability as it criticizes it. To be sure, Keohane rejects the crude version of the theory in order to bring out the autonomous significance of regimes. However, as we have seen (sect. 3.1), he also admits that hegemony often does play an important (though not essential) role in the formation of international regimes. What is more, he bases his argument for the robustness of regimes in part on the difficulties of "regime-creation in the absence of hegemony" (Keohane 1984: 100). Finally, it should not be forgotten that he was one of the first scholars to introduce arguments about the stabilizing effects of power concentration in world politics into the nascent study of international regimes – a marriage of ideas which he no doubt regarded as promising at the time (Keohane 1980).[5]

The origins of hegemonic stability theory

Part of these complexities may be rooted in the fact that the theory of hegemonic stability did not come into existence as one designed to account for international regimes. The theory originated in economist

[5] In fact, Keohane must be credited with the catchy term "theory of hegemonic stability," which has stuck, although not all scholars contributing to this agenda are perfectly happy with its associations (Kindleberger 1986; Lake 1993: 460, n. 1). As it is common in the literature, we use the terms "theory of hegemonic stability" and "hegemonic stability hypothesis" interchangeably. The latter term, though it is less often used, may actually be more appropriate, because it suggests that the proposition is not self-sufficient, but is backed up by a distinct and more general theory, in this case Olson's theory of collective action.

Charles Kindleberger's (1973: 305) work on the Great Depression of the late 1920s and the 1930s, in which he argued that "for the world economy to be stabilized, there has to be a stabilizer, *one* stabilizer" (emphasis added). Kindleberger's dependent variable was not the institutionalization of segments of international politics or the strength of regimes across issue-areas. Rather he focused on the creation and maintenance of what David Lake (1993: 462f.) has aptly termed "the international economic infrastructure," which includes a medium of exchange, sufficient liquidity, and a set of basic property rights. Kindleberger observed that stability in this sense is an international public (or collective) good.[6] This is a crucial step in the construction of his argument, because it allows him to locate his *explanandum*, stability in the world economy, within the broader context of Mancur Olson's (1965) theory of collective action. In fact, the theory of hegemonic stability is a special case of Olson's theory – or so it purports to be.

Olson sought to explain why groups of rational actors often cannot be expected to act on behalf of their common interest. Furthering the common interest of a group, he argued, amounts to providing it with a public good. *Public goods* are characterized by the attribute that exclusion of any member of the group from the consumption of the good is not economically feasible. The classic exemplar of a public good is the lighthouse. One collective good that Olson studies in greater detail is wage rates and working conditions under legislation which precludes discrimination among workers on the basis of their membership of the relevant unions. The impossibility of exclusion inherent in collective goods has most important implications for the incentives of (rationally motivated) group members to pay for the good and hence for the likelihood of it being provided in the first place. Olson's theory works out these implications for different contexts, with group size as the central contextual variable.[7]

[6] Throughout this book we treat the words "collective good" and "public good" as synonyms.

[7] "Pure" public goods are not only non-excludable, but also "in joint supply" meaning that additional consumers do not reduce the amount of the good that is available to the rest of the group. In other words, there are no "crowding effects." The core of Olson's theory does not depend on the desired group goods displaying jointness in supply, though. Therefore, he adopts the broader definition of "collective good" that we have paraphrased in the text. He notes, however, that most of the group goals he in fact considers in his study are to a large extent "joint" (Olson 1965: 14, n. 21). Moreover, his analysis of "inclusive" and "exclusive" groups is largely based on the jointness-characteristics of the collective goods at issue (Olson 1965: 36–43).

In a nutshell, Olson argues that large groups are *qualitatively* different from small ones. More specifically, in the absence of coercion or additional inducement besides the potential benefits of the public good itself, large groups will fail to produce what would be collective goods to them, whereas the prospects of smaller groups are much brighter in this regard. In particular, some small groups are *privileged* by the fact that (at least) one member of the group has a sufficiently strong interest in the good as to make it rational for her to provide (some amount of) the good even if no-one shares in the costs (Olson 1965: 49f.). Assuming that interest in the good increases with the "size" of the actor,[8] two conclusions follow immediately: (1) internal asymmetry works to the group's advantage; (2) since no member of the group can be excluded from the benefits of the collective good whether he helped to provide it or not, there is "a systematic tendency for 'exploitation' of the great by the small" (Olson 1965: 29): the smaller actors will take a "free ride" on the largest member's readiness to supply the good all by herself if necessary.

In essence, then, Kindleberger's thesis is that only the presence of an outstanding economic and political power which has the capacity (and the willingness) to lead can make the group of states who participate in the world economy a "privileged group" by supplying and supporting the infrastructure that permits comparatively smooth and mutually beneficial international exchange to take place. At different times in modern economic history, Britain and the United States played this essential part of a leader of the world economy. When the strength of the stabilizer wanes, however, the stability of the system is at risk as well. At the end of the day, no great power cooperation will be able to substitute for some one state shouldering the burden of leadership. Consequently, Kindleberger regards the relative decline of the United States since about the late 1960s as a development that causes difficulties not only for that particular country, but, in the final analysis, runs counter to the interests of the system as a whole (at least as long as no successor in leadership is in sight). "[T]he danger we face is not too much power, but too little, not an excess of domination, but a superfluity of would-be free riders, unwilling to mind the store, and waiting for a storekeeper to appear." (Kindleberger 1981: 253)

Hegemonic stability theory (as the term is used in this chapter)

[8] For example, larger firms, *ceteris paribus*, benefit more from a higher market price achieved through oligopolistic collusion than do smaller ones.

applies this reasoning to *international regimes* asserting that (1) regimes are established and maintained by actors who hold a preponderance of power resources (relevant to the issue-area in question) and that (2) regimes decline (i.e. decrease in strength or effectiveness) when power becomes more equally distributed among their members (Keohane 1980). The underlying assumption is that international regimes are (or involve) public goods for the states in the issue-area.

It should be noted that Kindleberger would probably not endorse this extended interpretation of his argument. Most of what he regards as the leader's responsibilities refers to immediate unilateral action to be taken by the stabilizer under given circumstances (e.g. providing a "market for distress goods" and a "steady if not countercyclical flow of capital") (Kindleberger 1981: 247). Regimes are mentioned only as an unpromising alternative to unilateral leadership (Kindleberger 1981: 252). Moreover, he is uneasy with the term "hegemon," which, in his view, carries misleading "overtones of force, threat, pressure," while in fact "it is possible to lead without arm-twisting, to act responsibly without pushing and shoving other countries" (Kindleberger 1986: 841f.).[9]

Benevolent and coercive hegemons

In his illuminating critique of the theory of hegemonic stability, Duncan Snidal (1985b: 285–90) distinguishes two strands of the theory, which differ in the way they describe the precise character of the hegemon's policies and in particular their distributional implications. The first variant, which Snidal refers to as the *benevolent leadership model*, depicts a hegemonic state which provides the collective good (in this case, an effective international regime) all by itself, while the other states basically are freed from the responsibility to help maintain the regime. Thus, this variant adheres (as does Kindleberger himself) to Olson's insight that, when public goods are at issue, the great tend to be "exploited" by the small. The formula "exploitation of the great by the small" does not imply that the hegemon's "advantage" (or net gain) is smaller than that received by the free-riders. Advantage is benefits (received from the good) minus costs (of provision of the good), and, by assumption, the largest actor's benefits are greater than those of the smaller ones. Thus,

[9] Besides Kindleberger, Gilpin (1972; 1975) made important early contributions to the then new research agenda; however, he failed to emphasize at that time the public good nature of his *explanandum*, international economic openness. In his more recent statements on hegemonic stability theory Gilpin (1981; 1987) has explicitly employed public good arguments.

depending both on the ratio of benefits to costs and on the distribution of actor size within the group, the hegemon's net gains may well exceed those of some or even all other states. What the formula does imply, though, is that the smaller actors effectively receive *rents* due to the hegemon's action.

The second variant, which Snidal calls the *coercive leadership model* and which he finds best represented in Robert Gilpin's (1981) study of war and hegemony, also assumes that a dominant state is required to produce the international public good. What is different in this model, though, is that the highly asymmetric "size" of the actors in the issue-area does not only (or primarily) mean that there is likely to be some one state whose individual *interest* in the good is so great that it is willing to supply it for itself and the rest of the group. Rather, the model assumes that the hegemon can and does use its superior *power* to force others to contribute as well, *de facto* "taxing" them for the collective good provided under his leadership. It is implicit in this perspective that the resulting distribution of burdens need not be proportional to actors' gains (or accord with any other notion of justice). In fact, the relationship between the "exploiting" and the "exploited" characteristic of the benevolent leadership model may easily be reversed – or rather put back on its feet, as many orthodox realists as well as many Marxists would argue.

Given this bifurcation, it might be argued that only one variant of hegemonic stability theory, the coercive leadership model, is genuinely power-based, whereas the other, the benevolent leadership model, is indeed interest-based and, consequently, had rather be subsumed under neoliberalism. Moreover, the fact that the benevolent hegemon puts up with its "exploitation" by the smaller actors might seem to be inconsistent with the realist tenet that states exhibit a low tolerance for relative losses. This argument has some force and reflects the close relationship between realism and neoliberalism as rationalist theories of regimes. Still, it is not cogent. First, in contrast with neoliberal theories, the distribution of interests highlighted by the benevolent leadership model is directly rooted in, and thus reducible to, a specific distribution of power resources. Second, as we shall see shortly, the exercise of power is likely to belong to the behavioral repertoire of the benevolent hegemon as well, blurring the distinction between a power-based and an interest-based model of hegemonic leadership even further. Third, as we have just observed, "exploitation of the great by the small" does not entail that the hegemon suffers a loss relative to others, although this *may* be the case in concrete instances of hegemonic cooperation. Moreover, tolerance for relative loss is not *per se* inconsistent with realist expectations. As we shall see below (sect. 4.3), realists assume that sensitivity to relative performance is a variable and hypothesize its value to be low if the power gap is so large that no conceivable asymmetry in gains from cooperation is likely to affect the relative power positions of states.

Snidal's typology is certainly useful. We agree, however, with commentators who have suggested that the two models had better be regarded as extremes of a continuum (Alt, Calvert, and Humes 1988: 447f., 462; Lake 1993: 467f.). At least, students of regimes should reckon with the possibility of a significant gray area. In fact, Snidal (1985b: 590) himself, pointing to studies by Keohane (1984) and Timothy McKeown (1983), concedes that "the two models are not logically incompatible," adding that "[s]ome combination of coercion and benevolence may obtain" (see also Yarbrough and Yarbrough 1987: 15f.). The same conclusion suggests itself when one looks somewhat more closely at what it means for an international regime to be "provided" and, consequently, for states to contribute to its provision. For this purpose, a distinction of two levels at which states may or may not cooperate in a regime context proves helpful.

First-order cooperation takes place whenever states adjust their policies with regard to certain substantive issues in a mutually beneficial way.[10] Usually, such cooperation is aided or structured by agreed-upon rules of conduct or regimes (although it does not strictly presuppose the existence of such rules: cooperation might be spontaneous and tacit). For example, in the issue-area of international trade, states may adopt and comply with common rules that prescribe the dismantling of certain barriers to free trade (tariffs, non-tariff barriers), thus reaping joint benefits in the form of efficiency gains and higher growth rates. What the concept of first-order cooperation leaves open is how the rules of cooperation come about (i.e. how rules are made) and why they are observed by self-interested actors, who sometimes must sacrifice greater short-term gains in order to act in accordance with the regime (i.e. how rules are enforced). This is where the notion of *second-order cooperation* comes in: both rule-making and rule-enforcement involve costs. These costs

[10] This formulation, of course, is patterned upon Keohane's (1984: 52) definition of the term "cooperation" (see sect. 3.1 above); however, he does not distinguish between two levels of regime-related cooperation.

may be either shared by several actors or borne entirely by one. Only in the first case (i.e. when the costs of rule-making and rule-enforcement *are* shared by at least some states) do we speak of second-order cooperation taking place within a regime.

The theory of hegemonic stability implicitly denies the ability of states to engage in (large-scale) collective action: no regime emerges in an issue-area, unless the group is privileged such that the collective good can be supplied by *independent* action. This skepticism about international cooperation is one of two features of the theory which place it squarely into the realist tradition (the other being its reliance on the distribution of power as its central explanatory variable) (Snidal 1985b: 593). We are now in a better position to see just what this skepticism means – and what it does not mean. Clearly, the theory of hegemonic stability *does not* rule out *first-order cooperation* at the international level, for the simple reason that it claims to explain the formation and demise of effective international regimes, which, in turn, imply cooperation among states with regard to the issues at stake (Keohane 1980: 132). To be sure, it is conceivable that rules might be imposed on a group of states which make some of them worse off. In this case we could not speak of cooperation which, by definition, requires mutual benefits (Keohane 1988: 380). Hegemonic stability theory, however, precludes this logical possibility by virtue of its interpretation of regimes as international *collective* goods. As a consequence, the theory's rejection of the possibility of collective action by states has to be understood in terms of the impossibility of *second-order cooperation* in the domains of rule-making and rule-enforcement. As a theory of regimes the theory of hegemonic stability does not and cannot claim that states are unable to cooperate. It does claim, though, that states cannot be expected to join forces in order to secure the *preconditions* for their mutual cooperation – a set of sufficiently clear and constraining rules and their reliable enforcement – in some issue-area.[11]

Having specified the sphere of hegemonic action in terms of rule-making and rule-enforcement, we can now re-examine the distinction between benevolent and coercive leadership. What distinguishes one from the other, according to Snidal (1985b: 588), is the hegemon's (in)ability "to induce others to share costs": coercive hegemons are

[11] Rule-making and rule-enforcement are sometimes also discussed as the *second-order problems* of supply and sanctioning, respectively (Axelrod and Keohane 1986: 255; Ostrom 1990: 42f.; Zangl 1994: 284–7).

capable of "taxing" the beneficiaries of their actions, whereas benevolent ones are not. While this criterion seems clear enough, it cannot be overlooked that it leaves ample room for graduation on either side of the line suggesting that benevolence in hegemony is not a binary variable. Thus, Snidal's criterion of benevolence is consistent with a hegemon who lacks the power to "tax" others, but is nevertheless not too weak to impose effective sanctions upon would-be free-riders (at the level of first-order cooperation), thus forcing them to comply with the regime. At the same time, there are likely to be other benevolent hegemons who are indeed too weak to implement such a policy, having to rely instead exclusively on persuasion and bribes. Clearly, whether or not a benevolent hegemon has this capacity of imposing sanctions does make a considerable difference for the nature of its "rule." Therefore, it is important not to mistake benevolent hegemony for a homogeneous category of behavior. And indeed, we should expect to find varying degrees of *coercion* on this side of Snidal's dividing line as well.[12]

One issue that appears to be in need of further clarification is the way in which the coercive hegemon collects its "taxes." Most likely, the hegemon will not want to rely on *ad hoc* compensations (the Gulf War model, so to speak), but will seek to *institutionalize* a steady flow of resources from the other actors in the issue-area by forcing upon them a regime which is distributionally biased in its favor. If this is correct, two additional observations can be made, one of a substantive, the other of a methodological nature. First, even for a coercive hegemon, opportunities for exploiting others are normally highly circumscribed. The reason is that institutionalizing higher degrees of inequality into the regime will not only increase the amount of compensation for the leader, but also decrease the legitimacy of the hegemonically sponsored order and thus increase both the expected frequency of challenges to this order and the overall sanctioning costs to be borne by the hegemon.[13] Second,

[12] It is not necessary to assume that a hegemon who is strong enough occasionally to put considerable pressure on rule-violators has also sufficient power to induce other states (especially middle-sized ones) to compensate it for its actions in favor of the long-term viability of the institution. Consequently, the fact that a hegemon is non-coercive in Snidal's terminology does not imply that "arm-twisting" does not belong to its behavioral repertoire. For an intriguing game-theoretic analysis of the incentives that objectively weak hegemons may have to use *costly* sanctions as a way of investing in their reputation (an investment which, in turn, can make future sanctions superfluous) see Alt, Calvert, and Humes (1988).

[13] This theme will crop up again in the next chapter (sect. 5.2), when we discuss Cox's concept of hegemony.

since, by definition, this strategy of diverting resources towards themselves must be unavailable to benevolent hegemons (who are unable to raise *any* taxes), scholars who seek a better understanding of these two basic forms of international leadership (their nature and determinants) should focus on the varying constraints dominant states face in their attempts at international *rule-making*.[14]

Objection 1: Are regimes really public goods?

At the theoretical level, two main criticisms have been directed towards the theory of hegemonic stability. The first questions the interpretation of international regimes as public goods. The second takes issue with hegemony theorists' one-sided reading of the (rationalist) collective action literature, which ignores the (however limited) opportunities for cooperation in the provision of public goods to which Olson and his successors have pointed. We discuss these two objections in turn.

Young (1989a: 21, n. 31) contends that "[i]nternational regimes, like other social institutions, will ordinarily exhibit the attributes of collective goods (that is, nonexcludability and jointness of supply) to a relatively high degree." This view is not generally accepted, though. Moreover, what is at stake in this disagreement is not trivial from a theoretical point of view. As we have seen, the theory of hegemonic stability relies heavily on Olson's analysis of the provision of public goods. Therefore, if Young's contention should turn out erroneous, the hegemonic stability hypothesis would suffer a major blow, as it would be deprived of its theoretical underpinnings. (The theory might still succeed as a predictive device, but we would not know why.) If it should turn out that only some but not all regimes have the attributes of public goods, the consequences need not be fatal. Proponents of hegemonic stability theory might be able to repair their account by delimiting the scope of the theory (i.e. the set of issue-areas it applies to) in a non-tautological fashion (see Snidal 1985b: 595–7). But this possibility merely underscores how important it is for those interested in this theory to give an account of the range of regimes that can be likened to public goods.

[14] Yarbrough and Yarbrough (1987: 14, 22f.) similarly associate the hegemon's role with rule-making and rule-enforcement. Moreover, they posit that different sides of the hegemon's "nature" correspond to these two successive stages of hegemonic cooperation: while in the negotiation stage (rule-making) the "carrot" is the predominant means of inducing cooperation, in the monitoring stage (rule-enforcement) the "stick" gains in significance.

One thing to be taken into consideration when assessing the plausibility of the view that international regimes are public goods is that it is quite common for such goods to exist only in relation to a particular group of actors. Indeed, what are collective goods to some, may be private goods to others. Olson's (1965: 14, n. 21) example is a parade "that is a collective good to all those who live in tall buildings overlooking the parade route, but which appears to be a private good to those who can see it only by buying tickets for a seat in the stands along the way." With this in mind, we can reject the argument sometimes put forth that regimes cannot be (very much like) public goods, because few (if any) benefit international society *as a whole*. Thus, we disagree with Snidal (1985b: 591, n. 23) who appears to find considerable force in this argument. We think he is right only insofar as the *normative* implications of limited publicness he points to are concerned: it is true, regimes that are but "restricted public goods" (because only a limited group of states are in a position to benefit from them) are likely to be more difficult to justify ethically than unrestricted ones. (Recall Keohane's observation that cooperation may consist in joint exploitation of third parties.) *Analytically*, however, i.e. in terms of the conditions under which regimes are created and maintained, whether or not the regime in question is (or would be) a restricted as opposed to a universal public good would not seem to be necessarily very consequential. At least, there is no obvious reason why the fact (assuming it is a fact) that most regimes are only restricted public goods should undermine the theory under scrutiny.[15]

The central issue, then, is whether international regimes display the attribute of *non-excludability*.[16] According to Snidal (1985b: 595–7), the extent to which regimes possess this attribute varies over issue-areas. More often than not, though, exclusion from the benefits they provide (to the relevant group) does not seem to be impossible, calling into question the theory's applicability to many issue-areas of international politics. In the issue-area of trade, for example, states that fail to live up

[15] As we shall see shortly, there may be a more concealed reason, though. If, on account of restricted publicness, group size (i.e. the number of states benefiting from a regime), generally or frequently, drops to the level of what Olson calls an "intermediate group," this property of regimes does have analytical implications as well.

[16] As we have noted above, Olson's general argument does not depend on the relevant group interests being pure public goods, which are not only non-excludable, but also joint in supply. Consequently, hegemony theorists would not seem to be committed to the view that there is no rivalry among states with respect to the benefits achieved through regime-based cooperation. For a differentiated critique of this view, see Snidal (1985b: 590–2).

to their promise to open their markets to foreign products certainly could be excluded from the advantages of the free trade regime. Other members might close their own markets to the products of those states, while continuing to practice openness in their mutual exchange relations. Historical experience abounds with examples of discriminatory trade practices, so there can be hardly any doubt about their possibility.

Thus, John Conybeare (1984: 8) has emphatically argued that free trade does not constitute a public good problem (although it may be a Prisoner's Dilemma). "The reason is that free trade exhibits excludability and rivalry, and is fundamentally a problem of predatory income transfers [as is characteristic of PD situations], whereas the public good situation centers on the problem of inducing free riders to contribute to the supply of the public good." Moreover, in the trade case those predatory income transfers take the form of an optimal tariff and it is a *hegemonic* state (if any) which has an interest in imposing such a tariff (technically speaking, whose optimal tariff is positive). As a consequence, and contrary to what proponents of hegemonic stability theory have tended to take for granted, the dominant power should *not* be expected to pursue free trade or to act as a political entrepreneur in favor of a free trade regime (Conybeare 1984: 11).

Conybeare bases his argument on the so-called pure theory of international trade. A state possesses a (positive) optimal tariff if it can improve its terms of trade (the relative price of its exports) and thus its overall welfare through the imposition of a tariff (Johnson 1954; see also Conybeare 1987: 22–8). Free trade may make every state better off, but it need not be the optimal outcome for any one country and, thus, may create a Prisoner's Dilemma pay-off structure (Conybeare 1984: 10). According to Conybeare (1984: 11), "hegemons should have more incentive than others to resort to restrictions, due to their greater capacity for diverting world income toward themselves (i.e., their perceived payoff from noncooperation is greater)." Indeed, the modal pay-off structure underlying a highly asymmetric trade relationship is not a PD, but a variant of the – even less cooperation-prone – suasion game (see sect. 3.2 above): the smaller state has the dominant strategy to cooperate (i.e. not to raise a tariff), which the hegemon can capitalize upon (Conybeare 1984: 19).

As Joanne Gowa (1989b: 314–16) has shown, though, hegemony theorists have a response to this criticism. The problem with non-excludability is that it produces individual disincentives to contribute to the provision of the public good and, therefore, is likely to result in the group interest not being furthered at all. Accordingly, in a regime context, the possibility of *exclusion* is important as a means of punishing non-compliant states (thus changing their incentive structure). However, imposing sanctions on free-riders in order to maintain or increase the level of cooperation in a regime is not cost-free. Moreover, sanctions (if successful) have effects that are beneficial to the whole membership of the regime *regardless of who shared in their costs and risks*. In other words, exclusion, as well as other kinds of enforcement such as issue-linkage, while often technically possible, may nevertheless fail to take place, because they involve collective action problems themselves. The fact, mentioned above, that trade discrimination is a familiar instrument of foreign economic policy does not *per se* invalidate this analysis even with respect to this particular issue-area. At any rate, we cannot draw this conclusion as long as we do not know how often such measures (1) are taken against partners of equal or greater power and (2) can be plausibly interpreted as attempts to improve compliance with a multilateral free trade arrangement. Consequently, the argument might still hold that effective regimes are unavailable to groups of states that are not privileged by a highly asymmetrical power distribution. In fact, that rule-enforcement is specific to the hegemon's sphere of action is precisely what we have stressed in our reconstruction of the theory (see also Lake 1993: 463).

There remains Conybeare's second argument that a hegemon is likely to have a positive optimal tariff and *therefore* cannot reasonably be expected to create and enforce a free trade regime (even when it has the power to do so). According to Gowa (1989b: 311–14), this argument is flawed, because it implicitly assumes a myopic hegemon who is insensitive to its longer-term interest. The hegemon's situation is analogous to that of a local monopolist. Just as theories of "limit pricing" predict that a rational monopolist may resist the temptation to maximize its prices in the short run in order not to attract competitors and thus to undermine its market position in the longer run, forward-looking hegemons may set tariffs below their optimal levels in the interest of the preservation of their (economic) power base. There may still be opportunity costs of forgoing one's optimal tariff, but they are likely to be much smaller than Conybeare's analysis suggests and may easily be offset by other, non-economic, gains. Thus, as Conybeare (1984: 12) acknowledges, "[p]owerful states may at times be moved to pursue free trade because of the potential for linking free trade to other purely political objectives." (Conybeare's example is the Cobden – Chevalier Treaty, concluded between Britain and France in 1860.)

The debate about the supposed public good characteristic of international regimes need not stop at this point, though. Neoliberals can argue that the proponents of the hegemonic stability hypothesis are ignoring at least two important considerations, which, at a minimum, should cause them to qualify their argument much more carefully. First, as situation-structuralists have pointed out, some types of international regimes (namely, those that are designed to cope with assurance and coordination problems) are largely self-enforcing (see sect. 3.2 above). Consequently, no hegemon is needed to provide the public good of confidence that would-be free-riders will be brought back in line. In many regimes free-riding simply is not an issue.[17] By contrast, the interpretation of international regimes as public goods implicitly assumes that regimes generally answer to what Stein (1983) has called "collaboration problems" and for which the Prisoner's Dilemma is the paradigmatic case.[18] Logic seems to require therefore that the range of application of hegemonic stability theory be explicitly restricted to a special kind of regime (or, alternatively, that it be shown that, empirically, assurance and coordination regimes are a negligible quantity).

Second, contractualists, while they would not in principle disagree with Gowa's argument concerning the public good character of enforcement of international norms, would nevertheless point out that this defense of hegemonic stability theory is too insensitive to the role played by international regimes themselves in reducing the costs of sanctioning. Regimes are not just abstract codes of conduct for certain issue-areas set up and enforced by hegemons, but sometimes quite elaborate institutions which reduce informational asymmetries by helping states to monitor each other's behavior. Regimes do not only de-legitimize certain forms of behavior, but often also legitimize, under specified conditions, sanctions to discourage such forms of behavior. Greater transparency and the partial replacement of self-help with collective forms of legitimization, in turn, work towards diminishing one of the most important cost factors of sanctioning: the fear of echo effects

[17] In coordination situations, hegemony may spur the process of rule-making, though, by facilitating the collective choice of a coordinating convention (Snidal 1985a: 940).

[18] As Hardin (1971; 1982: 25–8) has shown, Olson's problem of collective action essentially amounts to an *n*-person PD.

("feuds") resulting from behavior that is perceived by its target as provocative and hostile (Gowa 1989b: 314f.).[19]

Objection 2: Collective action by *k* states as a substitute for hegemonic leadership

The potential power of the foregoing argument is not fully obvious unless it is linked up with a second line of (theoretically oriented) criticism of the hegemonic stability hypothesis. The issue here is not whether regimes can be plausibly described as (involving) public goods – in this context this interpretation, which is fundamental to hegemonic stability theory,[20] is accepted as an assumption. Rather the debate focuses on the question of whether hegemonic stability theory's claim that only (hegemonically) privileged groups of states will be provided with international regimes can in fact be based on the theory of collective action.

Although Olson, for the most part, had framed his conclusions in terms of large vs. small groups, his analysis contained many elements of a more differentiated picture. Most important in this context, he introduced and briefly discussed a category of groups, which are not privileged, but may nevertheless succeed in achieving their common good. These groups, which he called "intermediate groups," are distinguished from large ones in that there is perceptible interdependence between at

[19] Still other arguments are available to scholars who are not committed to the rationalism that unites interest- and power-based approaches to analyzing regimes. Thus, from a strongly cognitivist (or sociological) point of view, compliance is based upon (beliefs of) legitimacy, ongoing and effective communication, processes of socialization (identity-formation), and a common ideology, rather than upon narrow and purely individualistic calculations of advantage that may be the target of hegemonic manipulation (see sect. 5.2 below).

[20] It should be noted that there are broader conceptions of hegemonic stability theory than the one that we, following Snidal's (1985b) example, have adopted in this book. Lake (1993), for example, uses the term "hegemonic stability theory" to refer to a "research program" which is composed of two different theories: one which he calls "leadership theory" and which is largely identical with what we discuss here under the label of "hegemonic stability theory," and another which he refers to as "hegemony theory" and which does not rely on public goods arguments. Hegemony theorists (in Lake's sense) do not seek to account for international stability or regimes, but for variations in international economic openness. Their explanatory focus is on the way in which different distributions of economic power affect the foreign economic policy preferences of differently situated states. The exemplar of this literature is Krasner (1976). A distinction very similar to Lake's is made by Webb and Krasner (1989: 184), who contrast a "collective goods version" and a "security version" of the theory of hegemonic stability (corresponding to Lake's leadership and hegemony theories, respectively).

least two members of the group. Within large groups interdependence is absent, because no member's decision has a noticeable effect on whether or not (some amount of) the public good is provided for the group. As a result, the group is trapped in a huge Prisoner's Dilemma, where each member has the dominant strategy not to contribute anything (his contribution being either useless or superfluous, but at any rate costly to himself) and, consequently, the common interest will not be furthered. The situation is radically altered and much more promising, though, for a group "which does not have so many members that no one member will notice whether any other member is or is not helping to provide the collective good" (Olson 1965: 50). In such intermediate groups bargaining and strategic interaction can be expected, which may (but may also fail to) result in the group pursuing its goal through collective action.

As Russell Hardin (1982: 41f.) has pointed out, though, Olson's emphasis on group size is somewhat misleading. In the final analysis, the prospects for groups, as regards the realization of their common interest, are not determined by the overall size of their membership, but rather by the minimum number of members that would benefit from cooperation amongst themselves. If this number, which is now commonly referred to simply as *k*, is relatively small, even nominally large groups can be provided with collective goods.[21] *Ceteris paribus k* will be smaller when group members are unequal in size: since, by assumption, larger actors receive greater benefits from the collective good, the cooperation of fewer actors is needed to provide the group with some amount of the good. Similarly, *k* tends to go down when costs of provision of the good are lowered (i.e. when the ratio of benefits to costs improves).

Snidal (1985b: 598–612) has used these important qualifications of the theory of collective action to challenge the hegemonic stability hypothesis on theoretical grounds. He argues that collective action of a *k*-group (with $k > 1$) may effectively substitute for hegemonic unilateral leadership. The possibility of this happening rests upon states' ability to think and act strategically, i.e. to take into account the likely reactions of others to their choices. On the basis of a numerical example (which

[21] The choice of the letter *k* and the corresponding term *k*-groups derives from Schelling's (1973) usage in an important early study of related problems. The basic idea underlying this concept is already present in Olson's (1965: 48) passing reference to the potential role of a "smaller subset of the group" in the provision of the public good through "oligopolistic interaction."

stylizes recent changes in the distribution of economic power among the United States, Japan, and Germany), Snidal demonstrates that post-hegemonic cooperation need not be attributed to some form of hegemonic afterglow or leadership lag, but can be accounted for in terms of the collaboration of a *k*-group (which includes the former hegemon). What is more, the very fact that, due to hegemonic decline, the group is no longer privileged helps to explain the emergence of stable coalitions, i.e. subsets of the group who join forces to create or maintain international regimes. Successful collective action is now more likely for two reasons. First, the opportunity costs of the alternative to collusion are much higher: since the group is no longer privileged, in the absence of (second-order) cooperation the regime would break down. Second, each member of the coalition knows that her decision to free-ride is likely to cause the collapse of the coalition – with the result that whatever gains seemed available from unilateral defection dissolve as well.

It may be added that, in at least two ways, (pre-existing) international regimes may be instrumental in the formation of *k*-groups. First, regimes (even hegemonic ones) create ongoing relationships among states and provide them with (material-institutional) negotiation fora and (intellectual) focal points, both of which should facilitate the formation of effective coalitions. Second, regimes reduce sanctioning costs – this is where the above mentioned argument comes in again – and hence *k*. Smaller groups, however, will, *ceteris paribus*, face lower transaction costs and therefore find it easier to cooperate to provide the collective good.[22]

Concluding remarks

Snidal's internal critique of the theory of hegemonic stability is powerful. It should be noted, though, that he does not conclude that the theory is useless. So it has proven correct (or, at least, has not been refuted by Snidal's argument) in its emphasis on asymmetry: unequal size distribution within a group may indeed be beneficial, even when the requirement of hegemony has turned out to be unwarranted. (This, of course, does not rule out that in some situations *k* happens to be 1 and that, consequently, second-order cooperation is unlikely.) Moreover, it is unclear to what extent Snidal's numerical example, which shows that, under a

[22] One of the most interesting aspects of Snidal's (1985b: 610) argument, though, is that, under specific circumstances, three-party post-hegemonic coalitions are more likely to form and be viable than two-party ones, even when the latter are broad enough to benefit from cooperation.

specific constellation, collective action is possible and even likely, really generalizes. Nor does Snidal's argument disconfirm the weaker claim implicit in hegemonic stability theory that privileged groups (issue-areas with a hegemon) are better off than intermediate ones (where $k > 1$ but still small): although the latter may sometimes succeed, the first may have clear advantages in terms of the likelihood of success. Thus, Gowa (1989b: 316–22) has come up with quite a long list of obstacles that may inhibit *k*-group cooperation. Moreover, she stresses that the game-theoretic solutions that are available in order to cope with these problems often do not appear relevant to real-world international politics. In her own critique of the hegemonic stability theory (insofar as it has been applied to the issue-area of international trade) she emphasizes a quite different point, which closely parallels Grieco's criticism of neoliberalism (see sect. 4.3 below): the theory's neglect of the security externalities of economic cooperation (Gowa 1989b: 322–4).

These caveats notwithstanding, most students of regimes would now seem to agree with the overall results of Snidal's critical analysis of the theory. The strong version of the theory of hegemonic stability which posits that regimes are neither created nor maintained unless there is hegemonic leadership in the issue-area is not tenable. Not only have its theoretical underpinnings been shaken, but also empirical studies (although they often fail to tie up their observations with the issues that are central to the theoretical debate) have come up with too many anomalies for the theory to remain intact. Thus, McKeown (1983) has challenged rather impressively the ability of the theory of hegemonic stability to account for observable patterns of trade policy in the nineteenth century. Similarly, two recent multi-case research projects focusing on regime formation have produced extremely disappointing findings for the hegemonic stability hypothesis: both in issue-areas pertaining to the Arctic (Young and Osherenko 1993b: 230) and to East–West relations (Rittberger and Zürn 1991: 176; Efinger, Mayer, and Schwarzer 1993: 269) various regimes could be identified in the unambiguous absence of hegemony. In the latter study a self-consciously behavioral definition of "regime" (see chapter 2 above) was applied (Rittberger 1990a: 3). It is therefore not possible to argue that its finding is of little relevance for the hegemonic stability hypothesis, which attempts to explain rule-based (first-order) cooperation, rather than merely the emergence of explicit normative agreements, which may or may not have behavioral consequences in the respective issue-area.

Nevertheless, we think students of regimes would be ill-advised to discard the theory completely at this stage. As indicated above, a more broadly conceived asymmetry theory might still prove to have considerable explanatory power, and even the *relative* advantages of hegemony may not have been sufficiently probed both theoretically and empirically. Moreover, there may be additional promising avenues for theoretical refinement. Thus, Beth and Robert Yarbrough (1987) have shown how the theory of hegemonic stability as an explanation for international trade relations might be further developed through an integration of theories of surplus capacity. Not only does their revised formulation add to the sophistication of the theory (by making its predictions conditional on the extent to which investments in trade are transaction-specific), it appears capable of dealing effectively with some of the empirical anomalies that have weakened scholarly confidence in the theory (Yarbrough and Yarbrough 1987: 19–26). Finally, if Snidal (1985b: 596) should turn out to be correct that few issue-areas of international politics meet the requirements implicit in the concept of public goods, the range of legitimate application of the theory would be much smaller than has been assumed hitherto by most regime theorists. The consequences of this line of argument for the theory are ambiguous. On the one hand, its explanatory power would be reduced. At the same time, however, its empirical standing (within its now limited domain of applicability) might be strongly enhanced: much of the alleged empirical counter-evidence might prove simply irrelevant. Lake (1993: 479–83) may turn out right in contending that the jury on the theory is still out, not least because very few (if any) *appropriate* tests have been conducted so far.

4.2 Battle of the Sexes versus Prisoner's Dilemma: Krasner's case for a power-oriented research program

Contractualism, as we have seen (sect. 3.1), describes the problem of international cooperation in terms of "market failure": even when states share substantial common interests they may fail to cooperate to realize these interests for fear of being cheated by their partners and ending up with the sucker's pay-off. Thus, in the absence of appropriate international institutions, a suboptimal (Pareto-inefficient) collective behavior may result. This, of course, is equivalent to saying that institutions (by way of reducing transaction costs) may help states to move to the Pareto frontier. Functional logic, then, has it that this effect of institutions, since it is valued by rational actors, also explains their existence. According to Stephen Krasner (1991; 1993a) this account is misleading, because the "basic issue [in the politics of regime formation] is where states will end up on the Pareto frontier, not how to reach the frontier in the first place" (Krasner 1993a: 140). This basic fact of politics – that it is about who gets what – is veiled by the PD with its single cooperative outcome, but is nicely captured by another, far less popular, game model: Battle of the Sexes. As a consequence, Krasner argues, Battle is a heuristically more fruitful point of departure in analyses of international regimes than PD.

As we have seen above (sect. 3.2, figure 3), Battle of the Sexes (in its basic form) is a coordination game with two Pareto-efficient Nash equilibria (representing the "cooperative" outcomes of the game), but, unlike in pure coordination games, the players have conflicting preferences regarding the two Pareto optima: the couple would rather spend the evening together than separately, but they disagree on where to go. Similarly, states often have an unambiguous preference for coordinating their activities in an issue-area such that mutual unilateralism is their "common aversion" (Stein 1983), but clash because they favor different institutional arrangements (i.e. different points of coordination).

Interpreting the problem of international cooperation in terms of Battle rather than PD has several important implications. Cheating no longer appears as the main problem hampering efforts to cooperate for mutual advantage. In fact, surreptitious deviation from the agreed-upon coordinating convention is outright irrational in Battle. Since all points along the Pareto frontier are Nash equilibria, changing one's mind unilaterally involves a loss of utility. By implication, Krasner (1991: 336, 362) points out, *intelligence* is devalued as a means of solving the cooperation problem (Axelrod and Keohane 1986: 231): the problem is *not* one of devising low-instrusive, but still effective compliance mechanisms. Instead, distributional conflicts and *power* as a means of deciding such conflicts come to the fore in processes of regime formation and reformation.

Krasner acknowledges that Keohane is not insensitive to power asymmetries and their consequences for bargaining outcomes within and without regimes. In fact, Keohane's (1984: 70f.) "constraint-choice approach" anticipates many of the themes that Krasner stresses in his own approach. As Krasner argues, though, there is both a "denotation" and a "connotation" to a research program. Research questions that are not ruled out by the explicit logic (the "denotation") of a research program may nevertheless be pushed to the background by its "connotation," which "suggests which questions are most important, what kind of evidence should be gathered, and, often tacitly, which issues should be ignored" (Krasner 1991: 361). The "connotation" of the contractualist research program, however, is clearly defined by the problems highlighted by PD and not those posed by Battle. Not only does Keohane (1984: 68) stress the particular relevance of PD for his argument, the very definition of "cooperation" that underlies his study – actors adjust their policies to each others' objectives (Keohane 1984: 52) – works well with PD (as well as with some other prominent games such as Assurance or Chicken[23]), but is inapplicable to Battle, where cooperation (coordination) is *not* achieved by mutual adjustment, but by one partner adjusting to the other.

Krasner (1991: 340) specifies three ways in which state power may be exercised in this connection:

> (1) Power may be used to determine who can play the game in the first place. In international relations less powerful actors are often never invited to the table.
> (2) Power may also be used to dictate the rules of the game, for instance, who gets to move first. In [Battle] the player who moves first can dictate the outcome, provided the other player is convinced that the first player's strategy is irrevocable.
> (3) Power may be used to change the payoff matrix.

Thus, by way of tactical issue-linkage (threats or promises) a state with more abundant resources (military, economic, or otherwise) may manipulate the other's preference ordering such that the game is effectively transformed into one in which there is only one Pareto-efficient equilibrium solution left: the one favored by the more powerful actor (Krasner 1991: 340f.). Finally, bargaining leverage may be derived from unequal opportunity costs of change: the actor less in need of cooperation (usually the one with the greater overall capabilities) can get his (or her) way by credibly threatening to walk away from the table if the other

[23] Chicken is a symmetrical game characterized by the preference ordering: DC>CC>CD>DD. Chicken poses a dilemma of common aversion (DD) with the peculiar feature that this dilemma can be solved by either coordination (CD or DC) or collaboration (CC) (Stein 1983: 131, n. 32). The Berlin blockade crisis of 1948 (Snyder and Diesing 1977: 113f.) and the Cuban missile crisis of 1962 (Zürn 1992: 187–90) have been analyzed as Chicken games.

side fails to be more forthcoming (Krasner 1976: 320; 1991: 363; see also Hirschman 1945).

In a manner very similar to Krasner, Geoffrey Garrett (1993) has recently criticized functional explanations of regimes and stressed the role of power as a coordinating mechanism. In a study devoted to the completion of the EC's internal market, Garrett (1993: 366f.) points out that functional accounts of cooperative arrangements in international politics are inadequate, because they are based on an assumption that is hardly ever justified empirically: that there is but a single Pareto-efficient solution to the collective action problem at hand. More often than not there are a variety of potential regimes which are not easily distinguished in terms of their aggregate welfare effects. Pointing to the functional benefits of a given regime, therefore, is most likely to be a highly underspecified explanation of this particular institution. Moreover, Garrett criticizes functional theory for downplaying both distributional conflict in processes of regime formation and the role of power asymmetries in "solving" these conflicts.

The significance of institutions

If asymmetrical information is no longer the core problem for states with an interest in cooperation, then what role is left for institutions? In a way not very different from that of radical critics of the regime-analytic research program (Strange 1983: 345), Krasner (1991: 362) notes that a power-oriented "analysis seeks to explain outcomes in terms of interests and relative capabilities rather than in terms of institutions designed to promote Pareto optimality." Still, he maintains that regimes are not insignificant. Regimes are necessary because of the common aversion to uncoordinated action and to "establish stability" (Krasner 1991: 337; see also Snidal 1985a: 937f.). Thus, in the case of global communications, which he uses to exemplify his argument, "[s]tates wanted some set of rules for the allocation of the electromagnetic spectrum and international communications including satellites, because the failure to coordinate policies on interference and on the compatibility of national networks would have left everyone worse off" (Krasner 1991: 362f.). The stability established by these regimes has been narrowly circumscribed, though, and is ultimately contingent on fairly stable external (in particular, technological) conditions: "Whereas previous institutional choices had not imposed much constraint, new interests and power capabilities conferred by new technologies had led to new institutional arrangements." (Krasner 1991: 337)

Regimes in this account exhibit little autonomy and robustness, but are often essential mediators between the distribution of power and concomitant interests, on the one hand, and outcomes in the issue-area, on the other. Moreover, although the autonomy attributed to regimes is arguably smaller than in interest- and knowledge-based theories, it is not negligible. This is implicit in the fact, acknowledged and even stressed by Krasner (1985: 7–9; 1991: 363), that regimes can be a source of power themselves. Thus, even structurally weak states can sometimes exert a modicum of influence on the collective policies in an issue-area due to the membership and voting rules of the international organization that administers the regime concerned. For example, in the case of the allocation of the electromagnetic spectrum (including the distribution of slots on the geostationary orbit) the demands of Third World states could not be completely ignored by the technologically much more advanced countries of the North, in part because those states could participate in collective decisionmaking through their membership in the International Telecommunications Union (ITU), an organization open to all states and operating on the basis of the "one-state-one-vote" rule derived from the principle of sovereign equality (Krasner 1991: 351–3).[24] If regimes did not have significant (distributional) consequences, actors would not bargain hard to determine their content and the "battle" would not so often continue to be fought even after the establishment of an institution.

In a book-length study of various issue-areas in satellite-based communications Kai-Uwe Schrogl (1993) has confirmed most of Krasner's somewhat more casual empirical observations. Stressing the possibility of deliberate "constructional faults" in regimes in the form of accepted *tensions* between principles, on the one hand, and norms and rules, on the other, he also finds, however, that substantive regime principles (as opposed to procedural rules regarding access) helped initially disadvantaged actors to bring about regime change by providing those states with a "rallying point" (Schrogl 1993: 14). This role of principles is ironic, because, according to Schrogl, their egalitarian content was

[24] While the autonomous causal significance of issue-specific *regimes* is rather limited in Krasner's account and tends to be trivialized by "structural variables" such as power and national interest, the importance of the *fundamental institution* of sovereignty is not easily overstated, as it defines who is an actor in international politics in the first place (Krasner 1988; 1991: 365; see also Ruggie 1986). This argument, as we shall see (sect. 5.2 below), is taken up and generalized by knowledge-based accounts of international institutions and regimes.

accepted by the dominant actors in the issue-area on the assumption that, in the final analysis, only norms and rules would be consequential in practical terms. At the same time, Schrogl makes it clear that principles can only *facilitate* change and that reforms would not have taken place had the material power position of the initially weaker actors not improved over time.[25]

Battle of the Sexes as well as Prisoner's Dilemma? Constructing a neoliberal reply

The plausibility of Krasner's argument would seem to depend, at least in part, on how well Battle of the Sexes characterizes issue-areas in international politics, particularly when compared with Prisoner's Dilemma. It would seem to presuppose that Battle is the rule, whereas PD is the exception in world politics. And, indeed, there are voices which can be adduced in support of this proposition. Fritz Scharpf (1989: 162) has pointed out that "the characteristics of Battle apply to an extremely wide range of real-life constellations" at all levels of social aggregation:

> Not only intimate partners, but also business firms engaged in joint ventures, unions and management in collective bargaining, inter-ministerial, federal-state and inter-European policy coordination or political parties in a coalition, and many similar joint undertakings, all are confronted with the same problem: while the benefits of cooperation are more attractive than the outcomes expected in the case of non-agreement, cooperation is seriously threatened by distributive conflict over the choice among cooperative solutions (or over the allocation of the costs and benefits of cooperation). *It is probably fair to say that in the great majority of ongoing relationships that is the major obstacle to cooperative solutions.* [emphasis added]

In the same vein, Gowa (1986: 172f.), in a review of Axelrod's (1984) seminal interest-based study of *The Evolution of Cooperation*, has cast doubt on the pervasiveness of PD situations at the inter-state level, quoting, *inter alia*, Bruce Russett (1983: 115) who has noted that "the true prisoner's dilemma is probably not a common situation in international

[25] Obviously, Schrogl could not have made this interesting *empirical* (not just conceptual) observation had he opted for the lean definition of international regimes. (At a minimum, it would have been much more difficult for him.) Proponents of the consensus definition, therefore, might cite analyses such as his as a vindication of their intuition that something would be lost if scholars no longer expected regimes to be complex and hierarchical normative structures.

politics." While such assessments by competent observers surely lend support to Krasner's general line of argument, it is no less sure that they cannot be regarded as decisive. It would not be difficult to cite countervailing impressionistic evidence gathered by scholars whose competence is likewise beyond doubt: the very popularity of PD in international relations theory suggests this possibility.[26] Moreover, Krasner (1991: 364) is probably right in warning that "[i]t is illusionary to suppose that this issue will be resolved on the basis of empirical studies."

But there is, of course, another possibility. We may be mistaken to try to *resolve* this issue in the first place, because both Battle and PD can be relevant for modeling issue-areas in international politics. Those neoliberals whom we have called situation-structuralists (see sect. 3.2 above) are most naturally inclined towards such a "compromise position." Scholars such as Stein (1983) have explicitly distinguished two types of international regimes: regimes that are a collective response to situations of (potential) market failure (*collaboration regimes*) and others which are created to cope with coordination problems such as Battle (*coordination regimes*). Moreover, situation-structuralists have described the respective natures of these two kinds of regimes in a way that is compatible not only with Keohane's account of collaboration regimes, but with Krasner's account of coordination regimes as well. Thus, Snidal (1985a: 935) has argued that in games such as Battle of the Sexes larger states (i.e. states with greater structural power), because of their decreased "need for coordination," are likely to get their way in negotiations over the coordination point.

From this vantage point, it would seem that Krasner's attack on the leading school of thought in regime analysis has been only partially successful at best: he has provided a valuable antidote to any "imperialist" aspirations there may be on the part of market failure theories of regimes. At the same time, he has discredited neither neoliberalism as a more broadly conceived research program nor a more modest form of contractualism which does not claim to hold unconditionally, but only in situations with PD-like characteristics (i.e. a functional theory that is embedded in a situation-structural perspective).[27]

[26] For a compilation of analyses using the PD, see Grieco (1988b: 604).

[27] It should be noted that there is yet another way of making compatible the perspectives on regimes favored by Keohane and Krasner, respectively, which may be more troublesome for standard neoliberal theory. Situation-structuralists may be wrong in suggesting that the set of issue-areas in international politics can be more or less neatly

But although Krasner focuses his criticism on Keohane (and indeed cites Stein and Snidal approvingly), this harmonizing conclusion may fall short of doing justice to his position. His basic concern, after all, is not with the frequency distribution of pay-off structures in international politics. What he argues is that Battle of the Sexes is heuristically more fruitful than PD, because it brings into the open central features of international politics in general: distributional conflict and the exertion of power. At least two components of his argument suggest that the power-oriented research program to which he wishes to contribute is more broadly conceived than is acknowledged by the neoliberal response we have just speculated about.

First, contrary to neoliberalism, the constellation of actors and interests (identifiable, for example, as a Battle of the Sexes game) is not the unproblematic starting point for the kind of analysis that Krasner has in mind. For, as we have seen, power, in this account, can be used not only to prevail in distributional conflict in a mixed-motives coordination situation; power may also be exerted to determine who is allowed to play the game in the first place, and it may even be employed to change one's opponents' preference orderings. Thus, the basic unit of analysis of situation-structuralism – the distribution of interests – is not strictly prior to power politics and in part is a function of the distribution of capabilities. As a consequence, Krasner's power-based approach cannot be subsumed under situation-structural theory.

Second, power-oriented analysis is also relevant for situations which are completely outside the purview of neoliberalism: zero-sum games, where one actor's gains are the other one's losses (Krasner 1991: 364). Situation-structural theories of regimes do not consider such situations

subdivided into Chicken situations, Assurance situations, Deadlock situations, and so forth. In particular, there may well be issue-areas which display properties of *both* PD and Battle and in which, consequently, both distributional conflict and the threat of market failure are prominent features. Analyzing the politics of the completion of the EC's internal market, Garrett and Weingast (1993: 184) have proposed a (still highly simplified) 2×3 pay-off matrix which exhibits a Battle of the Sexes game nested within a Prisoner's Dilemma. This hybrid game takes account of the fact that the trade liberalization envisaged in the "1992 Project" not only led to interested disagreement about which strategy to implement in order to achieve this broad goal, but involved familiar problems of monitoring compliance as well (Garrett 1993: 370f.). Indeed, if Zürn (1992: 203) is correct, such mixed situation structures are much more common than explicit situation-structural theorizing suggests. This might also explain Krasner's (1991: 364) observation that "[t]he literature [about regimes] now contains enough examples to suggest that both market failure and power-oriented research programs can present plausible analyses, *often about the same issue*" [emphasis added].

because they do not pose problems of collective action, which pit individual against collective rationality. In zero-sum games, conflict of interest is absolute and each potential outcome is Pareto-efficient. So there is no possibility of reaping joint gains through cooperation. Bringing to mind earlier speculations about "imposed regimes" (Young 1983: 100f.), Krasner (albeit implicitly) even departs from the neoliberal consensus that the concept of regime is useful only in mixed-motives situations and is intrinsically linked to the concept of inter-state cooperation. His power-oriented analysis of the formation and the fate of the various human rights *regimes* that have been established by great powers since the end of the Thirty Years' War makes it clear (although he renounces the use of game-theoretic language in this study) that he views, in each of these cases, the underlying pay-off structure as much closer to a pure conflict than to a mixed-motives situation (Krasner 1993a: 140f.).

Bargaining leverage versus structural power: on the limits of a power-oriented research program

The preceding caveats suggest that neoliberals may not be able to deal with Krasner's challenge as easily as it appears at first sight. Indeed, attempts to absorb the critical thrust of his arguments by way of subsuming them under a broader neoliberal framework may be misguided, and it may be necessary for adherents to an interest-based analysis of international regimes wishing to defend the paradigmatic status of their approach to confront the challenge of Krasner's power-oriented research program more squarely. Young (1994: ch. 5) has recently shown how this could be done. As will become obvious from our brief discussion of his analysis, though, a critique of a power-centric approach to regime formation is likely to be most compelling when it does not rely on interest-based arguments alone, but draws on the intellectual resources that are provided by the third school of thought in regime analysis, which we refer to as knowledge-based theories, as well.

Resuming considerations that informed his model of institutional bargaining (see sect. 3.4 above) and citing numerous empirical examples mainly from environmental issue-areas, Young argues that there is often a striking discrepancy between the distribution of *structural power* and actors' ability to exert significant influence on the outcomes of institutional bargaining, and that control over a great amount of material resources is only one determinant of *bargaining leverage* among several (although undoubtedly an important one). Young (1994: 120–34) points to a broad range of conditions and factors that, frequently or generally, constrain or even block the exercise of structural power during processes of regime formation, mentioning, *inter alia*, the constitutive principles of international society, internal dissensus, the leverage resulting from strategic position, the danger of coming to be regarded as an international bully, or pressures to respect principles of equity that emanate from the consensus rule and the need for domestic implementation of agreed-upon rules. Moreover, the conditions under which attempts to create international institutions normally take place (limited knowledge of the contract curve, presence of a veil of uncertainty) discourage or mitigate distributive bargaining in the first place. Ideas, which are beyond the control of any single actor and thus cannot be manipulated by even the most powerful one, heavily influence bargaining outcomes.[28] Finally, Young's insights into the often critical role of individual leadership in institutional bargaining can help to reverse the devaluation of intelligence as a means of solving problems of international cooperation implicit in Krasner's power-oriented perspective. This is rather obvious with intellectual and entrepreneurial leaders, but ultimately true of structural leaders as well (Young 1991: 290f.; 1994: 138). Young is aware that arguments such as these do not invalidate analyses that highlight the distribution of capabilities as a constraint on the interaction between states. Nevertheless, we agree with him that they should be weighed very carefully by proponents of a power-oriented research program, focusing attention once more on the nature and sources of power as control over outcomes in international politics (see also Baldwin 1993a: 15–22).

4.3 The meaning of anarchy: Grieco's modern realist perspective on regimes

In a series of publications in recent years, Joseph Grieco (1988a; 1990; 1993b) has subjected the neoliberal theory of cooperation and regimes to a thorough criticism. More specifically, he has argued that neoliberalism has *not* been successful in attempting to "show, on the basis of . . . [Realists'] own assumptions, that Realism's pessimism [about the prospects of international cooperation] does not follow" (Keohane

[28] In their study of the completion of the EC's internal market, Garrett and Weingast (1993) stress the role of ideas as focal points that help to select regimes in situations of multiple equilibria (see also sect. 5.1 below). Recall also Young's (1989b: 369) hypothesis that institutional bargaining is more likely to succeed if a salient solution or a focal point is available.

1984: 67). By means of a reconstruction and clarification of the supposedly authentic realist view on international cooperation as well as on the basis of carefully designed empirical research, Grieco has sought to demonstrate that realism provides a more adequate understanding of cooperation among nations than does its challenger, neoliberalism.

As a central element of this critique, Grieco has qualified, though not altogether rejected, neoliberalism's claim that international institutions play an important role in states' cooperative ventures. He has repeatedly confirmed the generally accepted view that the school of thought he identifies with, realism, places little confidence in international institutions, and neoliberal participants in the debate that has been sparked off by his response to the "newest liberal institutionalism" (Grieco 1988a) regard the simple term "institutionalism" as sufficient to characterize their own position, thus implying that their opponent discounts institutions (Snidal 1991b: 701; Keohane 1993b). Nevertheless, as we shall argue, it would be misleading to describe Grieco's position as downright anti-institutionalist. Indeed, his interpretation of the realist theory of international cooperation does have interesting positive implications for international institutions as well, some of which he has recently begun to work out in greater detail (Grieco 1995). This is not to say that Grieco has offered a fully fledged power-based theory of international regimes so far. Neither does he claim to have done so. Even so, some of the building blocks of this emerging theory are obvious enough in light of his critical analysis of the neoliberal view of institutions.

Grieco's critique of the neoliberal theory of cooperation

Neoliberals have employed rational choice analysis and economic theories of institutions (Stein 1983; Keohane 1984; Axelrod 1984; Axelrod and Keohane 1986) to show that realists, when stressing the – very narrow – structural limits to international cooperation, regularly make stronger claims than are justifiable on the grounds of realism's basic assumptions about the nature of states and their social environment. These assumptions, it is argued, are perfectly consistent with a range of effective policy coordination for mutual benefit considerably broader than realist theories of hegemony or alliances would make us believe. This is because, even in a "realist" world, states have incentives to create international institutions, which, in turn, help them to manage the risks of cooperation. In making their case neoliberals have emphasized two features of this realist world: anarchy or the lack of a central authority, and states' disposition to act as rational egoists. Yet, according to Grieco, neither of these features adequately represents the view of the world as actually held by realists. The concept of anarchy, of course, is indeed central to realist thinking about international politics, but neoliberals have failed to grasp its full meaning. This failure, in turn, has led them to misconstrue realism's understanding of the basic motivation of states as well: according to realism, states are *not* rational egoists. As a consequence, the neoliberal argument regarding realism's allegedly exaggerated pessimism about international cooperation is fundamentally flawed.

Grieco (1988a: 497) points out that in the neoliberal perspective *anarchy* boils down to a condition in which no central agency enforces promises. In the absence of appropriate institutions, therefore, states will often find it very difficult to cooperate for fear of being cheated by their partners. But, according to realism, there is more than this to international anarchy. Most important, the lack of common government means that no central agency guarantees states their survival as independent units of the system. The international system, therefore, is one in which self-help is the order of the day (Waltz 1979). As Grieco emphasizes, this does not rule out that states sometimes cooperate to further common objectives.[29] However, cooperation among states is less likely – more difficult to achieve and harder to maintain – than neoliberal theories suggest. For anarchy, properly understood, involves more than just the one obstacle to cooperation that neoliberals have specified: not only states' fear of being double-crossed, but also a structurally induced *intolerance for relative losses* circumscribes their ability to work together.

This position clashes with the behavioral model embraced by neoliberalism. Neoliberals have characterized states as *rational egoists* (Keohane 1984: 67), i.e. each state seeks to maximize a utility function that is independent of the utility function of any other. States (just like firms in microeconomic theory) "do not gain or lose utility simply because of the gains and losses of others" (Keohane 1984: 27). However, according to Grieco, rational egoism is not a behavioral disposition that meets the demands made by anarchy. Therefore, realists, while agreeing that (in formal terms) states may be described as utility-maximizers, sharply disagree with neoliberals as to the nature of their utility functions: in international politics the gains of another do detract from one's

[29] Incidentally, this view implies that there are situations in international politics which are not zero-sum. Consequently, Grieco departs in at least one important aspect from what Krasner (1991: 338, n. 4) calls "conventional realist thinking" and regards as exemplified in Waltz's (1979) work.

own level of satisfaction. Relative gains (or losses) count. In particular, this applies to situations in which states are engaged with others in cooperative undertakings or are considering whether or not to forgo unilateral policymaking on some issue. In such situations, states' decisions will depend not only on how well they are doing (or expect to be doing), but also on the (expected) pay-offs of their partners. The reasoning behind this proposition has been spelt out succinctly by Waltz (1979: 105):

> When faced with the possibility of cooperating for mutual gain, states that feel insecure must ask how the gain will be divided. They are compelled to ask not "Will both of us gain?" but "Who will gain more?" If an expected gain is to be divided, say, in the ratio of two to one, one state may use its disproportionate gain to implement a policy intended to damage or destroy the other. Even the prospect of large absolute gains for both parties does not elicit their cooperation as long as each fears how the other will use its increased capabilities. Notice that the impediments to collaboration may not lie in the character and the immediate intention of either party. Instead, the condition of insecurity – at the least, the uncertainty of each about the other's future intentions and actions – works against their cooperation.

Under anarchy each unit bears exclusive responsibility for safeguarding its own survival and independence. States, therefore, must protect (and possibly enhance) their capacity for self-help. This capacity is a function of their relative power capabilities. To the extent that gains resulting from collective action are likely to affect these capabilities, states, when contemplating cooperation in a given issue-area, must take into account not only the size of the absolute gains they are likely to achieve, but also the size of gains that are enjoyed by their partners. Such relative gains concerns can keep states from embarking on, or continuing to support, cooperative ventures with others, *even when* cheating is not (or no longer) a problem.

In her work on the "political correlates of a stable world market economy," Gowa (1989b: 307) has developed ideas which are very similar to those formulated by Grieco and Waltz. Thus, she argues that the major weakness of hegemonic stability theory is its insensitivity to the "security externalities of trade":

> [T]he most durable barrier to open international markets . . . may be the anarchic international system that makes two facts common knowledge among states: (1) each seeks to exploit the wealth of others to enhance its own power, and (2) trade is instrumental to this end. The

> structure of international politics, in short, may lead a state to prefer the status quo ante because it fears that any change may benefit others more than itself. (Gowa 1989b: 323)

Meanwhile, for relative gains concerns to be aroused it is not necessary that the state's survival is in immediate danger. Grieco (1988a: 500) stresses that the *uncertainty* inherent in the anarchical international system together with states' low tolerance for risk in matters of security cause these concerns never to disappear completely from the minds of central decisionmakers in their dealings with other states. States are uncertain about their partners' future intentions, for those in charge of foreign policy know that "[m]inds can be changed, new leaders can come to power, values can shift, new dangers and opportunities can arise" (Jervis 1978: 168). As a result, they are likely to keep an eye on the development of the relative capabilities of even those states that they are presently on friendly terms with. We have seen (sect. 3.1 above) that the concept of uncertainty plays a critical role in the neoliberal theory of cooperation as well, but note the differences as to the range of possibilities it refers to in both contexts (Grieco 1988a: 503). Contractualism centers upon states' uncertainty about others' issue-specific behavior: "If we agree to cooperate on this issue, will they honor their commitments?" By contrast, realists stress a kind of uncertainty that is much more existential and also not confined to a particular issue-area: "Will our partners (or our enemies) be prepared to use, or threaten to use, their relative power capabilities against us – relative capabilities we might inadvertently help them to build up through distributionally unbalanced mutual cooperation?"

Moreover, improving one's short- or long-term prospects of survival is not the only motive that makes states attentive to how well their partners do compared to themselves. States also fear that their partners may be able to turn their relative advantages into greater (non-military) bargaining power in the issue-area in question and beyond. This, in turn, would enable them to drive ever better bargains up to a point where the relatively disadvantaged partner's capacity for autonomous choice, at least in the issue-area at hand, may be seriously hampered (Grieco 1990: 29; 1993a: 734). Thus, states seek to avoid relative losses, not only because survival is their fundamental goal, but also because they value their independence and autonomy.

Three aspects of Grieco's position are worth stressing in this connection, because they have often been ignored by his critics. First, Grieco takes great pains to drive the point home that just because states are sensitive to the distribution of gains they are not necessarily relative gains *seekers*. Most realists, he points out, expect states to be highly concerned with preserving their relative power position, but much less so with increasing their capabilities at the expense of others. In Grieco's (1990: 37–40) own terms, states are not status-maximizers, but *"defensive positionalists."* Clearly, not all realists subscribe to this interpretation. John Mearsheimer (1995: 11f.), for example, holds that the basic behavioral disposition of states is more adequately described in terms of an *offensive positionalism*. According to Grieco, however, this is a minority view. Second, states do not exclusively care for relative gains (or losses), but absolute gains enter into their utility calculations as well. As a result, suffering a relative loss in a given relationship or interaction is not necessarily unacceptable to them and will not always keep them from cooperation. Under certain circumstances, relative losses may be outweighed by greater absolute gains. Third, Grieco argues that, although states are never completely indifferent to differences in gains, their *sensitivity to relative losses* varies.

The last two points are nicely captured in a formula devised by Grieco (1988a: 500) to describe the utility function of states as characterized by realists:

$$U = V - k(W - V) \text{ [with } k > 0\text{]},$$

where U is the state's utility, V its absolute gains, W its partner's (absolute) gains and k is the coefficent for that state's sensitivity to differences in pay-offs. (According to Grieco's reconstruction, the corresponding utility function as assumed by neoliberals is simply: $U = V$. The greater a state's expected absolute gains, the greater its interest in cooperation no matter how well or how badly others might do.)[30]

In a spirit similar to Krasner's (see sect. 4.2 above), but rather different in detail, Grieco (1988b) has criticized the conventional Prisoner's

[30] Grieco's formula reveals a notable difference between his and Gowa's analyses. According to Grieco, any gain for a partner affects a state's utility negatively: *ceteris paribus*, since k is always greater than zero, the greater W, the smaller is U. By contrast, Gowa (1989a: 1249; Gowa and Mansfield 1993) allows for *positive* security externalities of trade as well: the gains achieved by a state's trading partners may even add to its utility (here, security), if and when the free trade arrangement is embedded in a military alliance. Moreover, these positive externalities are the greater, the more stable the alliance. For this reason, Gowa argues, bipolar systems with their inherently greater stability (Waltz 1964; 1979: ch. 8) are more conducive to (intra-alliance) free trade than multipolar ones.

Dilemma representation of the cooperation problem for states for veiling the distributional implications of collaboration. Although the usual form of the PD in which the numerical values express ordinal rankings (see sect. 3.1, figure 1) is not inconsistent with a situation in which actors are interested in both absolute and relative gains, it fails to specify *how* absolute and relative gains add up to an actor's utility. To remedy this deficiency, Grieco has proposed to analyze problems of international cooperation with the aid of an Amended Prisoner's Dilemma based upon conventional PD and the (above) utility formula that, according to realists, describes the structure of state preferences (Grieco 1988b: 608).

According to Grieco (1988b: 610–13; 1990: 45f.), several contextual variables determine the degree to which, in a given situation, a state is sensitive to relative gains achieved by its partners. "In general, k is likely to increase as a state transits from relationships in what Deutsch terms a 'pluralistic security community' to those approximating a state of war." (Grieco 1990: 45) More specifically, the intolerance for relative losses is influenced by both the present and the past of the relationship concerned. It makes a difference whether one's (potential) cooperation partner is a longtime ally or a longtime foe. Relative gains concerns tend to be suppressed when the states in question share a common adversary or when the power difference between them is so large that no conceivable gap in pay-offs from cooperation is likely to affect their relative positions to a noticeable degree. States whose power base is generally shrinking tend to be more sensitive to relative losses than rising hegemons. Moreover, the nature of the issue has a bearing on the level of k. Thus, cooperation in economic issue-areas is less likely to be inhibited by relative gains concerns than security cooperation.[31] Also, states, *ceteris paribus*, are the more strongly concerned with how well their partners do as compared to themselves, the more easily the gains at stake are transformed into relative capabilities (military strength or bargaining power).

The modern realist theory of cooperation among nations

According to Grieco, realists accept the proposition underscored by neoliberalism that fear of cheating constitutes an obstacle that states must often overcome, before they can pursue common interests by

[31] For a thorough discussion of the unequal conduciveness to cooperative treatment of economic and security issues, see Lipson (1984).

means of policy coordination. However, they insist that this is not the only impediment to international cooperation in mixed-motives situations: in addition, states, being defensive positionalists, may eschew collaboration and thus forgo even sizeable absolute gains, when they expect their partners to reap even greater benefits and thus increase their relative capabilities. Grieco (1988a: 487) argues that, since this *relative gains problem for cooperation* has gone unrecognized by neoliberal authors and, in fact, could not have been accounted for by neoliberalism due to its depiction of states as rational egoists, "realism . . . offers a more complete understanding of the problem of international cooperation than does its latest liberal challenger." Furthermore, because of this additional major barrier to coordinated action for mutual benefit, realism's generally greater skepticism about international cooperation is well-founded.

This realist analysis of the cooperation problem does not only suggest a hypothesis about the likelihood of states working together for mutual advantage, but also one about the *form* that any collaboration that might be achieved is likely to take: defensive positionalism creates a tendency for states to cooperate on terms that ensure a *balanced (or equitable) distribution of gains*, i.e. one which "roughly maintains pre-cooperation balances of capabilities" (Grieco 1990: 47). Since such a distribution of benefits from cooperation often does not result "automatically,"[32] states regularly offer side-payments or other concessions to dissipate otherwise disadvantaged partners' concerns about relative losses. Conversely, if gains are unbalanced and attempts to redress this problem are not made or fail to take effect, ongoing cooperative ventures are likely to come under stress or even break down altogether.

In order to test the "more complete understanding of the problem of international cooperation" offered by realism, Grieco (1990) has conducted a study of the collective attempts to remove non-tariff barriers (NTBs) to trade undertaken during and subsequent to the Tokyo Round of the General Agreement on Tariffs and Trade (GATT). The design of the study is competitive, pitting realism against neoliberalism. Indeed, the case selection aims at conducting a "crucial experiment" (Stinchcombe 1968: 24–8; Eckstein 1975: 113–23), which "generates find-

[32] Recall the fact discussed in the preceding section (4.2) that there frequently exists a multitude of Pareto-efficient solutions to a collective action problem that differ sharply in their distributional consequences.

ings that simultaneously constitute strong disconfirming evidence for one theory (that is, refutation in circumstances highly biased in the theory's favor) and strong confirming evidence for another, competing theory (that is, failure to refute or even affirmation of the theory in circumstances least favorable to it)" (Grieco 1990: 14f.).

Grieco (1990: 12–14) chose the NTB case (which turns out, in practice, to consist of six cases) because of the presumption that it represents a hard case for realism, but an easy case for neoliberalism. Since the issue-area belongs to the economic rather than the security realm and the central actors are advanced democracies who are not only highly interdependent but often military allies as well, neoliberalism should have little difficulty coping with this case, whereas realism, due to its preoccupation with "high politics" and conflictual relationships, is likely to be less well equipped to shed light on the collective behavior to be observed in the case at hand.

The Tokyo Round, which was launched in 1973 and concluded in 1979, produced a regime which consists of six codes and – representing the procedural component of the regime – associated committees of signatories dealing with different kinds of NTBs. Codes were agreed upon covering customs-valuation methods, import-licensing procedures, technical barriers, anti-dumping practices, government procurement, and subsidies and countervailing measures. Grieco (1990: 18) finds that the effectiveness of these agreements varied considerably in the 1980s and that this variance is largely a function of the level of cooperation (or discord) between the European Community and the United States. His main results are twofold. First, neither cheating nor the variables that, according to neoliberalism, determine the likelihood of cheating can account for the varying level of EC–US cooperation. (The neoliberal variables that are taken into account are (i) the number of participants, (ii) the level of development of the partners, (iii) the degree of iteration, and (iv) the size of the benefits from cooperation.) (Grieco 1990: 19, ch. 6). Second, the distribution of success and failure among the codes is consistent with realist expectations centering upon states' intolerance for relative losses (Grieco 1990: ch. 7). Most important for the hypothesis advanced by realists are the (sub-)agreements concerning government procurement and technical barriers. According to Grieco (1990: 182–209), the effectiveness of these accords was reduced by conflicts that originated in the fears harbored by members of the EC that they might lose ground (in technologically critical sectors) to the United States and Japan, as a result of fully implementing an agreement which was beneficial to the Europeans in absolute terms but *even more so* to their overseas competitors.[33]

The role of international institutions

Neoliberals have based their theory of international regimes on a specific analysis of the problems that make cooperation difficult for states. Not surprisingly, then, Grieco's realist critique of this analysis has implications for the role to be played by international institutions as well. At first sight, these implications appear to be purely negative, yet closer inspection of Grieco's position reveals a more nuanced picture and a more favorable view of the significance of international regimes. The case for an anti-institutionalist interpretation of Grieco's argument is readily made: Grieco intends his argument as a *defense* of the realist view of international politics against the challenge posed by "neoliberal institutionalism" and believes himself to have shown that "realism is still the most powerful theory of international politics" (Grieco 1988a: 487).[34] According to *realism* (and contrary to what neoliberals think), however, international institutions "affect the prospects for cooperation only marginally" and are not "an independent force facilitating cooperation" (Grieco 1988a: 488, 494). Thus, Grieco would seem to be committed to rejecting the view that regimes matter.

Nonetheless, Grieco's (1990: 233f.) own conclusion is quite different:

> [I]nternational institutions *do* matter for states as they attempt to cooperate. Indeed realists would argue that the problem with neoliberal institutionalism is not that it stresses the importance of institutions but that it *understates* the range of functions that institutions must perform to help states work together. Realists would agree that international

[33] The other codes turn out far less relevant for Grieco's purpose of conducting a competitive theory test (see also Keck 1993: 55). In fact, the observable patterns in these cases are more or less consistent with both realism *and* neoliberalism. The codes (or sub-agreements) that achieved a high level of success generated absolute gains for all parties and no significant relative losses for either party (at least not for the EC, the partner to be expected to be more sensitive to relative performance). Finally, the one agreement that was a complete failure (subsidies) came to be seen by the EC as being not beneficial to it at all (whether in relative or absolute terms).

[34] Grieco (1990: 229f.) is aware that there are further theories of institutions that are even more fundamentally critical of the realist perspective on international politics. Moreover, he regards these approaches, which we refer to as knowledge-based theories of regimes (see ch. 5 below), as "the most serious liberal institutionalist challenge" to realism, suggesting, however, that the power- and anarchy-based argument he directed at the neoliberal account of cooperation and regimes might apply to those approaches as well.

> institutions are important because they reduce cheating; yet, realists would also argue, they must do much more than that if cooperation is to be achieved.

The fact that, in light of the realist understanding of anarchy, the neoliberal institutionalist analysis of the cooperation problem turns out to be incomplete does not entail that the solution strategy highlighted by neoliberalism – institution-building – is irrelevant for states in their attempts to overcome the full range of obstacles standing in the way of mutually beneficial collaboration. International regimes can be instrumental in mitigating not only the cheating problem, but the relative gains problem as well. Indeed, Grieco (1988b: 614–20; 1990: 234) suggests that regimes may be used to affect both of the variables that determine the severity of relative gains concerns: the size of the gap in pay-offs ($W - V$) and the sensitivity of actors to relative losses (k).

As regards gaps in gains, international regimes (as, for example, GATT) often include stipulations providing for differential treatment of weaker partners who are less well able to exploit the opportunities resulting from regime-based cooperation. Regimes may also serve as institutional frameworks to facilitate the arrangement of *side-payments* to improve the relative performance of otherwise dissatisfied actors. The regular review conferences prescribed by the procedural component of many regimes allow relatively disadvantaged states to voice their concerns about the skewed distribution of gains and to push for corrections. Formal opting-out clauses as exist in some regimes (e.g. the whaling regime) lower exit costs and thus work as additional "insurance against the development of otherwise politically unacceptable gaps in jointly produced gains" (Grieco 1988b: 620). As to actors' intolerance for relative losses, Grieco speculates about the possibility of institutions promoting a *norm* of reciprocity (again GATT is a case in point) which, to the extent that it is regarded as effective, makes it easier for states to accept relative losses in one period or on one issue, as they expect to be compensated in a later period or on another issue.[35]

More recently, Grieco (1995) has put forward a "voice-opportunity hypothesis" to explain why states, in contradiction to the realist expectation that the units in an anarchical system tend to "balance" rather than to "bandwagon," sometimes seek intensified cooperation with more powerful states (even including ones which might reach for

[35] Keohane's (1986c: 19–24) observations about diffuse and sequential reciprocity seem to be highly relevant in this connection.

regional hegemony). The "puzzle" that suggested this revision of realism's "essentially sceptical expectations about the importance assigned by states to international institutions" (Grieco 1995: 39) is the decision of states such as France and Italy to collaborate with the united Germany to launch a process that is meant to culminate in a European Monetary Union. Grieco (1995: 34) interprets this decision as an attempt on the part of these states to use a newly constructed institution (i.e. the European Currency Bank) to gain more opportunities for them to "voice their concerns and interests" in the field of European monetary policy and "thereby prevent or at least ameliorate their domination" by a stronger partner (i.e. Germany).

It may be added that even if institutions could not do anything to ameliorate the relative gains problem, Grieco's admission that the fear of cheating is a potentially important barrier to cooperation and that institutions can reduce that fear entails the neoliberal proposition that institutions can facilitate cooperation. Indeed, it would seem to follow that sometimes cooperation crucially depends on the availability of institutions: this will be the case whenever (in a PD situation) collaboration is *not* likely to produce unequal shares of gains but informational asymmetries are significant. In such a situation, states that do not worry about relative losses are likely not to cooperate for fear of being double-crossed by their partners, unless institutions to dissipate such fears are in place (or can be created at a reasonable cost).[36]

As already noted, Grieco does not claim to have presented a theory of international institutions so far. Indeed, he has called on realists to develop such a theory (Grieco 1993b: 335; 1995: 39). It is not surprising, therefore, that the enumeration of these additional "functions" of regimes leaves open numerous questions. The most pressing of these, of course, is *to what extent* these considerations suggest a revision of the realist tenet that "international institutions affect the prospects for cooperation only marginally" (Grieco 1988a: 488). (It seems inevitable, in light of Grieco's own analysis, to make *some* revision.) Any attempt to

[36] Note that here we follow Grieco's practice to treat cheating and relative gains as two analytically separate problems. This practice is questionable, however, because an actor who is being cheated at once suffers relative (as well as absolute) losses (Milner 1992: 486). Giving up this practice, though, would not alter the conclusion that the "more complete understanding" of the cooperation problem provided by realism implies a positive role for international institutions as long as it is acknowledged (as it is by Grieco) that regimes can reduce the relative gains concerns that arise from the possibility of cheating.

provide a convincing answer to this question would presumably include theoretical and, in particular, empirical investigations that aim at establishing how *effectively* regimes do perform these functions under varying conditions. What does it take for an institution to be capable of actually fulfilling these tasks? And are the conditions under which regimes seem to facilitate cooperation through the above mechanisms more or less identical with the conditions under which cooperation is likely even in the absence of an institution (as most realists would suspect they are)? But if so, why do states invest so much effort in establishing institutions in the first place? (Keohane and Martin 1995: 40f.)

The neorealist–neoliberal debate I: do relative gains concerns matter?

As mentioned earlier, Grieco's critical analysis of neoliberalism has triggered the latest round in the longstanding debate between realism and liberalism about the proper understanding of essential features of world politics (Baldwin 1993b; Keck 1993; Powell 1994). The controversy has paid little (if any) attention to Grieco's positive interpretation of international institutions, but has focused on the underpinnings of this (nascent) theory, i.e. Grieco's realist account of the cooperation problem for states. The dispute provoked by Grieco's challenge basically has taken place on two "fronts": one where conceptual and theoretical (deductive) arguments are being exchanged and one where the validity of Grieco's empirical argument is at issue. We cover both fronts in turn, starting with the deductive debate.

Assuming (for the sake of the argument) that states care for relative gains, Snidal (1991a; 1991b) has employed game-theoretic models to examine the proposition that relative gains concerns seriously inhibit the ability of states to cooperate in a decentralized setting. His results provide very limited support for the realist position other than in a tight bipolar world in which the two camps are highly sensitive to relative gains. Since Snidal's analysis is particularly interesting and sophisticated and is often regarded as a devastating critique of Grieco's position, we look at his argument in somewhat greater detail.

Snidal finds that, in a situation in which there are only *two actors*, relative gains concerns can indeed make cooperation significantly more difficult. If states care *only* about relative gains, the situation is zero-sum no matter how conducive to cooperation the underlying absolute gains situation structure. Thus, even the game of Harmony when played

		Actor B C	Actor B D
Actor A	C	$4,4_{P,N,M}$	2,3
	D	3,2	1,1

P = Pareto-efficient; N = Nash equilibrium;
M = maximin solution

Fig. 7. Harmony.

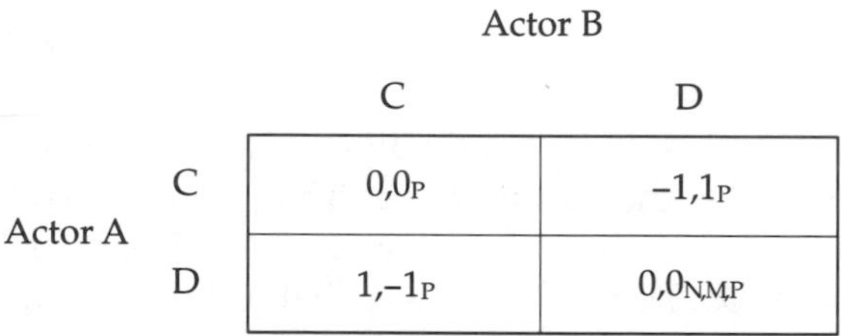

		Actor B C	Actor B D
Actor A	C	$0,0_{P}$	$-1,1_{P}$
	D	$1,-1_{P}$	$0,0_{N,M,P}$

P = Pareto-efficient; N = Nash equilibrium;
M = maximin solution

Fig. 8. Harmony played by pure relative gains seekers.

by pure relative gains seekers no longer sustains cooperation among rational actors (Snidal 1991b: 706). When actors pursue absolute gains, Harmony is highly conducive to cooperation, because each player has the dominant strategy to choose C, i.e. he is better off acting cooperatively no matter what his partner decides to do.[37] Things change dramatically, however, if actors are only interested in relative gains: Harmony gets transformed into a situation of pure conflict. (Here we assume that the numbers in the matrix do not only represent ordinal ranks but cardinal pay-offs as well.)

Pure relative gains seeking, however, is an extreme possibility. Therefore, Snidal goes on to explore situations in which states are inter-

[37] Stein (1990: 18) regards the view that Harmony is "the modal payoff environment in international politics" as characteristic of the classical liberal perspective on world politics. Since in a Harmony situation cooperation is the natural outcome, *laissez-faire* liberals face difficulties in accounting for international institutions (Stein 1990: 25f.). In the language of situation-structuralism, Harmony is *not* a problematic social situation.

ested in both absolute and relative gains. Varying the importance actors attach to relative performance Snidal (1991b: 708–13) shows that higher levels of relative gains concerns (short of pure relative gains seeking) make cooperation less likely by converting situation structures in which cooperation is comparatively easy to achieve into Prisoner's Dilemmas (albeit not very intense ones) and by making (the cooperation problems posed by) PDs more intense.

The other games besides Harmony that Snidal takes into consideration are Chicken, a coordination game similar to Battle of the Sexes, and two kinds of assurance games. The intensity of the cooperation problem is measured in terms of the minimum discount factor (describing the relative valuation of future benefits) that is required to support cooperation when the game is iterated infinitely. With one minor exception, this minimum discount factor is always higher in PD than in the other games. Consequently, results indicating a destructive effect of relative gains concerns on cooperation which are based on the assumption that the underlying absolute gains game is PD do not generalize to all strategic constellations – an observation that may be seen as underscoring the analytical value of a situation-structural approach (see sect. 3.2 above) to issues of international cooperation (Snidal 1991b: 712f.).

If the realist expectations regarding the effects of relative gains considerations on international cooperation are more or less confirmed by Snidal's analysis of the two-actor constellation, the same cannot be said about the obviously much more realistic situations in which three, four, or more players interact. To analyze the impact of relative gains orientations in the multiple-actor case Snidal (now focusing exclusively on the PD) develops a model that, *inter alia,* includes information about the general (system-wide) level of relative gains concerns and the varying importance states attach to relative performance in their dealings with particular other states (represented by specific weights, w_{ij}). The latter parameter is important, because (as Grieco had pointed out in his discussion of the determinants of k) states are likely to regard some partners as more frightening than others. This model is used to study how changes in the overall sensitivity to relative gains and in the number of actors affect the difficulty of cooperation. Again, the difficulty of cooperation is measured in terms of the minimum discount factor necessary to stabilize cooperation. The number of states in the system is factored in by means of its effect on the weights (w_{ij}) states attach to relative gains in their encounters with other states. For

Snidal (1991b: 716, 725, n. 31) assumes that (1) "states distribute their relative gains concerns across states" and that (2) "other states are weighted equally in terms of relative gains." (Obviously, the latter assumption is not unproblematic given that the explicit purpose of these weights is to "incorporate *different* evaluations of different states" (Snidal 1991b: 716 [emphasis added]).) The central result is that, even with fairly pronounced relative gains concerns, the cooperation-inhibiting effect decreases rapidly with increasing numbers of states in the system. Thus, adding a third party to a bipolar world of pure relative gains seekers is equivalent to halving the level of sensitivity to relative performance (Snidal 1991b: 719). If the number of actors is very large, relative gains seeking does not impede cooperation at all (Snidal 1991a).

A potentially serious limitation to Snidal's analysis is his assumption that cooperation between any two states[38] does not result in relative gains for either party. In his model relative gains can only be achieved through unilateral defection or with respect to third parties. Taking into account third parties is important, because relative gains concerns may induce not only additional reservations against collaboration, but also what Snidal (1991a: 401; 1991b: 722) refers to as "defensive cooperation," i.e. cooperation that is due to the awareness of states that they may also lose relatively by *refusing* to cooperate (e.g. because of unequal shares of absolute gains) if and when *others* cooperate among themselves. Still, Snidal's assumption of equal gains from cooperation[39] raises the question of whether he has not missed a crucial point of the realist argument, since, as we have seen, the distribution of gains within a specific cooperative undertaking which may, and often does, yield relative losses to some parties is precisely what Grieco's argument centers upon. Not surprisingly, therefore, Grieco has criticized Snidal's defense of the neoliberal theory of cooperation for solving "the relative gains problem by assumption" (Grieco 1993a: 730).

In a rejoinder, Snidal has rejected this criticism arguing that it is based on a "misunderstanding of the relative gains problem" which, according to Snidal, is primarily about *motivations* and the way they affect strategic incentives (e.g. by making PDs more intense) rather than about

[38] In a way similar to Axelrod (1984), Snidal studies cooperation in an *n*-actor setting as a form of strategic interaction that takes place in dyadic relationships.

[39] More precisely, Snidal (1991b: 714f.) assumes constant returns to scale for cooperating states and then shows that, given this assumption, states, *irrespective of their relative sizes,* achieve equal gains from their mutual cooperation.

outcomes. What is more, he provides a formal proof to show that his central results are independent of special assumptions concerning the distribution of gains in dyadic relationships (Snidal 1993: 739f., 741f.). Snidal's analysis, of course, might be flawed for different reasons. Otto Keck (1993: 53) has made the rather fundamental objection that "the realists' concern for relative gains . . . [does not seem to be] adequately modeled if averaging out of (weighted or unweighted) relative gains is allowed for" as is the case here. He explains his dissatisfaction by means of a numerical example: "[C]onsider a world with three states, each with an initial welfare of 10 units. According to Snidal's model, state 1 would be indifferent against a change which did not affect its own welfare and at the same time increased the welfare of state 2 to 20 and the welfare of state 3 to zero."[40]

Given this rather intricate situation, it is useful to look briefly at Keck's own critical analysis of the realist argument which addresses more directly the issues on which Grieco focuses. Using an indifference-curve approach and concentrating on the two-actor case (i.e. the constellation in which, according to both Grieco [1990: 228] and Snidal [1991b], the cooperation-inhibiting effect of relative gains concerns should be at its maximum), Keck (1993: 47–53) has shown that relative gains concerns (as long as actors take at least some interest in absolute gains as well) do not decrease the prospects of cooperation (as compared to an otherwise identical situation in which only absolute gains count) *unless some "very restrictive" conditions are met*. Collaboration is only impeded if three conditions hold simultaneously:

(1) the gains from cooperation are indivisible
(2) side-payments cannot be made
(3) (appropriate) issue-linkages are impossible.

Provided that the underlying absolute gains game is not constant-sum and relative gains concerns are not pure but mixed with an interest in absolute gains for their own sake, there is a set of possible agreements that would make both actors better off. What is more, since this set is a genuine subset of the set of Pareto-superior agreements possible for pure absolute gains seekers, a concern for relative gains may even have the paradoxical effect of facilitating bargaining and thus

[40] Note, however, that the reason Grieco (1990: 228) gives for why realists expect states to prefer collaboration with many partners over collaboration with few appears to endorse precisely this interpretation!

cooperation by reducing the number of feasible settling points (Keck 1993: 49).[41]

There may, of course, be legitimate *disagreement* about how restrictive Keck's three conditions really are and, consequently, how strongly relative gains concerns impede cooperation in practice.[42] Hence, the neoliberal–neorealist dispute might well continue along these lines. Perhaps more interesting, however, are the *similarities* between Keck's result and Grieco's own reflections about the prerequisites of cooperation in a "realist" world. Indeed, Keck's analysis, which is presented as a vindication of the neoliberal case, may be seen as directly feeding into the (nascent) *realist theory of institutions* we have discussed above, *if and to the extent that* institutions are likely to facilitate the operation of the mechanisms this analysis points to (redistribution of gains, side-payments, issue-linkage). And indeed, both Grieco and Keck (as well as other theorists of regimes) suggest that this *is* a plausible hypothesis. Not surprisingly, then, Keck's (1993: 52, see also 58) conclusion is strongly reminiscent of the extended quote from Grieco (1990: 233f.) we have given above: "This [Keck's] analysis of the relative-gains problem implies the counter-intuitive result that with increasing emphasis on relative gains the need for international institutions and their potential contribution increases rather than decreases." It seems to us that this is an interesting convergence, indeed, and one that, although it need not be seen as erasing all differences among neoliberal and realist approaches to regimes,[43] does suggest that a more constructive dialogue

[41] This argument assumes, however, that cheating is not a problem. Factoring out the cheating problem may be justified in this connection, as Grieco himself treats the relative gains problem and the cheating problem as analytically separate issues. However, substantively, this move is problematic and suggests a possibly important limitation to Keck's otherwise elegant analysis. Thus, Snidal (1993: 739) has taken Grieco to task for not realizing that "the relative-gains argument is intertwined with considerations of cheating" adding that relative gains "do their work by increasing the incentives to cheat while decreasing the benefits of cooperation." Another assumption in Keck's analysis that might be criticized as (empirically) inadequate is that the zone of agreement is fully specified and known to the actors (Young 1989b). Note, however, that, according to Young, relaxing this assumption should only further improve the prospects of cooperation (see sect. 3.4 above).

[42] For an argument stressing the difficulties of equalizing distributional outcomes by means of side-payments, see Gowa (1989b: 318).

[43] For example, realists might argue that analyses such as Keck's do not take account of the *uncertainties* of states regarding how large asymmetries in outcomes will be in reality and to what uses they may be put. And realists may also point out that neoliberals understate the *risk-aversive* nature of states that guarantees that such considerations will loom large in their calculations (Grieco 1993a: 733–5).

between these important schools of thought is not only desirable but feasible as well.

The neorealist-neoliberal debate II: are states concerned with relative gains?

While the conceptual-theoretical part of the controversy triggered by Grieco's challenge to neoliberalism has focused on the question of whether, and if so when and to what extent, relative gains concerns diminish the likelihood of cooperation between states, the empirical part has centered upon Grieco's claim to have demonstrated, in his study of the Tokyo Round agreements on NTBs, that states actually care for relative gains. Grieco's critics have pointed out that his argument is inconclusive because of a "fundamental ambiguity" that it cannot resolve: what Grieco essentially bases his conclusion upon is the observation of tough bargaining, but tough bargaining (including the breakdown of negotiations) may *just as well* result from absolute gains maximizing as from concerns about relative losses (Keohane 1993b: 280, 283; see also Keck 1993: 56). These critics are correct insofar as Grieco does tend to attribute any intense distributional conflict (particularly when it undermines the effectiveness of a code) to relative gains concerns. Two qualifications are in order, though.

First, Grieco does not just provide *any* evidence for distributional conflict (and its detrimental effects on cooperation). His observations are more specific and more closely in touch with his theoretically derived expectations. Thus, Grieco (1990: 182–8) reports numerous instances in which negotiators rejected proposals the implementation of which would have been likely to make all better off (in absolute terms) with reference to the *asymmetrical* (inequitable, unbalanced, etc.) distribution of gains and burdens (i.e. opportunities and costly obligations) they would produce. To be sure, as Snidal (1991b: 703, n. 29) has pointed out, "[u]nequal gains diminish the incentives of one side to cooperate (and increase the incentives of the other side) for *both* absolute and relative gains reasons" [emphasis added]. So the "fundamental ambiguity" would seem to be preserved. Still, there seems to be a "surplus" in Grieco's observation that is not well accounted for in terms of absolute gains maximizing: *whence the saliency of symmetrical gains?* Why is it that only those states demand a greater share for themselves whose satisfaction would depend on the distribution of gains becoming more equal?

Neoliberals seem to have two possible answers to this. They might modify their motivational assumption suggesting that states are not really maximizing, but satisficing actors (Simon 1972). But, obviously, this answer has its own difficulties. Not only might it appear as though neoliberals, in their debate with realism, change the rules as they go along. (True, Keohane [1984: 110–16] could point out that he had sought to integrate concepts of bounded rationality and satisficing behavior into his theory right from the beginning. Yet, this part of his theory seems to have had little influence on the ensuing debate and has been ignored by other neoliberals.) Even more important, realists might ask for an explanation of *why* states seem to link their "aspiration level" so closely to a symmetrical distribution of gains, and they might add that only realism has such an explanation: defensive positionalism.[44]

Neoliberals might therefore advance a different argument. They might point out that defensive positionalism is not the only possible explanation for the observed saliency of symmetrical gains, thus varying their theme that the realist argument suffers from an unresolved ambiguity. More specifically, they might argue that the divergence in the behavior of relatively advantaged and relatively disadvantaged actors might also be put down to the operation of a *norm of reciprocity* (or equity) at the international level (Keohane 1989c: 4).[45] Such a norm would affect the costs of bargaining for greater shares differently for differently situated actors: while the relatively disadvantaged (at a given point in time) would find it easier to advance their position, the relatively advantaged would find it more difficult to do so. However, this answer, too, could be challenged. For one thing, it is unclear how the existence (and effectiveness) of such a generalized norm fits in with the rationalist framework that both neoliberalism and realism adhere to. For another, to the extent that norms *can* be accounted for in rationalist terms it may again turn out that realism holds a key to such an account whereas neoliberalism does not. Thus, from a realist perspective, "it may be possible to argue that states . . . seek in their

[44] Note, in this connection, that Grieco's formula describing the calculations of advantage made by states, $U = V - k(W - V)$, is not well suited to express his idea of *defensive* positionalism: according to this formula states do attain greater utility through *relative gains* and it is not clear why in this case they should prefer less utility to more. What this indicates is that the defensive positionalism thesis, which, if Grieco is correct, is accepted by most modern realists, suggests that the characterization of realism as a rationalist theory should be qualified: in as far as states are depicted as satisficing rather than maximizing actors, realists endorse a procedural (or subjective) rather than the more common substantive conception of rationality (Simon 1972; 1985).

[45] Keohane (1986c: 5–8) defines the concept of reciprocity in terms of contingency of behavior and *equivalence* (symmetry) of benefits.

ongoing interactions to develop commonly shared norms . . . that reflect their concerns about anarchy but nevertheless allow for cooperative endeavors" (Grieco 1990: 230).[46]

A second qualification which is in order is that, contrary to what some of his critics have suggested, the ambiguity of tough bargaining or distributional conflict has not escaped Grieco altogether. He is well aware that the best way to make his case would be to come up with situations in which states pursued greater symmetry *even at the price* of smaller absolute gains for themselves (Grieco 1990: 20, 169). The question is, though, how many such situations he really has been able to report in his study. Our impression is that evidence of *this* kind is scarce in his (otherwise very carefully argued) book and that the few situations that can be plausibly interpreted this way hardly provide a basis broad enough to decide an issue as fundamental as that of the *nature* of state motivations.

Perhaps Grieco's best case is the dispute about the regulation of basic price systems under the Code on Anti-Dumping Practices, where some countries at first *blocked* a proposed interpretation of the agreement with reference to distributional asymmetries inherent in the proposal and then *accepted* a modified interpretation which not only addressed some of these asymmetries, but also promised *smaller* absolute gains to the group of opposing countries than the original one (Grieco 1990: 209–14). In addition, two other events might be regarded as supporting Grieco's case relatively well: the EC's rejection of the proposal made by Switzerland and strongly backed by the United States to extend the Government Procurement Code to government-owned enterprises, and the politics of the EC with regard to product-testing as an item to be dealt with under the Code on Technical Barriers to Trade (Grieco 1990: 198–200, 194–6). It should be emphasized, though, that neither case is clear-cut: the alternative explanation that the reluctant parties were simply holding out to get a better deal cannot be ruled out with any great degree of certainty.

Thus, it would be difficult to argue that Grieco has successfully made his empirical case for the pervasiveness of relative gains concerns. This said, a proposition is not refuted just because attempts to prove it have

46 If evocation of a norm of reciprocity should turn out to be a self-defeating move for the neoliberal case, there may be no need to make it in the first place. There may be alternatives. For example, neoliberals might point to the "veil of uncertainty" that Young sees in operation in most instances of institutional bargaining (see sect. 3.4 above) as a non-normative, non-realist mechanism that might account for the tendency (assuming there is one) of – absolute-gains maximizing, but risk-sensitive – states to settle upon regime-constituting contracts that can be described as "equitable" and balanced.

failed. Consequently, Grieco's critics have been careful not to claim that his study has strengthened their absolute gains interpretation of state action. All they could claim is that it has not weakened it. Moreover, they now concede that "the issue of relative gains . . . has been underemphasized . . . by liberal or neoliberal commentators on the world economy" (Keohane 1993b: 283).[47] Snidal (1991b: 702, 720f.) has even *used* the relative gains thesis to explain (albeit provisionally) a number of "stylized facts" about the postwar international system (the tendency of the great to be exploited by the small, hegemonic cooperation and decline, and cooperation patterns in a loose bipolar world). Finally, explanations being based on hypotheses, Snidal's empirical applications bring back to mind that there is yet another and possibly more fruitful way of evaluating empirically realist and neoliberal propositions about state motivations: rather than seeking to establish *directly* that states do or do not care for relative gains (the path chosen by Grieco), scholars interested in this issue may also make efforts to derive and test contrasting hypotheses about various aspects of the collective behavior of states. Grieco (1988a: 504–6) himself has made a promising start along these lines, but stopped short of executing the actual hypothesis tests. For example, according to Grieco, realists would hypothesize that states, speculating that relative losses *vis-à-vis* some partners might be compensated for by relative gains *vis-à-vis* others, find it easier to cooperate with many partners than with few. By contrast, neoliberals would hypothesize that just the opposite holds, because a greater number of actors decreases transparency and therefore exacerbates the cheating problem (Oye 1986b: 18–22). Meanwhile, as deserving as an adequate testing of such pairs of competing hypotheses might be, it must not be overlooked that it would also be fraught with difficulties because of the rather stringent requirements it places on case selection.

"Trench warfare" or cooperation? The future of the debate

These unexploited opportunities for testing competing hypotheses notwithstanding, continuing to focus on what divides neoliberals and

[47] Keohane talks of "underemphasizing" rather than "missing," because in *After Hegemony* he did note the possibility that states might be concerned with relative gains and that this attitude can hamper cooperation. However, the two occasions on which this possibility is briefly mentioned (Keohane 1984: 54, 123, n. 9) give the impression that Keohane then regarded negative altruism on the part of states as an extreme case not deserving of extensive theoretical treatment (see also Young 1989a: 210, n. 53) – a view which he has clearly abandoned since (Keohane 1993b: 274–8).

realists need not be the most fruitful approach to advancing the cause of regime analysis, or international relations theory more generally, in the years to come. To be sure, the "politics of difference" that have characterized a substantial part of this debate have encouraged scholars to sharpen their ideas and to explore the consequences of their assumptions more thoroughly. Still, we feel that a point has been reached where the marginal utility of the contest approach to promoting theoretical progress appears to be diminishing rapidly and more attention should be given to the commonalities of the two perspectives and the potential they hold for some sort of synthesis. In particular, as we have demonstrated above, realists and neoliberals are no longer easily distinguished by the significance they attribute to international institutions. At a minimum, the question is no longer one of "yes" or "no." Taking states' concerns about relative gains more seriously does not preclude a positive role for international institutions. Not only do earlier arguments about cheating remain in force, the relative gains problem of cooperation highlights possible functions of regimes that hitherto have gone unnoticed. Empirical research is needed to establish whether these functions are in fact performed and how effective regimes can be in mitigating this problem. Another promising avenue for future research, as well as a possible lever for furthering synthesis, is the conditions under which relative gains concerns are likely to be pronounced (i.e. the determinants of Grieco's k coefficient). These conditions should affect both the likelihood of cooperation (at least in small-n settings) and the *form* of institutions that may be created to facilitate collective action. At the same time they suggest when realist *or* neoliberal expectations are more appropriate. Thus, we believe, with Snidal (1993: 741), that "[t]he two perspectives share much in common and reach similar conclusions regarding many matters. Even when dealing with contentious issues such as relative gains, it is more productive to investigate how the different arguments work together than to seek to establish either liberalism or realism as a clear victor." What is needed, therefore, are steps "towards a contextually richer theory that is able to explain international politics better than either vulgar realism or vulgar liberalism in isolation."[48]

[48] This point is elaborated in the concluding chapter.

5 Knowledge-based theories: ideas, arguments, and social identities

Cognitivist approaches to the study of international politics stress ideas and knowledge as explanatory variables. Cognitivists are critical of rationalist theories of international politics, whether of neoliberal or realist provenance. The common flaw of these theories, from a cognitivist point of view, is that they treat states' identities and interests as exogenously given, i.e. as non-theorized initial conditions in explanations of international phenomena such as international regimes. Proponents of knowledge-based approaches point out that by blackboxing the processes which produce the self-understandings of particular states (i.e. their identities) as well as the objectives which they pursue in their foreign policy (i.e. what they perceive to be in their interest), a significant source of variation in international behavior and outcomes is ignored and *ipso facto* trivialized. Cognitivists argue that these processes are shaped by the normative and causal beliefs that decisionmakers hold and that, consequently, changes in belief systems can trigger changes in policy. Hence, rationalist (neoliberal or realist) explanations of international regimes are at best incomplete and need to be supplemented or even supplanted by a mode of analysis which focuses on the way the "distribution of knowledge" (Alfred Schütz) constitutes the identities, and shapes the preferences as well as the perceived options, of state actors (Schaber and Ulbert 1994).

Knowledge-based approaches to international regimes share a dissatisfaction with the model of the *homo œconomicus* which informs rationalist theorizing, bringing back in, as it were, the *homo sapiens* by stressing the knowledge-dependence of international behavior. Meanwhile, there are significant differences among cognitivists themselves as to how radical a critique of rationalism they deem necessary. There are, in other words, "weak" and "strong" cognitivists. While weak cognitivists regard the problem of mainstream (i.e. neoliberal and realist) approaches to the study of international regimes as one of (essential) incompleteness, strong cognitivists challenge the rationalist mode of analysis in international relations theory (and other branches of social inquiry) more fundamentally, suggesting a replacement of the *homo œconomicus* by the *homo sociologicus* as the microanalytical foundation of social theorizing. That is, while weak cognitivists focus on the origins and dynamics of rational actors' understandings of the world, strong cognitivists inquire into the origins and dynamics of social actors' self-understandings in the world.[1]

Weak cognitivists, whose perspective we address in section 5.1, argue that the demand for regimes in international relations depends on actors' perception of international problems, which is, in part, produced by their causal and normative beliefs. These beliefs, in turn, are considered partially independent of actors' material environment (e.g. the distribution of power and wealth), which makes both the origins of these beliefs and the mechanics of their impact on international decisionmaking worth studying. Owing to their focus on "the prevailing forms of reason by which actors identify their preferences, and the available choices [i.e. options] facing them" (P. Haas 1993: 170), the concerns of weak cognitivists can thus be seen as *complementary* to mainstream rationalist accounts of regimes, which, as we have noted, take preferences and options as exogenously given. Weak cognitivism in the study of regimes is an attempt to fill a gap in interest-based theorizing by supplying a theory of interest change. Therefore, in the final analysis, weak cognitivists are still comfortable with a conceptualization of states as rational utility-maximizers, provided it is admitted that the perception of utility depends on knowledge and that knowledge is irreducible to material structures (and thus possesses the status of an autonomous variable).

Characteristically, the criticism articulated by *strong cognitivists*, whose contribution is discussed in section 5.2, runs deeper. Strong cognitivists make the case for an *alternative* rather than a supplement to extant theorizing about regimes. These scholars are not so much concerned with the impact of new knowledge on states' perceptions of

[1] To be quite clear, weakness and strength, in this connection, is measured by the distance of the respective research program from rationalism, not by the quality of the arguments that it is based upon. In other words, to claim that the weak cognitivists have advanced stronger arguments than their strong counterparts would not amount to producing a contradiction in terms.

interest (against a backdrop of more or less stable identities) as with problematizing the existence and nature of states as competent actors in international politics. As we shall see, strong cognitivists hold that knowledge as a factor in international politics is not adequately conceptualized as a variable merely intervening between structural constraints, on the one hand, and behavioral outcomes, on the other, leaving the basic dispositions of actors unaffected. Rather, knowledge has to be appreciated as operating at a more fundamental level, indeed constituting states and enabling them to engage in both power games and cooperative ventures. This is because the concept of knowledge encompasses the shared understandings that shape the role identities of states, i.e. their fundamental self-understandings in relation to others. Strong cognitivists posit the existence of an *international society* which is structured by institutions.[2] Ultimately, these institutions are cognitive entities (mutual expectations, beliefs about appropriate and inappropriate behavior, etc.), although they depend on corresponding practices for their continuity. Strong cognitivists, thus, advocate a sociological turn in the study of international regimes (and of international relations more generally) to reflect their basic insight that knowledge not only affects states' interests but is constitutive of their identities: states as the central actors in international relations do not merely hold a certain stock of knowledge (e.g. scientific expertise) which influences their choices in specific situations, but they *are* states (and states of a particular kind) only by virtue of a shared knowledge which spans international relations as a social space.

This sheds new light on the meaning of rules in international life including those incorporated in international regimes. If international institutions can be regarded as embodying the cognitive structures that underpin international society and make possible meaningful action within that society, the nature of these institutions must escape the – instrumental – logic of rationalist approaches. For the latter, as we have seen in the preceding chapters, regimes boil down to useful but (from

[2] We use the terms "international society" and "international community" interchangeably and agree with Bull's (1977: 13) definition according to which a "society of states (or international society) exists when a group of states, conscious of certain common interests and common values, form a society in the sense that they conceive themselves to be bound by a common set of rules in their relations with one another, and share in the working of common institutions." In an international society (or community), states are recognized members whose legitimate interests are mutually respected. That is, the concept refers to a particular practice of states relying on principles of justice and "no harm."

the actors' point of view) contingent problem-solving devices which are put in place by self-interested states (who either do not or identify only negatively with one another). From a strongly cognitivist point of view, by contrast, international institutions appear as necessary features of international politics because they are prerequisites for, rather than consequences of, rational choices. As a result, the robustness of international institutions would seem to be considerably greater than neoliberals suggest, who can point out factors that drive up the price of opportunistic behavior, but are unable to appreciate the repercussions of institutionalized cooperation on actors' identities.

5.1 Weak cognitivism: ideas, learning, and the role of epistemic communities

In order to bring out the significance of weakly cognitivist arguments for the study of international regimes we proceed as follows. After outlining the central assumptions of this research program, we briefly review recent work focusing on the role of *ideas* (i.e. causal and normative beliefs held by individuals) in international politics. Although this work has obvious implications for the study of international regimes (justifying its inclusion in this book), its immediate concern is with establishing the need for a cognitive research agenda as a remedy for theoretical shortcomings of the dominant rationalism in the study of foreign policy. Subsequently, we turn to an argument which is more specifically concerned with the impact of cognitive change on international regime dynamics. Proposing to reconstruct processes of regime formation and change in terms of *learning*, this approach seeks to illuminate how new knowledge can influence the demand for rule-based cooperation among states (sect. 5.1.1). Finally, we examine research which addresses the issue of how new policy-relevant knowledge spreads and, in particular, makes its way to central decisionmakers. Recent work in this field has stressed the role of scientists and other experts who not only generate new insights into causal relationships but actively (and often effectively) promote those changes in public policy at the national and international levels which they believe are necessitated by these insights. More specifically, contributors to this body of literature have sought to shed light on when and how knowledge-based transnational networks, which they refer to as *epistemic communities*, come to affect processes of agenda-setting and regime formation (sect. 5.1.2).

Three central assumptions of the weakly cognitivist research program

Weak cognitivists emphasize that "between international structures and human volition lies interpretation. Before choices involving cooperation can be made, circumstances must be assessed and interests identified" (Adler and Haas 1992: 367; see also P. Haas 1992b: 2). Interpretation, in turn, is assumed to depend on the body of knowledge actors hold at a given time and place. This body of knowledge shapes the perception of reality and informs decisionmakers about linkages between causes and effects and, thus, between means and ends. Without at least implicit theories which the actors take to be valid (or plausible) representations of reality, genuine choices would be impossible. As a consequence, weak cognitivists argue, it is misleading to regard actors' interests as something that is simply "given"; rather, preferences are to be seen *and to be treated analytically* as contingent on how actors understand the natural and social world. Thus, weak cognitivists share the assumption "that the knowledge actors carry in their heads and project in their international encounters significantly shapes their behavior and expectations" (E. Haas 1990: 7), and conclude that students of international relations should seek to integrate knowledge structures and dynamics into their theoretical models.

Another assumption constitutive of the weakly cognitivist research program refers to the growing demand on the part of decisionmakers for scientific information and other supposedly reliable knowledge. Under the conditions of complex interdependence and because of the increasingly technical nature of international issues, decisionmakers experience enduring uncertainties about their interests and how to realize them (Adler and Haas 1992: 369; P. Haas 1992b: 14f.; Goldstein and Keohane 1993a: 16). Technological innovations devalue traditional strategies, and social change redefines the parameters of international relations. In such a situation, political priorities as well as strategies relating means to ends have to be reconsidered continually. State actors therefore are not only "power and wealth pursuers" – as realism and neoliberalism suggest – but also "uncertainty reducers" (P. Haas 1992b: 4). In order to make intelligent choices in unfamiliar situations decisionmakers need (and often demand) high-quality information and expert advice. Those who are in a position to supply the desired knowledge, therefore, can exert considerable influence on the choices made by policymakers.

As we have seen (sect. 3.1 above), *uncertainty* is also highlighted by contractualist theory. Moreover, since the central function of regimes, according to this theory, is to reduce uncertainty (which may lead to suboptimal collective behavior), Keohane's (1983) neoliberal demand-for-regimes argument has the implication that states can be described, or often act, as uncertainty reducers. Still, the differences between the two perspectives should not be overlooked. Contractualism's notion of uncertainty refers to states' lack of reliable information about the behavior and intentions of other states. Regimes are useful precisely because they help reduce this kind of uncertainty. By contrast, when weak cognitivists talk of decisionmakers' uncertainty, what they have in mind is the inability of politicians to assess the likely consequences of their decisions (or non-decisions) (e.g. on the natural environment). Scientists and other experts are often in a position to reduce (but also to create or intensify) this kind of uncertainty. Regimes are also relevant in this connection, but their causal role is an indirect one: for example, they may help spread policy-relevant scientific information (Keohane, Haas, and Levy 1993). In some respect, Young's (1989b: 358–62) notion of uncertainty is more similar to that of the weak cognitivists, as both depict decisionmakers as uncertain about what is in their interest. However, Young and the weak cognitivists tend to assess the relationship between uncertainty and international cooperation in opposing ways. While for Young a "veil of uncertainty" *improves* the prospects of regime formation (see sect. 3.4 above), weak cognitivists tend to associate the *reduction* of uncertainty due to the activities of epistemic communities with higher levels of cooperation.

A third assumption which is widely held among cognitivists refers to the importance of intersubjectively shared meanings for both regime formation and regime performance. As Peter Haas (1992b: 29) puts it: "Before states can agree on whether and how to deal collectively with a specific problem, they must reach some consensus about the nature and the scope of the problem and also about the manner in which the problem relates to other concerns in the same and additional issue-areas." Thus, a minimum of collective understanding concerning the issues at stake is supposed to be a necessary condition for the choice of a substantive body of rules. Otherwise, convergent expectations among independent actors in an international issue-area would be impossible, and cooperation would be doomed to failure. It is a question of particular interest to students of regimes as to where these expectations originate (Haggard and Simmons 1987: 509–13; E. Haas 1990: 20–8, 164; Adler and Haas 1992: 371; Jönsson 1993: 219f.).

5.1.1 *Creating a "knowledge-oriented research program": cognition as an explanatory variable*

Road maps, focal points, and institutions: how ideas matter

The impact of ideas on foreign policy has recently been probed in a volume edited by Judith Goldstein and Robert Keohane (1993b). The contributors to this volume gather evidence for the need to go beyond the rationalist mode of analysis, which in the past ten years or so has taken such firm roots in the study of international relations in general and in regime analysis in particular. Hence, the case studies that form the empirical backbone of the volume depart from the null hypothesis "that the actions described can be understood on the basis of egoistic interests in the context of power realities: that variations of interests are not accounted for by variations in the character of the ideas that people have" (Goldstein and Keohane 1993a: 26f.). Note that the sentence following the colon is not just a paraphrase of the first one. The null hypothesis is a double one: it implies, first, that – *given* a set of "egoistic interests" – behavior can be explained without reference to ideas (e.g. normative beliefs about right and wrong behavior) which might be thought to *intervene*; and, second, interests do not *change* as a result of changes in beliefs that actors hold (i.e., in relation to interest, ideas do not function as an *independent* variable). Analyzing a number of important changes in the history of international relations, the authors find that rationalist reasoning based on this twofold null hypothesis, time and again, proves ill-equipped to provide convincing explanations.

Two examples may serve to illustrate this. Scrutinizing the construction of an open world economy in the aftermath of World War II , John Ikenberry (1993: 58) points out that the impact of a set of policy ideas inspired by Keynesianism "was crucial in defining government *conceptions* of postwar interests" [emphasis added], even when underlying power realities and fundamental economic interests did affect the negotiations. According to Ikenberry, without allowing for the causal significance of this "new thinking" advocated by a highly respected group of officials and economists, the final outcome cannot be explained. "In effect, the 'new thinking' of these experts transformed the way people thought of or framed the issue of postwar economic order and, as a consequence, changed the outcome." (Ikenberry 1993: 59)

Another case in point is the abolition of colonialism and the institutionalization of the norm of national self-determination in the course of this century. Robert Jackson (1993: 128) points to a "fundamental shift of normative ideas" which has to be taken into consideration if the collapse of colonialism is to be accounted for. Reviewing the history of this far-reaching process, he concludes that "[d]ecolonization was above all an international change of ideas about legitimate and illegitimate rule and not a change in the balance of power or the economic utilities of imperialism" (Jackson 1993: 130).

With reference to such empirical anomalies from the perspective of conventional approaches, Goldstein and Keohane argue that changes in behavior, to some extent, can be explained by variations in principled (normative) or causal beliefs. *Principled beliefs* consist of "normative ideas that specify criteria for distinguishing right from wrong and just from unjust"; *causal beliefs* are defined as "beliefs about cause – effect relationships which derive authority from shared consensus of recognized elites . . . [and] provide guides for individuals on how to achieve their objectives." (Goldstein and Keohane 1993a: 9, 10) Although Goldstein and Keohane (1993a: 25; see also Levy 1994: 300; Nye 1987: 381) argue that new ideas "become politically efficacious only in conjunction with other changes, either in material interests or in power constellations," this cannot detract from the necessity to integrate moral concerns and scientific knowledge as explanatory factors into international relations theory.[3] At least in periods in which power relations are in flux and interests and strategies are unclear "new thinking" may have a considerable impact on the course of international politics (Goldstein and Keohane 1993a: 26). Under such conditions "ideas serve the purpose of guiding behavior . . . by stipulating causal patterns or by providing compelling ethical or moral motivations for action" (Goldstein and Keohane 1993a: 16).

More specifically, the influence of ideas works through one of three "causal pathways" (Goldstein and Keohane 1993a: 8–24). First, beliefs may serve as *road maps*. Out of the universe of possible actions decisionmakers select those which fit best with their normative and analytic understandings. Principled beliefs help define actors' goals

[3] For a recent study on the role of "moral vision" in foreign policy and, in particular, the policy of foreign aid, see Lumsdaine (1993).

(preferences), while causal beliefs strongly influence the choice of means to achieve these ends. Different choices under otherwise similar material circumstances can thus be explained by differences in the belief systems of actors. Second, widely shared ideas may facilitate cooperation in the absence of a unique equilibrium, serving as *focal points* which help define acceptable solutions to collective action problems. Third, the impact of ideas is often mediated and enhanced by international norms and rules which are created under the influence of particular widely shared beliefs. Once ideas have become *embodied in institutional frameworks*, they constrain public policy as long as they are not effectively undermined by new scientific discoveries or normative change.

The last two of these causal pathways, in particular, are clearly related to international regimes. Not only is the coordinating function of ideas relevant for explaining the content of specific regimes. Their implications are much more fundamental: as Geoffrey Garrett and Barry Weingast (1993) explain, in the absence of ideas as focal points regimes may often not be formed at all. Where there are several Pareto-optimal equilibria over which actors have divergent preferences (as in Battle of the Sexes), attempts at regime creation are often doomed to failure unless some compelling coordinating device is at hand. The third pathway, finally, sheds light on a specific effect of international regimes. This effect both presupposes and confirms the notion of institutional robustness, which may even superimpose in a somewhat paradoxical way the effectiveness of ideas as beliefs held by people: for, as Goldstein and Keohane (1993a: 20) observe, through the intervention of institutions "the impact of ideas may be prolonged for decades or even generations . . . [such that] ideas can have an influence even when no-one genuinely believes in them as principled or causal statements." With the help of institutions ideas have assumed a life of their own.

Note that both the arguments being discussed here have "materialistic" analogs within the study of regimes. With regard to the first of these, ideas as focal points have the same coordinating function in processes of regime formation that Krasner's "power-oriented research program" attributes to power (see sect. 4.2 above), and one might talk of focal points and power asymmetries as functional equivalents. The analogy is strengthened by the fact that both Krasner's materialistic and Garrett and Weingast's (1993: 175–7) idealistic perspectives have similar critical implications for the sort of functional argument which Keohane advanced in *After Hegemony*. Both criticize Keohane's functionalism for ignoring the fact that there is normally more than one Pareto-superior collective behavior and hence more than one possible constitutional contract states may agree upon. As a result, pointing out that regime-building makes all better off is insufficient as an explanation for any given regime that is created.

With regard to the second argument, the notion that institutions may prolong the impact of ideas corresponds to what Krasner (1983b: 356–8) referred to as the tectonic-plates version of the theory of hegemonic stability. The characteristic feature of this variant of the hegemonic stability hypothesis is that it allows for a substantial "leadership lag" to occur, i.e. for a period in which the leader has departed, but not, for the present, the order which the leader created. Proponents of this version of hegemonic stability theory, in other words, depart from the "crude" version in that they attribute a measure of robustness to (post-)hegemonic regimes.

Learning cooperation

Changes in beliefs may or may not induce behavioral change. If they do, this process *can* be referred to as learning (Nye 1987: 378–82; E. Haas 1990: 2–6; P. Haas 1993: 175).[4] Here we will look at an approach concerned with the role of learning in international regime dynamics. Learning can take one of two forms: new understandings of their social and political environment may prompt decisionmakers either to alter their strategies to achieve basically unchanged goals or to redefine the very content of the national interest, which involves selecting new goals and searching for appropriate strategies. While, in the first case, (intertemporally) identical actors behave differently to realize unchanged interests, in the second, identical actors behave differently owing to new goals.[5] To capture this difference conceptually Joseph Nye (1987: 380) has distinguished "simple" from "complex" learning:

> Simple learning uses new information merely to adapt the means, without altering any deeper goals in the ends – means chain. The actor simply uses a different instrument to attain the same goal. Complex learning, by contrast, involves recognition of conflicts among means and goals in causally complicated situations, and leads to new priorities and trade-offs.

[4] For a critique of this behavioral definition of learning, see Levy (1994: 289–91) who argues that cognitive change and behavioral change have to be distinguished more sharply and that only the first should be referred to as learning.

[5] We understand Nye, whose analysis of regime-related learning we focus on in this section, to assume that actors' social identities remain unaltered. This sets him apart from the strong cognitivists' emphasis on socialization (see sect. 5.2 below).

A distinction very similar to Nye's, yet referring more specifically to the policies of international organizations, has been suggested by Ernst Haas (1990: 23f., 34f.):

> By "learning" I mean the process by which consensual knowledge is used to specify causal relationships in new ways so that the result affects the content of public policy. Learning in and by an international organization implies that the organization's members are induced to question earlier beliefs about the appropriateness of ends of action and to think about the selection of new ones . . . Adaptation, in our context, is the ability to change one's behavior so as to meet challenges in the form of new demands without having to reevaluate one's entire program and the reasoning on which that program depends for its legitimacy . . . Because ultimate ends are not questioned, the change in behavior takes the form of a search for more adequate means to meet the new demands.

Thus, Haas's terms "adaptation" and "learning" are roughly equivalent to Nye's "simple learning" and "complex learning," respectively.

It is the second type of learning (Nye's complex learning) which is particularly important for cognitivists because, even from a conventional theoretical point of view, it is not surprising that states sometimes alter the strategies by which they pursue their interests. This fact is sufficiently well understood by rationalist approaches, which maintain that "states learn by responding to structural changes in their environment, or, to put it in game theory terms, they adjust their behavior to changes in the pay-off matrix" (Nye 1987: 372; see also Levy 1994: 297f.). New information is received and leads to a behavioral response, but this information is about a change in the material environment (which the subsequent change in behavior merely reflects) and does not call into question the objectives of actors. Therefore, the task of explaining "how interests themselves may be redefined" (Nye 1987: 373) has still to be accomplished. As we have seen at the beginning of chapter 3, rationalists, who, for methodological reasons assume that states' interests and preferences are stable over time, lack the means to do this. And even when they recognize that interests and preferences are not immutable, the systemic ontology that they subscribe to requires them to attribute such changes to structural dynamics rather than (complex) cognitive change. Therefore, a compelling demonstration that states sometimes redefine their interests and alter their preferences *without* a shift in the distribution of power and wealth would pose a major challenge to rationalism (Smith 1987: 280f.; P. Haas 1992b: 21.).

Nye (1987) finds remarkable instances of complex learning in the bilateral relationship of the postwar superpowers. According to his interpretation, US – Soviet cooperation in highly sensitive issue-areas such as strategic arms control and nuclear non-proliferation became possible only after the United States and the Soviet Union had changed their initial beliefs about the usability of atomic weapons and the mechanics of nuclear deterrence. Both sides became more fully aware of the destructive power of nuclear arms and the impossibility of protecting one's population unilaterally from the horrors of an all-out nuclear war. They learned the need for crisis management to minimize the dangers of escalation and for robust command and control systems to help central decisionmakers control escalation. And they came to acknowledge the dangers of nuclear proliferation, which might destabilize the precarious balance-of-threat and increase the likelihood of nuclear war (see also Smith 1987: 277f.). New information about the destructiveness of nuclear arms as well as about the consequences of nuclear warfare (such as apocalyptic scenarios of a "nuclear winter") gave rise to a shared *concept of national security* which ultimately rested upon the inescapable paradox of mutually assured destruction. The consensual knowledge both sides had acquired over time led them to accept that nuclear risks could only be managed by a change from (purely) unilateral to (more) cooperative security strategies. In other words, new information, although it did not affect the distribution of material capabilities in the issue-area, transformed a (sharply competitive) zero-sum game into a mixed-motive game, in which *both* sides could gain security through cooperation. The subsequent development of international institutions (such as the nuclear non-proliferation regime and the SALT/ABM-based regime for the control of nuclear armament) designed to solve the remaining collective action problems thus rested on the emergence of (new) consensual knowledge between the superpowers. Regimes were formed in response to a change of mind which made the world look different from before and not in response to a change in the material world which forced a "new thinking" on the actors.

So far, regimes have been in the picture only as a dependent variable: it has been argued that the emergence of consensual knowledge works as a driving force of regime formation. The causal relationship between knowledge and regimes is more complex, however. As an instance of what Krasner (1983b: 361) has referred to as "feed-back," regimes themselves make a difference to actors' beliefs by helping to "lock in" and to further develop the learning that had prompted their creation (Nye 1987: 385; see also Goldstein and Keohane 1993a: 20–2). By stabilizing actors' mutual expectations in an issue-area regimes can reshape their perceived self-interest.

> More specifically, the institutionalization of regimes can 1) change standard operating procedures for national bureaucracies; 2) present new coalition opportunities for subnational actors and improved access for third parties; 3) change participants' attitudes through contacts within the framework of institutions; and 4) provide means to dissociate a particular issue from changes in the overall political relationship by regular, formal meetings (Nye 1987: 400).

Thus, once rule-conforming behavior is taken for granted, states are in a position to partially re-allocate their resources according to their changed expectations. Regimes then form part of the political environment of actors and thus affect the way states define and pursue their interests in the issue-area (Krasner 1983b: 362–4).

It must not be overlooked, though, that much in the same way that learning can lead to a change from unilateral to multilateral politics, newly acquired beliefs may also destabilize existing patterns of cooperation (Nye 1987: 379; P. Haas 1992b: 30). Alterations of established rules and procedures according to new knowledge may take place, and learning may even undermine the foundations of regime-based cooperation altogether. Since a high measure of institutional robustness is widely regarded as desirable for a social system lacking a central authority to regulate the interaction of its units, it would be important to know more about the conditions underlying evolutionary regime change and the role played by new knowledge in such processes.

The same can be said with regard to regime formation. As Nye (1987: 379) points out, "[n]ew information affects prior beliefs, but its reception and interpretation are also affected by those prior beliefs. The extent and accuracy of learning depends upon the strength of the prior beliefs and the quantity and quality of the new information." Unfortunately, he does not specify how to assess the robustness of existing cognitive patterns and under what conditions one should expect the impact of new knowledge on foreign policy decisionmaking to prevail. To make progress on this agenda, students of international regimes should therefore ask questions about those parameters of both new information and prior beliefs that affect the likelihood of governmental learning. Moreover, they should not forget that not only prior beliefs, but also structures of power can have a bearing upon actors' receptivity to new information. As Karl Deutsch (1963: 111) once observed, power, "[i]n a sense . . . is the ability to afford not to learn." It therefore appears central to attempt to factor this variable into the emergent cognitive theories of international regimes and cooperation.

5.1.2 *Consensual knowledge, epistemic communities, and regime formation and change*

For knowledge to have an impact on regime formation it must be widely shared by key policymakers (Krasner 1983c: 19). There must be a common understanding of both the nature of the problem to be solved by rule-governed cooperation and appropriate means to attain the valued ends. Building on this basic insight, a group of scholars brought together by Peter Haas (1992c) has focused on the process by which the views of specialists gain acceptance among, and are acted upon by, decisionmakers. They argue that *epistemic communities* are crucial "channels through which new ideas circulate from societies to governments as well as from country to country" (P. Haas 1992b: 27).

Epistemic communities are defined as "network[s] of professionals with recognized expertise and competence in a particular domain and an authoritative claim to policy-relevant knowledge within that domain or issue-area" (P. Haas 1992b: 3). This claim rests on a theoretically informed vision of reality and a notion of scientific validity which consists of internally formulated truth tests. The members of such a community share a common understanding of particular problems in their field of research *as well as* an awareness of, and a preference for, a set of technical solutions to these problems. Most important, they are not content with the essentially passive role of providers of information who speak out only at the request of decisionmakers. Rather, they have an idea of a better public policy which they actively strive to bring about by seeking to get access to governing institutions.[6]

With the benefit of modern communications and a relatively free flow of information these networks of specialists often operate transnationally. New findings are conveyed and discussed across national borders. As long as the members of an epistemic community can reach consensus on important issues in their field of study they can establish a relatively independent source of scientific evidence and authority. Epistemic communities may thus be considered respected guardians of

[6] Further discussion of the concept of epistemic community may be found in Ruggie (1975: 569f.), P. Haas (1989: 384; 1992b: 16–20), and E. Haas (1990: 40–6).

policy-relevant knowledge in a world of ever-increasing complexity. If innovative ways of drawing linkages between causes and effects and means and ends are sanctioned by the consensus of a transnational epistemic community, this can serve as a central source and vehicle of learning at the inter-state level.

Seeking to explicate the "causal logic of epistemic policy coordination" Peter Haas (1992b: 3f.) has established analytically three central requirements for knowledge as provided by scientists and other experts to have an impact on processes of international cooperation. Thus epistemic policy coordination is only likely to occur in the presence of (1) a high degree of uncertainty among policymakers, (2) a high degree of consensus among scientists, and (3) a high degree of institutionalization of scientific advice.

Considering the first condition, Peter Haas argues that the increasing complexities of problems of global concern give rise to demands for scientific information. Policymakers come to acknowledge that their understanding of current problems is limited and hence perceive the need for scientific advice. Since decisionmakers do not always realize that their grasp of complex issues and causal linkages is insufficient, however, it often takes a crisis or a shock "to overcome institutional inertia and habit to spur them to seek help from an epistemic community" (P. Haas 1992b: 14; see also 1993: 187).[7]

With regard to the second condition, scientists or other experts with knowledge relevant to the issue-area have to organize themselves as an epistemic community within which beliefs about cause-and-effect relationships and appropriate means to solve the problems at hand are shared. In short, no coherent policy advice can be given unless there is a high measure of consensual knowledge among experts about the appropriate solutions to particular problems (P. Haas 1989: 384; 1992b: 23; Adler and Haas 1992: 371). Conversely, in cases in which "scientific evidence is ambiguous and the experts themselves are split into contending factions, issues have tended to be resolved less on their technical merits than on their political ones" (P. Haas 1992b: 11).

Finally, the members of the epistemic community must gain political power (Adler and Haas 1992: 374; P. Haas 1992b: 27; 1993: 179). In order

[7] This observation brings to mind Young's hypothesis that regime formation becomes more likely in the event of shocks or crises exogenous to institutional bargaining (see sect. 3.4 above). Both assessments of the role of this factor are compatible, since it is normally assumed that epistemic community influence works in favor of international regime-building and cooperation.

to influence the process of both regime formation and regime implementation they have to become part of the bureaucratic apparatus. As Peter Haas (1989: 398) has observed with reference to the regime for the protection of the Mediterranean Sea: "Persuasion did account for a small amount of the regime's broadened scope to include more sources and forms of pollution, but national compliance came from the *power* acquired by a new group of actors [i.e. the epistemic community that had emerged in the issue-area]." (emphasis added)

Drawing on the evidence gathered in a number of case studies (P. Haas 1992c), Emanuel Adler and Peter Haas (1992: 372–85) argue that the influence of epistemic communities on international regime creation and maintenance can be exerted in four phases of the policy process: policy innovation, policy diffusion, policy selection, and policy persistence. At each of these four stages knowledge provided by recognized experts may decisively shape the perception of political actors, making them prone to choose one set of norms and rules rather than another.

With regard to *policy innovation*, epistemic communities can influence the framing of issues for collective debate. Subsequent negotiations are then conditioned by the information initially provided by the epistemic community. The framing function of epistemic communities has been investigated by means of case studies including ones of trade in services (Drake and Nicolaïdis 1992), nuclear arms control (Adler 1992), management of whaling (Peterson 1992), protection of the stratospheric ozone layer (P. Haas 1992a; Breitmeier 1996), and protection of the Mediterranean Sea (P. Haas 1989; 1990; 1993). Furthermore, in situations of pronounced uncertainty epistemic communities may not only succeed in exerting strong influence on a debate, but also help states identify their very interests in a particular situation. In the case of trade in services, for example, policymakers were initially largely unfamiliar with the subject. They therefore had to turn to services experts to ask for clarification about the precise nature of the stakes (Drake and Nicolaïdis 1992).

Epistemic communities are also important agents of *policy diffusion*. Because of their transnational links, experts can communicate new ideas and policy innovations to their colleagues in other countries who in turn influence their governments. The process of policy diffusion has been traced by Adler (1992) in the case of nuclear arms control. He found that an American epistemic community played a key role in creating the internationally shared understanding and practice of nuclear arms control. The members of the community were able to influence not only the US government but also – through their Soviet counterparts – the Soviet government to the extent that their ideas were finally embodied in the ABM Treaty. Similarly, Thomas Risse-Kappen (1994) has recently pointed to a transnational network linking a community of Western experts who were supportive of common security and non-offensive defense concepts, on the one hand, and scientists and "institutniks" at the United States of America and Canada Institute in Moscow, on the other. He argues that some of the ideas that informed the reconceptualization of Soviet security interests in the late 1980s originated in that Western liberal internationalist community (Risse-Kappen 1994: 186).

By contrast, *policy selection* is a highly political stage in the policy process and one with regard to which the impact of an epistemic community is particularly difficult to assess. Still, there is some evidence that epistemic communities can exert considerable influence at this stage as well, particularly when they are able to provide integrative formulas in complex negotiations (Adler and Haas 1992: 383).

Finally, epistemic communities may operate as effective advocates of established regimes by defending them as the best-suited means to eliminate or alleviate the problems which have prompted their creation. The impact of an established epistemic community on *policy persistence* depends on the degree of consensus among community members and the persuasive force of competing science networks. As Adler and Haas (1992: 385) put it: "When an epistemic community loses its consensus, its authority is diminished and decisionmakers tend to pay less attention to its advice." According to Peter Haas (1993; 1989), this loss of scientists' standing with the decisionmakers may even contribute to regime collapse.

Some open questions

Most students of regimes now seem to acknowledge the importance of consensual knowledge and ideas for international cooperation (Krasner 1983a: 368; Keohane 1984: 131f.; Young 1994: 39–42, 125f.), and there seems to be no fundamental objection to attempting to integrate the concept of epistemic community into the theoretical framework of regime analysis. Weak cognitivists have come up with convincing evidence to support their claim that knowledge-based networks of experts are a source of complex learning and subsequent decisionmaking in international relations. Nevertheless, more research is needed in order to move forward from the insight that epistemic communities *can* have an impact on political outcomes to an understanding of *when and how* they are able to influence policy coordination (Sebenius 1992).

As Oran Young and Gail Osherenko (1993d: 237) have pointed out, consensual knowledge is not a guarantee for the emergence of international cooperation. Conversely, Peter Haas himself has observed that knowledge does not have to be shared by all actors to have an impact on regime formation. The pattern of "follow-the-leader" (P. Haas 1993: 187f.) that he describes suggests that, for cooperation to arise, it may be sufficient that a hegemon in an issue-area is influenced by the new knowledge. Moreover, an increasingly complex world not only results in decisionmakers more frequently feeling uncertain about the choice to make, but also it can be expected to cause a proliferation of competing epistemic communities, who all claim to provide scientifically sound policy advice in a particular issue-area. To the extent that this happens, however, the buck once again stops with the politicians.

From a normative point of view, it is worth stressing that, as Adler (1992: 124) has remarked with respect to the case of nuclear arms control, it is not necessarily the best ideas (however scientific in origin) that are selected and implemented. More often than not those ideas are turned into policy which best tie in with the interests of policymakers and, additionally, conform to the constraints engendered by domestic politics. Therefore, it is certainly not enough to hypothesize "that the greater the extent to which epistemic communities are mobilized and are able to gain influence in their respective nation-states, the greater [is] the likelihood that these nation-states will in turn exert power on behalf of the values and practices promoted by the epistemic community and will thus help in their international institutionalization" (Adler and Haas 1992: 371f.). Leaving aside the question whether or not such a hypothesis has empirical content, we need to know more about the selection process in the course of which a particular epistemic community prevails over its competitors. In order to assess the independent impact of learning and new knowledge on international politics, we must not be concerned merely with "the winning epistemic community" (Adler and Haas 1992: 372), but should seek to understand what makes a specific epistemic community gain the upper hand and whether its success is due to historically contingent factors (Adler 1992: 106) or can be traced back to the endogenous dynamics of the evolution of knowledge.

Finally, it should be kept in mind that Nye's distinction between simple and complex learning is not as straightforward as it might appear at first sight. Although the underlying idea is plausible enough, its operationalization is likely to prove very difficult. When is a change in behavior prompted by a change of interests and when are new instruments applied to pursue the same national interests as before? Was the move, in superpowers' security relations, from unilateral strategies to more cooperative ones a result of newly perceived interests due to a new understanding of the risks inherent in nuclear deterrence or only a change of strategy to realize unaltered security interests? These questions, once again, point to the fact that weak cognitivists still "lack a systematic theory of how such changes occur" (Wendt 1992a: 393). The relationship between knowledge and reality as well as the interdependence of scientific advice, social exigencies, and new experiences is much more complicated than the simple distinction between cognitive change and structural change, either of which might lead to a change of actors' interests, suggests.

5.2 Strong cognitivism: the sociological turn

In the preceding section (5.1), we discussed scholarly work which is united in the endeavor to illuminate the process of interest and preference formation prior to rational decisionmaking in strategic situations. By problematizing (and not just establishing and then evaluating) the pay-off structures that constitute international games, by investigating the emergence of the options that actors perceive (rather than treating them as contingent "givens" from the point of view of theory), and by demonstrating the importance of causal and normative beliefs for the framing of political conflicts and their solutions, these *weakly cognitivist* critics of conventional rationalist perspectives in the study of international institutions seek to integrate a larger segment of the causal chain leading to regime formation and transformation into regime theory. While such calls for a broadened research agenda certainly reveal dissatisfaction with the analytical foci of the dominant schools of thought in regime analysis and in international relations theory more generally, the amended models designed to fill the perceived theoretical lacunae hardly represent a fundamental challenge to the regime-analytical mainstream. In the final analysis, the contribution of weak cognitivism is best characterized as a necessary and fruitful *supplement* to the established body of theory, leaving intact the utilitarian core and the ontological assumptions of rationalist approaches, including their conception

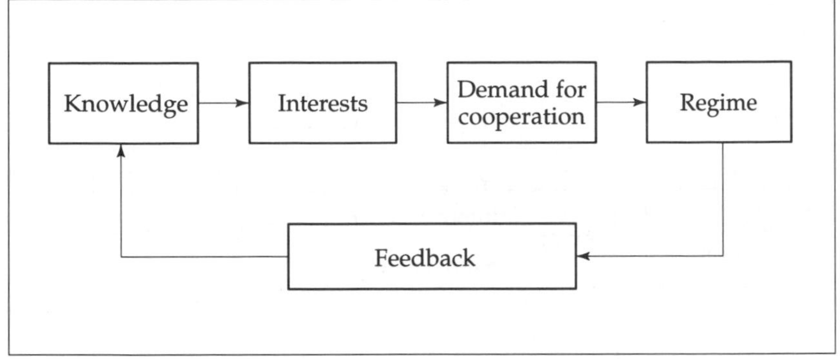

Fig. 9. The ontology of weak cognitivism.

of norms and rules as functional responses of rational actors to perceived collective action problems (Goldstein and Keohane 1993a: 5; Jönsson 1993: 221).

In this section, we feature attempts to make sense of regimes and other international institutions which are based on a more radical opposition to the theoretical mainstream and for which we use the descriptor *strong cognitivism*. Authors such as Thomas Franck, Friedrich Kratochwil, Harald Müller, John Gerard Ruggie, Alexander Wendt, and Robert Cox have each made important contributions in this regard. In different ways they (together with a growing number of others) have questioned the appropriateness of the rationalist perspective for studying international regimes. They argue that international regimes are embedded in the broader normative structures of an international society and that these structures, in turn, escape rationalist theorizing because utilitarian approaches do not problematize the capacity of rational actors to engage in optimizing behavior. In particular, these approaches ignore that individual rationality always presupposes sociality, that there is no optimization without prior socialization.

Strong cognitivists reject the rationalist interpretation of state behavior in terms of utility-maximizing in favor of a conception of states as role-players. The idea of role-playing is nicely captured by a model of political behavior which James March and Johan Olsen (1989: 21–6, 160–2) summarize as the "logic of appropriateness" and contrast with the utilitarian "logic of consequentiality." Actors following the logic of appropriateness do not examine their individual goals and preferences and then calculate which course of action would have the

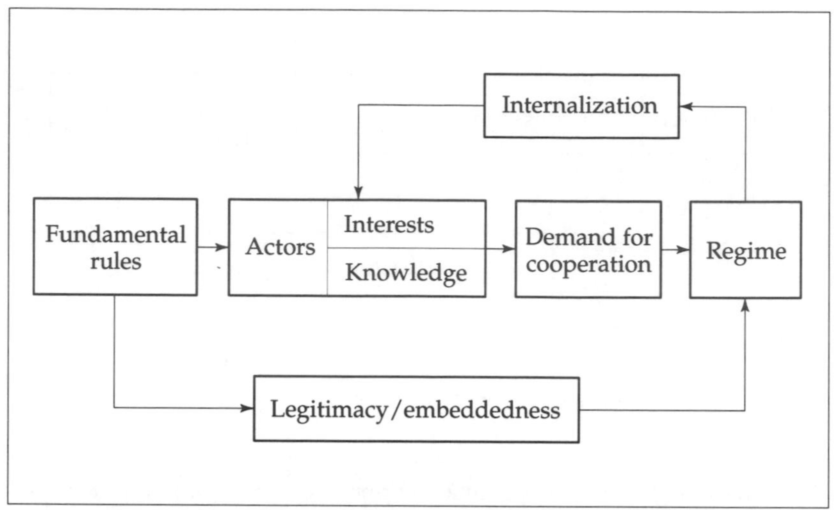

Fig. 10. The ontology of strong cognitivism: the basic model.

best consequences in the light of these goals. Rather, the software program that determines their behavior can be specified by the following considerations: "1) What kind of situation is this? 2) Who am I? [i.e. what is my role in society or which of my several roles is called upon in this situation?] 3) How appropriate are different actions for me [as an occupant of this role] in this situation?" (March and Olsen 1989: 23) Thus, other than actors who conform to the logic of consequentiality they do not merely take rules into account; their behavior is *rule-driven*:

> To describe behavior as driven by rules is to see action as a matching of a situation to the demands of a position. Rules define relationships among roles in terms of what an incumbent of one role owes to incumbents of other roles . . . The terminology is one of duties and obligations rather than anticipatory, consequential decison making. Political actors associate specific actions with specific situations by rules of appropriateness. What is appropriate for a particular person in a particular situation is defined by political and social institutions and transmitted through socialization. (March and Olsen 1989: 23)

The notion that behavior is rule-driven is consistent with the possibility that, in a given situation, actors have to make choices between different rules. Moreover, acting in accordance with the logic of appropriateness must not be mistaken for simple-mindedness. The specification and application of the appropriate rule is seldom a trivial, quasi-mechanical process. (Indeed, Kant associated with this process a separate cognitive faculty, which he referred to as *Urteilskraft* [judgment].)[8]

Proponents of a strong cognitivism in regime analysis subscribe to an ontology which emphazises the dependency of state identities and cognitions on international institutions and relates the formation and maintenance of particular international regimes to these pre-established identities. Thus, a "shadow of institutions" comes to join forces with the famous "shadow of the future" (see sect. 3.1 above) in producing cooperation. According to strong cognitivism, states are significantly less free to ignore institutional commitments than mainstream approaches suggest. Correspondingly, international regimes, due to their being nested within broader normative networks, exhibit a considerably higher degree of robustness than utilitarian reasoning predicts. Consequently, self-interest (even if broadly defined) is considered an unreliable "signpost" when it comes to understanding regime maintenance. Better insights into this phenomenon, strong cognitivists argue, can be gained from focusing on questions of the legitimacy of normative injunctions, the importance of intersubjectively shared meanings and the role of communication in their formation and reformation, the process of identity formation in international relations, and the conservative power of historical structures. In one way or another all of these concepts refer to the operation of "social facts" (Emile Durkheim) which are not only beyond the reach of individual manipulation, but are necessary conditions for individuality and autonomy in international politics. These social facts have to be considered if one wants to come to a more adequate understanding of the emergence and persistence of regimes in international society.

In this section we proceed as follows. We will first address the metatheoretical criticism raised by strong cognitivists about rational choice approaches. In a nutshell, strong cognitivists argue that rationalist approaches, due to their positivist epistemology and their adherence to an ontology that gives actors priority over rules, are unable to grasp essential features of rule-governed cooperation under anarchy (sect. 5.2.1). Subsequently, we will give an account of some of the theoretical proposals strong cognitivists have come up with in their attempts to advance alternative understandings of the significance and dynamics of regimes and other institutions in international politics (sect. 5.2.2).

[8] For a similar explication of the idea of role-playing in terms of Rawls's (1955) concept of practice, see Young (1989a: 211f.).

5.2.1 *Strong cognitivism's critique of rationalist approaches to the study of international regimes*

Blind spots of an atomistic ontology

Rational choice approaches as used in regime analysis take the preferences and powers of state actors as the unproblematic starting point for explaining rule-governed cooperation in international relations. The world they study is populated by sovereign states facing numerous collective action problems, some of which they solve by creating and maintaining regimes. From an ontological point of view, this account of norms and rules as problem-solving devices which are designed to manage international relations in particular issue-areas implies that states are conceptualized as prior to the regimes which they negotiate, create, maintain, comply with, or ignore according to their individual utility calculations. To put it differently: rationalist approaches treat international regimes as derivatives of instrumental rationality and hence individualistic in origin. Their emergence and functioning is made completely dependent on the will of pre-existing states (Ashley 1984: 243f.).

This implicit ontology of agents and rules in international relations has been criticized by scholars who favor a more "institution-centric approach" (Wendt and Duvall 1989: 67). Proponents of this approach argue that the behavior of states, as any social behavior, presupposes normative structures which cannot be explained from the vantage point of rational actors but have to be analyzed in their own right (Ashley 1984: 242–8; Wendt 1987: 361–9; Dessler 1989: 451–8; Behnke 1993: 33). Individual choices, in this alternative ontology, are structurally shaped in the sense that they are deeply and essentially influenced by social institutions. Social institutions and the corresponding practices are a "condition of the possibility" of individual choice. Without them rational behavior would be unthinkable.

To illustrate their theoretical claims, proponents of an institution-centric approach regularly make reference to such fundamental institutions of international society as sovereignty, diplomacy, or international law. According to Alexander Wendt and Raymond Duvall (1989: 53) "these institutions *constitute* state actors as subjects of international life in the sense that they make meaningful interaction by the latter possible" (emphasis added). For instance, the norms and rules that make up the institution of sovereignty define intersubjectively who can lay claim to the status of an actor in international politics and what rights and duties each actor bears in principle. Without such norms and rules it would make no sense to speak of either illegal intervention or legitimate self-defense. Moreover, as Andreas Behnke (1993) has demonstrated with regard to cases of security cooperation in both Europe and Eastern Asia, the reciprocal recognition of sovereignty is a necessary condition for more issue-area specific arrangements to come about (see also Dessler 1989: 469). Thus, for the Korean case, Behnke (1993: 53–7) could show that, as long as at least two opponents in a regionally defined security complex are not prepared to grant each other the status of a legitimate actor in international politics, no sustained policy coordination can emerge even when there are considerable joint gains to be realized through cooperation. Similarly, the norms and rules specifying the legal principle of *pacta sunt servanda* define what counts as a treaty and determine the conditions under which a treaty has to be regarded as binding the future volition of the participants. If these injunctions and specifications were not generally accepted the notion of an international treaty would be devoid of meaning. And this is more than a semantic statement: in the absence of such rules, *practices* such as treaty-oriented negotiating or treaty-stabilized cooperation would not exist as well.

Pointing to such underresearched structural preconditions of purposive agency at the inter-state level, strong cognitivists call for a broadening of the regime-analytical agenda. It is not enough to tackle the question "why do states cooperate?"; equally important and indeed more fundamental is another one: "how is cooperation between states possible?" (Wendt 1987: 363). Elsewhere, Wendt (1991: 390) elaborates on this distinction and explains:

> By explicating the rules governing social contexts a *constitutive* approach [i.e. an approach that inquires into the structural preconditions of individual action and choice] shows how it is possible that in those contexts certain actors are empowered to engage in certain practices and others are not, and it also shows how those practices – when performed – in turn instantiate (or fail to instantiate) the rules. *Causal* theories, in contrast, show why actors engage in particular kinds of practice and how these practices help produce and transform both the actors themselves and social institutions.[9] [emphasis added]

International rules cannot be reduced to mere devices for problem-solving. To do so amounts to overlooking that states as actors are

[9] For a critical assessment of this distinction, see Hollis and Smith (1991: 406).

themselves dependent on established normative frameworks (Krasner 1988: 89f.; Wendt and Duvall 1989; Buzan 1993: 350). Therefore, it is a central task for the study of international cooperation (as well as for International Relations in general) to uncover the nature and the workings of the norms and rules which "constitute or empower those agents in the first place" (Wendt 1987: 369).

Given that such calls for a constitutive approach are usually accompanied by attacks on rationalism's too narrow perspective on international rules, it is noteworthy that many, perhaps most students of regimes who regard rationalism as the correct point of departure for purposes of theory-building readily admit that a more complete account of international regimes would have to take into consideration the normative features of international life which strong cognitivism focuses on. Thus, for instance, Snidal (1986: 45) makes it clear that "the international system, with its established patterns of practice and rules, is significant for defining the individual game model and for deriving conclusions from it." This norm-constituted system establishes a frame of reference which is taken for granted by state actors, since "even the definition of issues, actors, and choices depends on the preexisting international order." Similarly, Keohane (1988: 390) acknowledges that "at some point one must embed the analysis in institutions that are not plausibly viewed as the product of human calculation and bargaining."[10]

But while rationalists seem to have come to accept the central tenet of strong cognitivism concerning the dependence of state actors on fundamental social structures, they nevertheless maintain that the creation and maintenance of *international regimes* as well as the patterns of international cooperation more generally can be perfectly well explained in terms of individual utility-maximization. As Keohane (1988: 380) has put it in an oft-quoted dictum:

> International cooperation does not necessarily depend on altruism, idealism, personal honor, common purpose, internalized norms, or

[10] Similar awareness of the significance of "extra-rational" factors can be found in authors who have contributed to the rationalist research program at the level of general social theory. Hardin (1982: 101) notes that "under the logic of collective action, we should expect to see very little large-scale collective action motivated by narrow self-interest," implying that the frequency of such action in reality belies at least the most ambitious aspirations of the rationalist agenda. Elster (1989: 125, 15) makes a similar point when he argues for "the reality of norms and for their autonomy." Neither the prescriptive force (effectiveness) nor the persistence (robustness) of norms, according to Elster, can be reduced "to rationality or any other form of optimizing mechanism."

> shared beliefs in a set of values embedded in a culture. At various times and places any of these factors of human motivation may indeed play a role in processes of international cooperation: *but cooperation can be understood without reference to any of them.* [emphasis added]

This seeming paradox clears up when we take into account the rationalist strategy of *separating* the constitution of states as central actors in international politics from issue-area specific institutional choices. While it appears to be accepted that states are ultimately constituted by the fundamental norms and rules of an international society, the same states are expected to proceed as utility-maximizers once they have to decide on the creation and maintenance of international regimes. To put it differently: socialization sets states free to engage in rational behavior when it comes to solving collective action problems, and as long as the deep normative structures of an international society remain unchanged they will not have any further impact on particular choices.

The result of this strategy might well be that mainstream scholars, after acknowledging with gratitude the points made by their strongly cognitivist critics, feel perfectly justified to continue as though nothing had happened. Therefore, if strong cognitivists want to avoid their marginalization in the field of regime analysis, they have to engage the rationalist separation thesis. They have to develop theoretical models to establish a connection between the more fundamental normative structures of international society, on the one hand, and (issue-area specific) international regimes, on the other. And they have to point out empirical methods suitable for validating their theoretical claims. In James Caporaso's words (1993: 82f.), the fundamental challenge facing strong cognitivism is "to explain institutions and sociality given some data on extant and prior institutions and sociality." As we will see in the following, until now strong cognitivism appears to have been much stronger in arguing the need for, and (to a lesser extent) in drawing up, theoretical alternatives to rationalism than in subjecting these alternatives to rigorous empirical tests.

Blind spots of positivism as a theory of explanation

Positivism as an epistemology of social science rests on the assumption that there are observable regularities in the social world, which can be analyzed with the same methods which have proven successful in deciphering the natural world. Social interaction is regarded as governed by objective forces, the causal workings of which can be formulated in general laws which hold independently of human subjectivity. These laws (together with statements about the initial conditions which contain the causally relevant specifics of the situation at hand) allow for explanations (as well as predictions) of social outcomes (Hempel and Oppenheim 1948). For the social sciences this supposed methodological unity of science involves a clear separation of subject and object on the one hand and a strong commitment to empirical validation of hypotheses on the other. Indeed, it "goes to the root of the Positivist ideas that hypotheses can be tested one at a time by comparing their implications with objective, neutral facts of experience" (Hollis and Smith 1990: 54).

The affinity of the rational choice perspective in international relations theory to the positivist conception of science can now be spelt out. By definition, rationalist approaches assume that states (or other relevant actors) are self-interested, goal-seeking actors whose choices are guided by instrumental rationality, i.e. states always choose the course of action that promises to maximize their (pre-established) utility function. On the basis of this assumption rationalist approaches advance a positivist explanation of social interactions, which appears as a "timeless account of what rational individuals can be expected to do in certain conditions" (Hollis and Smith 1990: 129). The hypotheses derived from this rationality axiom (as well as from additional auxiliary assumptions), in turn, can be evaluated in light of the historical evidence. The observable conduct of states thus serves as an essential point of reference in the process of building a theory of international relations. It is taken for granted that the causes of behavior (represented by the "initial conditions" in positivist explanations) and the behavior that is caused (the *explanandum*) can be isolated and operationalized. Moreover, it is assumed that the scientific community and its objects of research can be separated, i.e. the discovered laws of social interaction of rational actors are taken to be objectively true, to be independent of both the subjective viewpoint of the observer and the historical contingencies of the situations observed. Both assumptions are criticized by a growing number of scholars. We will first turn to the assimilation of social rules to (efficient) causes and then briefly report on the criticism directed against the separation of subject and object in social research.

Adopting a positivist model of explanation, mainstream students of international regimes are inclined to regard institutional arrangements as objectively influencing the behavior of state actors by affecting their calculations of interest. Norms and rules are likened to external causes of international conduct, the impact of which can be specified and tested by predicting state behavior on their basis. However, as Kratochwil and Ruggie (1986: 767) suggest, this interpretation of the effectiveness of regime injunctions is too simple and misses central dimensions of the operation of norms and rules in social interaction:

> Unlike the initial conditions in positivist explanations, norms can be thought of only with great difficulty as "causing" occurrences. Norms may "guide" behavior, they may "inspire" behavior, they may "rationalize" or "justify" behavior, they may express "mutual expectations" about behavior, or they may be ignored. But they do not effect cause in the sense that a bullet through the heart causes death or an uncontrolled surge in the money supply causes price inflation.

In order to come to a better understanding of issue-area specific normative arrangements in international politics, strong cognitivists advise scholars to take the intersubjective quality of international regimes, as suggested by the reference made in the consensus definition to convergent expectations, more seriously (Kratochwil and Ruggie 1986: 764; see also Gehring 1994: 321 as well as ch. 2 above). Accordingly, regimes are more than mere incentive-manipulators affecting the utility calculations of rational actors. They comprise understandings shared by the members concerning the right conduct in circumscribed situations. Not only do they prescribe certain actions in defined circumstances, they also serve as commonly used points of reference for the determination and the assessment of individual behavior. International regimes therefore can be conceptualized as "principled and shared understandings of desirable and acceptable forms of social behavior" (Kratochwil and Ruggie 1986: 764). They embody shared social knowledge, and they have both a *regulative* and a *constitutive* dimension: that is, on the one hand, they operate as imperatives requiring states to behave in accordance with certain principles, norms, and rules; on the other hand, they help create a common social world by fixing the meaning of behavior.

To illustrate the notion of regimes as constituting practices rather than merely regulating behavior, strong cognitivists sometimes draw an analogy between the workings of normative institutions in world politics and the rules of games such as chess or football. Such rules, as Dessler (1989: 455–8) and Kratochwil (1993b: 449f.) among others have noticed, cannot be interpreted as causing particular moves within the play. Rather, by defining the admissible behavior and the consequences (i.e. the meaning) of individual moves, they enable the actors to play the game in the first place. They provide the actors with the knowledge necessary for assessing a particular action and responding to it in an adequate fashion. Rules of the game enable actors to respond to each other's moves in a meaningful way.

By the same token international regimes define inappropriate behavior. Within a regime context uncooperative or otherwise harmful behavior can be retaliated against (and thus reduced) with a smaller risk of one's reaction being mistaken for an unprovoked "unfriendly act." Müller (1993b) highlights this important quality of international regimes. Analyzing security cooperation between the Soviet Union and the United States he writes:

> For the Soviets, the amount of learning [initiated by interaction within the regime context] was gigantic. Security cooperation with the United States has convinced a considerable part of the Soviet foreign policy élite and the security apparatus that their manichaean image of the world was wrong . . . They now could interpret hostile steps by the United States as responses to Soviet actions. (Müller 1993b: 384)

The regime had shaped the way actors interpreted one another's actions.

The ascription to regimes of a constitutive dimension is problematic for rationalists because it blurs the distinction between cause and effect. While regulative rules may be thought of as causing state behavior in a sense that is consistent with positivism, constitutive rules cannot. Rather, constitutive rules can be likened to what philosophers, following Aristotle, have traditionally called "material causes" (Dessler 1989: 453). They do not *make* states act in a particular way; they make it *possible* for them to pursue whatever purpose they choose. Consequently, the rationalist focus on causes, which is actually a focus on *efficient* causes (in the traditional philosophical sense), leads to a truncated picture of the "effectiveness" or, more broadly speaking, the significance of international norms and rules.

Moreover, if it is accepted that international regimes encompass a regulative as well as a constitutive dimension, then their effectiveness cannot be assessed in terms of overt compliance alone. The rules of chess as well as the norms of free trade are not *ipso facto* invalidated if they are partially or temporarily ignored by the relevant actors. Rather, it is a characteristic feature of social norms that they are to a certain degree "counterfactually valid" (Kratochwil and Ruggie 1986: 76; see also Gehring 1994: 370). Some or – depending on the circumstances – even many instances of deviant behavior thus do not allow for the conclusion that the norm in question is no longer valid. This general feature of social rules (including international regimes) certainly raises the difficult question of at what point in time and under what conditions deviant behavior does signal the breakdown of a regime. Nevertheless, the point is that rationalists owing to their epistemological stance are ill-equipped to even notice the difference between validity and (behavioral) effectiveness of international norms.

One might argue that rationalists need not care. What they are interested in is not actors' attitudes towards a set of norms, but whether (and when) regimes make a difference to behavior. To this, strong cognitivists might respond that, even though behavioral effectiveness and normative validity (i.e. actors' recognition that the norm in question continues to be binding) are not perfectly correlated, it is plausible to assume that the behavioral effectiveness of some written agreement is not independent of whether or not its stipulations are still regarded as valid by the parties (Kratochwil and Ruggie 1986: 773; Kratochwil 1989: 184). Consequently, rationalists *should* care for normative validity and hence intersubjective meaning, even when all they want to understand is the effects of norms on state behavior.

Thus, according to strong cognitivists, international regimes add up to a "web of meaning" (Neufeld 1993: 43) which makes sense of state conduct in specific issue-areas and establishes understandable linkages between otherwise unconnected sequences of action. To reduce regimes to technical ordering devices therefore is highly misleading. In order to correct for this shortcoming of positivist accounts of rule-governed cooperation strong cognitivists advocate opening "the positivist epistemology to more *interpretive* strains, more closely attuned to the reality of regimes" (Kratochwil and Ruggie 1986: 766 [emphasis added]; see also Hurrell 1993: 64). Scholars should not concentrate on cause–effect relationships alone, but also study the emergence and dynamics of the common understandings that strong cognitivists believe to be intrinsically linked to the emergence and dynamics of international institutions.

A second line of criticism takes issue on the notion that, in regime analysis as in social research generally, the observing subject can and should distance itself from the observed object. This doctrine is rejected as both illusory and socially harmful. According to these critics, theory-building in the social sciences inevitably has both social origins and social consequences and therefore goes beyond simply describing and explaining an independently given reality. Theory is never a neutral image of society, but itself a causal factor in ongoing social conflicts which either supports the existing order or promotes change. As Cox (1986: 207) has put it:

> Theory is always *for* someone and *for* some purpose. All theories have a perspective. Perspectives derive from a position in time and space, specifically social and political time and space. The world is seen from a standpoint definable in terms of nation or social class, of dominance or subordination, of rising or declining power, of a sense of immobility or of present crisis, of past experience, and of hopes and expectations for the future. . . There is, accordingly, no such thing as theory in itself, divorced from a standpoint in time and space.

By contrast, scholars committed to the positivist ideal tend to lose sight of the fact that their professional activity is part of a larger social process and, in turn, affects this process. Since theories (as ideas in general) are not part of their ontology, these scholars are averse to any self-critical application of reason. They conceive of the world "as a set of ready-made facts awaiting discovery through the application of scientific methodology, with the perception of these 'facts' being quite independent of the social framework in which perception takes place" (Hoffmann 1987: 233; see also Neufeld 1994: 14f.). Positivistically oriented scholars are disinclined to take into account the social consequences of their research because, according to their epistemology, the process of scientific investigation unveils an independently existing reality which is not itself affected by this process.[11]

Often this criticism then takes another twist: not only has research informed by the positivist philosophy of science social consequences that are not reflected by those who produce them; beyond this, the character of these consequences is socially conservative, and research that is conducted along positivist lines tends to inhibit (potentially desirable) social change. This is because, in their pursuit of time-less accounts of social behavior, positivists *ipso facto* privilege one particular historical perspective over possible alternatives. Claiming merely to describe and explain reality as it is, they, in fact, help stabilize the current order of things by declaring it natural (discouraging those who have an interest in revolutionary change) and/or providing it with a legitimizing ideology (Cox 1986: 208f., 243f.). To avoid the pitfalls of positivism, theory must become "critical," i.e. it must systematically reflect its own impact on the social world. It has to analyze its genesis and to understand what social purposes it serves. Scholars should recognize that "knowledge is

[11] This does not rule out that, in a separate process, scientific insights are used to manipulate reality. On the contrary, according to positivists, this is possible precisely because the results of scientific research – the laws describing social regularities – are objectively true (if they are true at all).

. . . not independent of our existence, but is integral to social relations and has a social function"; and this is why "theory must be able to give an account of itself" (Hoffmann 1987: 232f., 237) and has to become itself part of the explicit ontology of social research.

5.2.2 Approaches to a strongly cognitivist theory of international regimes

Although in the writings of strong cognitivists the critical aspect of the collective enterprise that is called social science all too often seems to dominate the constructive one (Keohane 1988), authors of this persuasion have come up with some interesting work that gives an idea of the specific content of what would be strongly cognitivist theories of regimes. In the following we look at four of these contributions more closely. Each of them emerges naturally from one or more of the critical themes we have introduced on the preceding pages. To begin with, a group of theorists perhaps most prominently represented by Thomas Franck and Andrew Hurrell have elaborated on what Franck has called the *power of legitimacy* in international politics. They rely heavily on the notion that, at a fundamental level, states are dependent on the existence of a rule-governed international society and suggest that the degree of correspondence between the specific norms and rules that constitute regimes and the broader normative structures underlying the international society strongly affects cooperative ventures between states. A second group of scholars including Kratochwil, Ruggie, and Müller concentrate on the importance of intersubjective meanings for international cooperation. More specifically, they have embarked upon an investigation into the communicative dynamics of rule-interpretation and rule-application, practices which they regard as inseparable from international regimes. In this connection, they highlight the *power of arguments* for collective choice at the international level. A third perspective is provided by Wendt (1992a; 1994) when he emphazises the *power of identity* in international politics (see also Krasner 1988: 73–7). In Wendt's formulation, identities – which are defined as "role-specific understandings and expectations about self" (Wendt 1992a: 397) – are at the same time constitutive of rational choices and shaped by the normative patterns of international politics. In this sense and by analogy to persons, Wendt talks of the socialization of states and the internalization of norms and rules over time, processes which are ignored by rationalists, although they must have significant repercussions on the robustness of international institutions. Finally, Cox stresses the *power of history* both in international politics and in academic theorizing. He argues that the identities and the behavior of states in the postwar era have been deeply affected by an encompassing hegemonic structure or world order of which international regimes form an integral part. This world order, as any social order, emerged from, and will break down in, historic conflicts. The hegemonic structure is a contested one, and those who are privileged by it defend it while those who are disadvantaged try to change it. As we shall see, Cox regards neoliberal regime theory as a part of the conservative project. It serves the purpose of maintaining and defending the existing hegemonic structure. Neoliberal regime theory takes sides in a historic conflict and, in doing so, has *itself* causal importance. It serves to stabilize the existing world order. Thus, according to Cox, the regime-analytic mainstream has a practical mission which goes beyond simply giving policy advice for the cooperative management of global problems. It attempts to stabilize a particular structure the distributive implications of which Cox considers grossly unjust.

A double concern is shared by all of these theorists. *First*, the functioning of individual norms and rules is analyzed in the context of broader normative structures which are seen as constitutive of international politics. For this purpose, the relationship between rules and choice, as it is described or presupposed by mainstream theorists of regimes, has to be rectified along the lines of a "more socialized ontology" (Wendt and Duvall 1989: 59). *Second*, their preference for an institution-centric approach notwithstanding, strong cognitivists are aware of the dangers of reification inherent in this option. Wendt (1987), in particular, has dealt at length with this problem. Reifying social structures (i.e. likening them to objects in the physical world) is not less problematic than ignoring their irreducible impact on social behavior (the error of the rationalists). In other words, theorists of international politics must avoid both the fallacy of holism and the fallacy of individualism. Strong cognitivists' preferred strategy to escape the danger of reification usually takes the form of a transcendental argument, i.e. analysts point to the indispensible preconditions of rational choices and argue that these preconditions are normative in nature. In one way or another, each of the following themes – the rule-impregnated "community of states," "intersubjectively shared meanings," the "social identity of actors," and "the long shadow of a historical structure" – represents a particular variant of this strategy.

Wendt pictures holism and individualism as extreme and ultimately untenable solutions to the so-called agent – structure problem in international relations theory (and in social theory more generally). This problem arises from "two uncontentious truths about social life: first, that human agency is the only moving force behind actions, events, and outcomes of the social world; and second, that human agency can be realized only in concrete historical circumstances that condition the possibilities for action and influence its course" (Dessler 1989: 443; see also Wendt 1987: 337f.; Onuf 1989: 52–65). The problem is how to conceptualize the relationship between structures and agents in a way that does justice to both truths. Neither human agency nor social structures should be given ontological priority. Rather, the relationship between the two has to be analyzed in terms of a "codetermined irreducibility" (Wendt and Duvall 1989: 59).[12]

The international society approach, or the power of legitimacy

The theoretical and methodological unease with rationalist accounts of rule-governed cooperation, the sources of which we have described in the preceding section (sect. 5.1), has given rise to demands for connecting regime analysis to the broader traditions of thought focusing on the normative foundations of international society (Hurrell 1993: 49). This focus is characteristic of the so-called English School in international relations theory, seminal contributions to which are due to Martin Wight, Hedley Bull, and R. J. Vincent among others. It comes as no surprise therefore that it has been a longstanding criticism of authors sympathetic to this body of ideas that "the literature on international regimes overwhelmingly focuses on formally negotiated international agreements and tends to ignore the social and political processes that underpin them" (Evans and Wilson 1992: 341). Others concede that "regime theory has made considerable progress in its own right," but add that the study of regimes "could now benefit from being reconnected to the older traditions of international society that both puts it into a broader context (systematically and historically) and connects it to the underlying political-legal framework of the modern international system" (Buzan 1993: 328; see also Hurrell 1993: 54–65). In particular, it is argued that rationalist approaches, although they correctly predict a substantial measure of resilience of agreed-upon norms and rules to

[12] Substantiating this ontological requirement is the central task that the "theory of structuration" (Giddens 1982) has set itself.

external changes, are ultimately lacking appropriate theoretical means to explain this phenomenon.

In search of a more adequate approach, a number of scholars have rediscovered the works of Louis Henkin (1968: 42) who observed that "it is probably the case that almost all nations observe almost all principles of international law and almost all their obligations almost all of the time." This famous statement is most closely associated with Henkin's (1968: 36) conviction that states feel compelled to comply with agreed-upon norms and rules, even when they have both incentives to break them and the capacity for doing so. This is explained with reference to a "sense of obligation" which induces states to respect international agreements independently of positive or negative sanctions. It is in this sense that norms and rules can be said to exert a "compliance pull of their own" (Franck 1990): their binding force is irreducible to the instrumental rationality of interacting agents. Consequently, to ignore this independent source of compliance cannot help but produce a distorted picture of international relations.

Such a perspective on international norms and rules is especially noteworthy not least because it has considerable policy implications (Chayes and Chayes 1993: 201). For instance, the existence of an autonomous binding force of norms and rules at the international level suggests that problems of cheating and free-riding need not attract too much attention in international negotiations. This does not mean that further research along these lines (even if its fundamental premises can be substantiated) is likely to produce the finding that efforts at devising effective compliance mechanisms are totally pointless: no-one assumes that obligation always trumps temptation. However, it might suggest that rationalist models, if taken at face value, can have misleading practical implications and, indeed, may even help cause the disease (distrust) they purport to cure.

There are two central topics on which strong cognitivists who are attracted to this line of thought concentrate when analyzing the autonomous "compliance pull" of norms and rules. First, they try to give a theoretical account of the postulated "sense of obligation" by pointing to the embeddedness of states in the international society. Their basic argument here is that states tend to comply even with inconvenient norms and rules because acting opportunistically would involve the risk of undermining their own existence in the long run. Second, they are looking for determinants which account for the varying strength of the compliance pull of different norms and rules. In this connection, they distinguish legitimate from illegitimate agreements and argue that the binding force of norms and rules depends on the degree of their legitimacy.

Concerning the first topic, the nature of the sense of obligation that is said to motivate states, one central argument was already elaborated by Henkin (1968: 32) himself who maintained that the general respect for norms and rules is "the price of membership in international society and having relations with other nations." According to Henkin, governments recognize their dependence on a normatively organized international system, the principles of which make a peaceful and orderly exchange of goods and ideas possible. Since states are in need of an international society they respect the needs of this society. Among these, the observance of treaties is of crucial importance, as no society can exist without the generalized confidence that obligations incurred by its members are honored (Bull 1977). Therefore, nations and those who govern them have "a common interest in keeping the society running and keeping international relations orderly" (Henkin 1968: 48; see also Franck 1990: 37; Hurrell 1993: 59).

Up to this point, the argument sounds as if the respect for normative arrangements were explained once again by reference to converging national interests. Such an understanding would miss a crucial point, however. To be sure, strong cognitivists such as Henkin or Hurrell talk of interests but these are interests of a very special kind. The interest that states have in the international society, where a set of basic norms such as the respect for sovereignty and the binding nature of treaties are taken for granted, is a necessary one: for without an international society there would be no sovereign states. In the words of German philosopher Otfried Höffe (1987: 391), the interest of states in the (viability of) international society belongs to the category of "transcendental interests," i.e. interests which are not a matter of choice to actors because they must pursue them so long as they (want to be able to) pursue any interests at all. As Henkin (1968: 48) has put it, the observance of the basic principles which are laid down in international law is an "assumption built into international relations." It is in keeping with this perspective when Franck (1990: 192) points out that most governments are fully aware of their duties and respect them in their foreign policy decisions. "[I]t is . . . demonstrable that there *are* obligations owed by states *which they widely recognize as concomitants of community membership and which are accurate predictors of actual state behavior*."

With regard to the second research topic we have mentioned, both

Franck (1990) and Hurrell (1993) have recently argued that only norms and rules which are perceived by state actors as legitimate can be attributed a compliance pull of their own. Conversely, regimes which are considered illegitimate can be upheld only by positive or negative sanctions. *Legitimacy* can be thus conceptualized as a quality of prescriptions which makes state actors abide by them voluntarily. This quality varies across norms and rules and, according to Franck, is dependent on four dimensions which he refers to as determinacy, symbolic validation, coherence, and adherence. The central hypothesis of this approach runs as follows:

> [T]o the extent a rule, or a rule-process, exhibits . . . [the] four properties [of determinacy, symbolic validation, coherence, and adherence] it will exert a strong pull on states to comply. To the extent these properties are not present, the institution will be easier to ignore and the rule easier to avoid by a state tempted to pursue its short-term self-interest. (Franck 1990: 49)

In this connection, *determinacy* refers to the textual clarity with which the content of a rule is communicated. *Symbolic validation* refers to rituals of recognition that express the extent to which a given rule has taken root in the traditions of international society. (Franck [1990: 103] points, as an example, to the "venerable ritual practices" surrounding the rules of diplomacy.) Even more important, however, are the other two dimensions, adherence and coherence, both of which are defined in terms of the relationship of the rules in question to broader normative patterns of relevance to international society. A rule has the property of *adherence* if and to the exent that "it is validated by an infrastructure of rules about rules . . . that define[s] how rules are to be made, interpreted, and applied" (Franck 1990: 184). The concept of *coherence* refers to the interconnectedness of individual rules through higher-order principles. Coherence thus expresses how closely a rule is related to the "underlying rule-skein which connects disparate *ad hoc* arrangements into a network of rules 'governing' a community of states, the members of which perceive the coherent rule system's powerful pull towards voluntary compliance" (Franck 1990: 181).

It is thus the correspondence between individual norms and rules and the underlying normative structure of the international society which determines the tendency of governments to observe specific injunctions. According to Franck, this is the case because breaking legitimate normative arrangements would send shock waves into the heart of the society of states and would shake its normative building blocks. This, however, is incompatible with the necessary interests of states. It is in this sense that states regard the respect for legitimate normative arrangements as an obligation they owe to the international society.

One corollary of the operation of a "sense of obligation" in the international system is that governments are not indifferent to the rule-breaking of third parties. At a minimum, they see their transcendental interest in the existence of an intact international society as affected. The breach of legitimate norms and rules is perceived as a potential threat to "the fabric of the community's rule system as a whole" (Franck 1990: 151). Therefore, respect for legitimate normative arrangements is considered indivisible and a government that intends to challenge such an arrangement has to reckon with negative sanctions by the community of states as a whole. This is another reason why legitimate norms and rules are more robust than rules which depend only on contingent interests of the cooperating parties.

Strong cognitivists elaborating on the "power of legitimacy" in international relations take the solidarity of states as a fact and assume a "sense of we-ness" (Buzan 1993: 335) which motivates governments to respect the fundamental principles and norms of international society. They argue that there is an interest in the system which, to a large extent, is congruent with self-interest yet cannot be reduced to self-interest, because the pursuit of one's *individual* interests as defined by rationalist theories presupposes statehood, and statehood depends on membership in a functioning *community* of states. This stance, however, brings them into sharp opposition to rationalist theorists such as Kenneth Waltz who vigorously denies an interest of states in the system.[13] According to Waltz (1979: 91) states have to be conceptualized as strictly self-regarding units. The system, then, is only the unintended consequence of their interaction. Although it constrains the interacting units, it does so not by means of obligations actors enter into but by virtue of its anarchical structure and the weight it confers to relative power capabilities.

Such arguments about the power of legitimacy are provocative not only to realists but also to most students of international relations today. Those strong cognitivists who propose to draw from this body of ideas should therefore make every effort to go beyond the confines of an

[13] Only under very restrictive conditions (i.e. in periods of bipolarity) does Waltz (1979: 195–9) consider a congruence between individual interests and the "interests of the system" possible.

almost exclusively theoretical argument and engage in empirical research that aims at assessing the concrete impact on foreign policy decisionmaking of the assumed autonomous compliance pull of legitimate norms and rules. The best way to make their case would be to come up with much more detailed and systematic observations which at the same time constitute serious puzzles for the rationalist research tradition *and* can be explained in a convincing manner by their own approach. Unfortunately, however, as Henkin (1968: 43f.; see also Franck 1990: 45–7; Chayes and Chayes 1993: 177) has already pointed out very clearly, empirical evidence to decide between the two competing visions of international rules is difficult to obtain. How could we decide whether an observable tendency for states to comply with agreed-upon international rules results from the workings of a "sense of obligation" rather than from utilitarian calculations involving considerations of sunk costs or reputation?

As mentioned above (sect. 3.1), supposed reputational concerns of governments play a major role in the contractualist account of rule compliance. The argument says that rational actors often refrain from violating rules that have become inconvenient for them, because they expect such an action to make it more difficult for them to realize gains through cooperation in the future (Keohane 1984: 99–107; Stein 1990: 52). Strong cognitivists have at least two objections at their disposal. The first objection contends that the argument that reputational concerns will (often) prevent states from following their short-term interest of non-compliance rests on unrealistic situational assumptions. The second is in a sense more fundamental, questioning the compatibility of this argument with the premises of rationalism itself.

Representing the first strand of criticism, Philip Heymann (1973) has argued that the "benefits of coordination frequently depend upon trust that agreed freedom of action will be honored in spite of conflicting temptations," adding that "the effects of reputation provide some basis for such trust only when a limiting set of conditions is met [:] any violation must be known; it must be known by a party whose reactions to the violations are important to the violator; and the expected cost to the violator must exceed the benefits of giving in to the conflicting temptation." Kratochwil (1989: 109) has quoted Heymann's analysis with approval, suggesting that this "set of conditions" is so restrictive that it amounts to a refutation of the rationalists' explanation of compliance with inconvenient obligations.

To this criticism rationalists can respond that it is precisely for the provision of those conditions that international regimes are created: authors such as Keohane have always emphasized that one of the most important functions of regimes is the reduction of asymmetrical information. Much seems to depend, therefore, on the empirical validation of this latter assertion. To make it plausible, presumably, one would have to show that regimes usually exhibit elaborate verification schemes (or rather verification schemes which are elaborate enough to create a sufficient degree of transparency). Moreover, given that rules are not always complied with, the conditions under which considerations of reputation take effect need further specification. Otherwise, there is a significant danger that the reputation argument degenerates to a theoretically useless passe-partout. Meanwhile, this danger is not limited to the rationalist argument: reference to a supposed sense of obligation might be just as arbitrary and problematic unless the nature of this disposition and the conditions of its efficacy are further explored.[14]

Given this open situation, strong cognitivists may advance an even more fundamental argument. They may point out that it is not evident why reputational concerns should trouble rational egoists at all (see Gowa 1989b: 319f.; Mercer 1996). If a good reputation is important for cooperation it should be so in situations in which states are unable to monitor one another's actions properly. However, the rational institutionalists' core thesis says that states cooperate through regimes and that regimes reduce informational asymmetries effectively. Hence it is unclear why states should ask for the "credentials" of their would-be partners before entering into a regime with them. Conversely, if regimes create transparency (and rule violations are likely, albeit not certain, to be sanctioned), they should, contrary to Keohane's claim, *not* be appropriate arenas for states to acquire a reputation for trustworthiness: rational actors are *likely* to behave cooperatively under such conditions; hence, no inferences are possible with regard to their behavioral

[14] There is yet another sense in which the information provided by regimes may be insufficient to substantiate the reputation argument. As both Garrett and Weingast (1993: 180–3) and Kratochwil (1993a: 76–83) have pointed out, international regimes usually rely on so-called "incomplete contracts" or "imperfect treaties." Rule-guided cooperation evolves in a dynamic environment and there will always be unanticipated contingencies which are not explicitly covered by the regime. Therefore, in many cases, "what is required by the rule of the game cannot be determined uniquely" (Garrett and Weingast 1993: 181). It is not clear, then, why rational actors should not seize upon any opportunity to exploit such loopholes, particularly since, owing to the ambiguity of the situation, they need not fear causing substantial damage to their reputation in this way.

dispositions in situations in which other conditions (i.e. less transparency) prevail.

The communicative action approach, or the power of arguments

For scholars belonging to the communicative action strand of strong cognitivism, such as Kratochwil (1989) and Müller (1994), regimes fundamentally depend on the success of practical discourses between states. A practical discourse is a debate conducted by members of a community aiming at establishing or re-establishing a consensus on common norms of conduct as well as on their interpretation and proper application in concrete situations. Theorists of that stamp hold that there is a permanent need for communication in international relations in order to produce and maintain the convergence in expectations that regimes live by. Conversely, persistent lack of success in regime-oriented discourses is expected inevitably to lead to the collapse of rule-governed cooperation.

Following Jürgen Habermas (1981 vol. I: 126–35; 1983: 144f.), Kratochwil and Müller make a fundamental distinction between communicative action and strategic action as alternative mechanisms of social coordination. *Strategic action* can be defined as the selection of appropriate means to control, in an efficient way, the social environment of actors so that they are induced to respect a normative arrangement. Strategic action is success-oriented (consequentialist) and, in a regime context, aims at keeping the behavior of others in line with agreed-upon norms and rules by establishing a system of positive and negative incentives. Successful coordination is achieved through external constraints, and social actors behave in accordance with norms and rules as long as it is in their interest to do so (which includes situations in which actors lack the power to improve an agreement they no longer regard as satisfactory, but still as preferable to generalized self-help behavior). This, of course, is basically how rationalist approaches analyze international regimes (Stein 1983: 137; Keohane 1988: 387).

Communicative action, by contrast, is oriented toward mutual understanding, aiming at coordinating social behavior by persuasive arguments. According to this model, the parties to a conflict enter a discourse where they first try to bring about agreement concerning the relevant features of a social situation and then advance reasons why a certain behavior has to be avoided. These reasons – as far as they are convincing – internally motivate the parties to behave in accordance with the previously elaborated interpretation and the justified expectations of others. Behavior is thus not coordinated by external incentives but by common understandings of what a given situation requires social actors to do. As Richard Bernstein (1985: 19) observed, "ideally, the only force that should prevail in such a discourse is the 'force of the better argument'." The objective is to convince the other participants and to make them see things as oneself sees them.

Strong cognitivists argue that rationalist approaches to international regimes with their focus on strategic action have systematically underestimated the role of discourses between states (Kratochwil 1989: 12; Müller 1994: 24–30). This neglect is increasingly less acceptable in a world which is characterized by growing interdependence and an ever greater complexity of international issues. As Keohane and Nye (1977) had already pointed out in the mid-1970s, rising levels of interdependence have devalued military power resources as a means of social coordination in important segments of international politics. However, not only has military power been marginalized in a growing number of issue-areas, but also the dramatically increased complexities of international problems are a cause for agonizing uncertainties on the part of political decisionmakers who find it ever more difficult to assess the national interests at stake and to identify the appropriate means to further them. As negotiation analysts (Young 1989b: 357–9; Sebenius 1992: 349) have argued, real-world diplomats often act under a "veil of uncertainty" because they find it extremely difficult to assess the likely effects on their nations of different institutional options (see also sect. 3.4 above). Moreover, they often find themselves in the uncomfortable situation of confronting a plurality of conflicting interpretations and advice recommending different and incompatible policies. Divergent understandings of reality, however, if they cannot be settled through communicative action, make rule-governed cooperation impossible, since even agreed-upon norms and rules must collapse if they are applied inconsistently by actors who follow their individual interpretations of what a particular situation is and what it requires them to do.

Given these trends, the question arises how it is possible for governments time and again to succeed in developing common interpretations of reality and in reaching consensus on certain proposals. In this context, strong cognitivists have pointed out that a crucial means available to policymakers of bringing about an agreement is the existence of convincing arguments. Such arguments reasonably support a particular

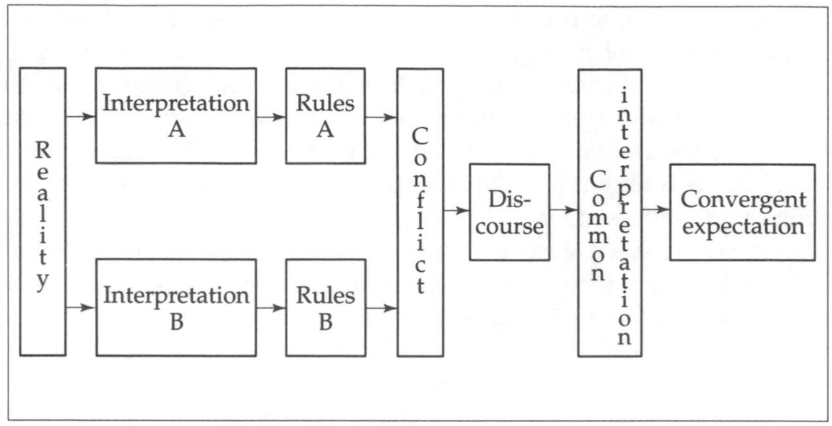

Fig. 11. The dependence on discourses of convergent expectations.

interpretation of the situation and its necessities which then can serve as foundation for the formation and maintenance of a particular set of rules expressing actors' convergent expectations about the right conduct in a particular issue-area. Thus, strong cognitivists hypothesize that in situations of power-inefficiency and when complex issues are at stake, persuasion tends to replace compulsion as the medium of policy coordination (Müller 1994: 28).

According to this line of reasoning, taking the "power of arguments" seriously sheds new light on the phenomenon that states often put up with apparent violations of agreed-upon norms and rules without engaging in sanctioning behavior (Kratochwil and Ruggie 1986: 765; Chayes and Chayes 1993: 187–97). From a conventional point of view, this seeming passivity is explained with reference either to the insufficient capabilities of the would-be regime defenders or to a second-order collective action problem which prevents each individual actor from taking the initiative and bearing the costs of sanctioning. Though difficult to refute in its own terms, this account is considered unsatisfactory by strong cognitivists, as it is not well attuned to the phenomenology of the behavior under consideration: in particular, the notion implied by this account that states, just because they do not retaliate, "do nothing" is criticized as highly misleading.

Confronting a *prima facie* defection, states habitually ask that the offender give reasons for its failure to live up to its obligation. They evaluate the reasons that are advanced in the light of principled and shared understandings of what the regime under consideration requires its members to do under certain circumstances. This may lead them to accept that conforming to a particular injunction would have been unduly hard for the *prima facie* offender such that it could not reasonably be expected to comply in this situation (Kratochwil and Ruggie 1986: 765). On other occasions of apparent non-compliance, states may come to the conclusion that the rule at issue needs reformulating to continue to be in accordance with the original purposes of the regime (Kratochwil 1988: 277f.). On still other occasions, they will reject the proffered justifications and engage in some sort of sanctioning. According to Kratochwil and Ruggie (1986: 774), this variety of possible reactions to instances of formal non-compliance with norms and rules indicates that "what constitutes a breach of an obligation undertaken within a regime is not simply an 'objective description' of a fact but an intersubjective appraisal."

In each case, it is argued that the principled and shared understandings underpinning the norms and rules at issue are of paramount importance for the evaluation of action and the choice of reaction. In a sense, therefore, the distinction between compliance and non-compliance turns out to be a communicative phenomenon, and the *reasons* which can legitimately be put forward to justify a given act or course of behavior advance to an important factor in the decisions of states whether or not to tolerate the deviance at issue. Consequently, "communicative dynamics may tell us far more about how robust a regime is than overt behavior alone . . . only where noncompliance is widespread, persistent, and unexcused – that is, presumably, in limiting cases – will an explanatory model that rests on overt behavior alone suffice" (Kratochwil and Ruggie 1986: 768).

From this point of view, international regimes are never an objectively given set of principles, norms, rules, and procedures but are "the product of an on-going process of community self-interpretation and self-definition in response to changing context" (Neufeld 1993: 55, n. 55), or, as Kratochwil (1989: 101f.) has put it: "In international relations, . . . the parties themselves must interpret each other's moves and constantly renegotiate the reality in which they operate." This makes normative arrangements essentially dynamic phenomena which depend on evolving international discourses (Smith 1989; Gehring 1994). Thus, scholarly research faces the task of inquiring into the nature and the logic of such *practical discourses* between states (Kratochwil 1989; Müller 1994; Schimmelfennig 1995).

In explaining the success and failure of international discourses, strong cognitivists emphazise the importance of two factors, one formal and the other material: (1) A set of basic norms which are considered constitutive features of the practice of argumentation has to be respected by the parties; and (2) success in practical discourses depends on the embeddedness of particular arguments in a framework of uncontested background knowledge concerning the right conduct of states in international relations.

(1) In contrast to strategic action with its focus on external (and sometimes forceful) motivation, communicative action aims at reorganizing the cognitions and attitudes of the parties by means of argumentation. To engage in communicative action as a mode of policy coordination requires that the parties respect certain basic norms of social interaction. When they enter into the practice of arguing, they have to recognize each other as equal, they must accept the principle of no harm and they have to respect the binding nature of agreements based on good reasons. Finally, as Kratochwil (1989: 36; see also Müller 1994: 27) has put it, they are obliged "to argue the 'merits' of their case and, in doing so, their argument must be cast in terms of universalizable rules." If these commitments are not widely accepted, practical discourses between states are impossible and the analytical distinction between persuasion and compulsion (or bribe) is pointless.

(2) Under the condition that these constitutive norms are respected, discourses between states can be described as an iterative process involving the interpretation and the evaluation of particular actions. Arguments are put forward to classify a move in a rule-governed context *and* claims are made concerning the legitimacy of this move. The two dimensions of this "reasoning process" (Kratochwil 1989: 11) are intrinsically linked. They form part of an encompassing communicative activity that is not only guided by norms and rules, but essentially and permanently involves explicit and discursive examination of these norms and rules in cases of disputed validity. By this very practice the actors necessarily transcend the narrow confines of purely prudential action which is properly analyzed using the tools of rational choice theory. Since convincing arguments cannot be built upon idiosyncratic grounds, they have to be grounded in general principles und common understandings, i.e. in what argumentation theory traditionally refers to as *topics* (Kratochwil 1989: 212–48).

Consider, for example, the principle that "ought implies can" or the principle of "embedded liberalism" which are both of particular relevance to (contemporary) international relations. The first principle is appealed to when an actor seeks to justify his behavior by pointing out that he lacks the capacity to fulfill incurred liabilities (Chayes and Chayes 1993: 193–5). The case at hand may be one of "involuntary defection" (Putnam 1988: 438) forced upon the government by (unexpectedly) strong domestic opposition to parts or the whole of an international agreement. In the second case, a government would argue that its international obligations do not fit the requirements of domestic stability anymore (Ruggie 1983: 215). According to Ruggie (1983: 227), it is accepted wisdom at least among the OECD nations that under such conditions imports could be temporarily suspended or restricted even if this involves a formal breach of rules that form part of the trade regime. Other important topics of international practical discourse are the principles of equity and reciprocity or the principle that contractual promises extracted through duress, fraud, or undue influence need not be observed (Yarbrough and Yarbrough 1987: 1). What all of these principles have in common is that they provide the participants in a discourse with recognized starting points for a sequence of arguments designed to convince other parties of a particular interpretation of a social phenomenon. While such general principles and understandings are not immune to self-interested manipulation, strong cognitivists maintain that they nevertheless restrict the set of arguments which can be convincingly put forward in international discourses (Kratochwil 1989: 241–3; 1993a: 92; Hurrell 1993: 61; Koslowski and Kratochwil 1994: 225).

The more explicit and the more clearly formulated the rules of international conduct in an issue-area, the easier is an intersubjectively shared specification of behavior. According to Kratochwil (1993a: 84–93), clarity enhances the compliance pull of rules, because actors can no longer use ambiguities in formulations of rules to mask the regime-adverse character of their behavior. The problem, however, is that often a further specification of norms and rules in international politics entails considerable costs. Overregulation may seriously hamper smooth rule management (Chayes and Chayes 1993: 189). Moreover, the dynamics and inherent unpredictability of international politics seem to require more generally formulated norms and rules which can be expected to cover a wider range of unforeseen situations (Cowhey 1993: 158f.). These considerations lead theorists to conclude that agreed-upon dispute settlement mechanisms which operate on the basis of commonly accepted principles can be most important for the compliance pull of regimes. This, of course, only reaffirms the importance of "principled and shared understandings of desirable and acceptable forms of social behavior" in international relations. There seems to be no way out of the continuous interpretation and evaluation of action by decisionmakers.

Though primarily concerned with the domestic side of regime-oriented discourses, Müller (1993a; 1993b) has made a notable contribution to this perspective. In so doing, he has taken up and reinforced an unease with rationalist explanations which has recently gained ground in the field of international security. Several case studies have raised serious questions regarding the usefulness of rationalist approaches for explaining the formation as well as the maintenance of security regimes. More specifically, the authors of these studies have suggested that the conceptual tools of mainstream regime analysis are insufficient, since they are unable to take account of important features of international politics such as the "complex web of enduring practices which exists between and among states" (Smith 1987: 280), "internationally shared cultural norms" (Brzoska 1991: 49), or the internalization of "mutually reinforcing attitudes and assumptions" (Duffield 1992: 844).

Müller's (1993b) focus is on the politics of compliance with inconvenient regime injunctions in three security cases: the challenges to the Anti-Ballistic Missile (ABM) Treaty as part of the strategic nuclear weapons control regime posed by the US government's Strategic Defense Initiative (SDI) and by the Soviet Union's deployment of an early-warning radar in Krasnoyarsk (treated as two separate cases by Müller), and West Germany's nuclear export control policy which, for several years, was incompatible with the non-proliferation regime. In each case the government, influential parts of the administration, or the military sought to implement measures, or already pursued a policy, which would have violated, or actually did violate, central regime norms. Müller finds that in each case the regime concerned proved to be a critical resource to those domestic groups which were opposed to the measures or decisions in question and enabled them to get the upper hand in the subsequent controversy. This observation leads Müller (1993b: 383) to the general conclusion, that "regimes exert pressure on governments, even on those with reservations about the regime. Not only are regimes powerful behavior-guides because it is so costly to construct alternatives: the sheer existence of regimes puts an 'extra' burden of proof on regime opponents."

Three of Müller's results are particularly noteworthy. First, he provides evidence that the regimes themselves, by virtue of their connection with both international and domestic law, provided substantial barriers to non-compliance, which could be utilized by their domestic defenders. Second, he shows that not only the regime defenders, but also the proponents of a policy change did not deny the obligation to keep treaties (*pacta sunt servanda*). In fact, there was a common understanding that treaties are binding. The public dispute therefore centered upon the question of how to interpret the stipulations of the treaty correctly, and the conflict between advocates and opponents of change took the form of a practical discourse. In other words, the situation could not adequately be analyzed in terms of strategic behavior, because *argumentation* played a central role in the process that drove and ultimately decided the conflict. In this discourse the norms and rules of the regime were the common points of reference. Third, Müller's results suggest that breaches of particular agreements are regarded as acceptable by the community of states provided they can be justified with reference to shared higher-order principles which would be violated if the particular agreements were implemented. When the West German government eventually acknowledged in 1985 that its nuclear export policy was not in accordance with the nuclear non-proliferation regime in that Germany's customers included countries which did not accept full-scope safeguards, it decided to suspend the corresponding trade agreements (Müller 1993b: 379). While this decision clearly implied a breach of previous supply commitments, not surprisingly West Germany was not accused by the community of states of disregarding international treaties. Rather, this policy shift was generally approved of with reference to the principles and norms of the nuclear non-proliferation regime, which were regarded to be of paramount importance for international security.

Strong cognitivists focusing on discourses between states are certainly right in pointing to a growing demand for communication in international relations. Moreover, few scholars of any persuasion would deny that a minimum of communicative action is needed to uphold international regimes under conditions of growing interdependence and increasing complexity and interconnectedness of international issues. But while strong cognitivists are asking the right questions, they do not seem to have come up with many convincing answers yet. At least four unresolved problems have to be mentioned.

(1) As Kratochwil (1989: 254) admits, the international political process is "often characterized by bargaining and coercive moves rather

than by persuasion and by appeals to common standards, shared values, and accepted solutions." To assess the concrete role of arguments under these conditions is a daunting and, so far, unresolved task. If, as Habermas (1981 vol. II: 115; 1983: 72) has remarked, under real-world conditions actors are motivated by a complex mixture of empirical pressure and argumentative persuasion, how can we establish when and to what extent policy decisions are driven by arguments and are the result of practical discourse? An answer to this question is necessary for a further specification of what counts as a good argument and what *topoi* are used in international practical discourses. As long as we cannot specify the impact of reasons on decisions we are in principle unable to transcend the general observation that the practice of discourses involves the respect for certain basic norms. It is also evident – and representatives of the communicative action approach concede this (Müller 1994: 38) – that a further sophistication of interpretative methods is required to make progress on this important issue. Thus, it is certainly not enough to point to "the hermeneutic circle" as the "methodology appropriate to an interpretative approach" (Neufeld 1993: 47–9) without giving at least some criteria for the validation of different interpretations – a problem which is, of course, familiar to interpretativists (Taylor 1985: 18–21, 24).[15]

(2) As has frequently been reported in the literature on international negotiations, states often fail to engage in communicative action, even when they realize that strategic behavior is likely to lead to a breakdown of the talks (Sebenius 1992: 334–7). This observation suggests that a "demand for communication" is not enough to motivate actors to change their mode of action. In addition, they have to trust each other, i.e. to have confidence that their legitimate interests will be respected not only in the final settlement, but in the implementation process as well (Jönsson 1993: 205–8). Otherwise, engaging in argumentation would hardly make much sense: the final outcome would still be dictated by the distribution of power and interests. This, however, is just another way of saying that (genuine) discourses between states presuppose an international morality which motivates actors to respect the results of collective normative choice as binding, even when they have the power to ignore them. Therefore, strong cognitivists concerned with communicative action at the international level should seek a better

[15] For a critique of the hermeneutic circle as a scientific methodology, see Haussmann (1991: 164–6).

understanding of the (interrelated) phenomena of trust and morality in international relations.

(3) A third point which is in need of further clarification is ontological in character and refers to the relationship between regimes and arguments in international discourses. On the one hand, scholars such as Kratochwil (1989: 11) maintain that "human action in general is 'rule-governed', which means that . . . it becomes understandable against the background of norms embodied in conventions and rules which give meaning to an action." Analyzed in this perspective, international regimes are likened to constitutive rules, which enable actors to act and to communicate in a socially meaningful way. Regimes are part of the *uncontested* and *assumed* social background knowledge which makes international politics possible. On the other hand, Kratochwil (1989: 34, 97, 101) repeatedly has pointed to the fundamental *dependence* of international regimes on arguments. He contends that social situations are always in need of interpretation such that debating "which set of rules applies in a concrete case is part of the mutual sense-making among actors." From *this* perspective, however, regimes no longer appear as part of the unproblematic basis for meaningful action, but as conditioned in their very content by common understandings which provide starting points for convincing sequences of arguments. Our point is not that these two perspectives of regimes are necessarily inconsistent, but that this somewhat unexpected *gestalt switch* indicates the need for further clarification of the ontological relationship between rules and arguments.

(4) There is a certain tension between the basic function of international regimes – namely to stabilize mutual expectations – and the thesis of Kratochwil (1989: 101f.) and Mark Neufeld (1993: 55, n. 59) that the international reality is in constant need of renegotiation. If the latter is true, then the validity of normative injunctions is permanently challengeable implying that actors cannot rely on them. To put it differently: if interpretations are in permanent flux, convergent expectations are impossible. Conversely, if it is accepted that the argumentative resources for rule obedience are robust enough to assure social actors that justifiable exemptions are rare, then the theoretical expectations of rationalist approaches and communicative approaches when talking about effective regimes converge. In this case, the critique of strong cognitivism that rationalism falls short of understanding international regimes, because it is preoccupied with overt behavior when analyzing the effectiveness of rules in international relations, loses most of its bite.

Constructivism, or the power of identity

Another line of reasoning pursued to shed light on the binding power of norms and rules challenges the rationalist practice of treating egoistic identities and interests of state actors as unproblematic and immutable starting points for the explanation of international regimes. Wendt (1994: 386), in particular, has argued that both actors' conceptions of self and other and their goals "are always in process during interaction." Therefore, identities and interests should be treated as dependent variables rather than pre-theoretical givens, the origins of which, whether they lie in human nature or domestic politics, are irrelevant for purposes of analysis (Wendt 1994: 385).

For Wendt, identities cannot be defined in substantive terms, i.e. in isolation from the social context. By contrast, they are "inherently relational" and have to be regarded as "sets of meanings that an actor attributes to itself while taking the perspective of others, that is, as a social object" (Wendt 1992a: 397; 1994: 386). Social identities represent particular conceptions of self in relation to other actors, thereby generating particular interests and shaping policy decisions. It makes a great difference for interaction whether *ego* considers himself a friend or a foe of *alter*. In the first case *ego* will respect the interests of *alter*, while in the second case he will only take them into account. Elaborating on this difference, Wendt develops two opposing ideal-types which form the poles of a continuum ranging from positive to negative identification with the welfare and the security of other actors. On the one hand, identities can be collective, that is other-regarding. *Alter* is seen "as a cognitive extension of self, rather than independent" (Wendt 1994: 386). She cannot be treated instrumentally. Collective identification, so understood, implies empathy and solidarity. Actors respect each other as members of a community where decisions are taken consensually. On the other hand, identities can be egoistic, that is self-regarding. *Alter* is "viewed as an object to be manipulated for the gratification of self" (Wendt 1994: 386). This conception of identity underlies the rationalist interpretation of international cooperation. It correlates with strategic action. The interests of *ego* are defined and pursued independently of the interests of *alter*, which are taken into consideration only as part of *ego*'s decision environment.

While Wendt does not deny that rationalists have a lot to say about "cooperation among egoists," he adds that, once established, rule-governed cooperation can change egoists into more altruistically orientated actors. An "evolution of cooperation might lead to an evolution of community" (Wendt 1994: 390), where actors at least partially identify with the legitimate interests of each other and respect them in their decisions. Egoistic motivations may play an important role in the early stages of regime-building, but, over time and with the proliferation of cooperative institutions in world politics, the parties acquire more collective identities: a process which "discourages free-riding by increasing diffuse reciprocity and the willingness to bear costs without selective incentives" (Wendt 1994: 386) is taking place. Therefore, cooperative institutions in international politics are not adequately analyzed in terms of functional responses to collective action problems, unless functional approaches find a way of integrating the evolution and internalization of new identities and interests which comes with the habitualized observance of agreed-upon norms and rules (Wendt 1992a: 399; 1994: 390f.).

To illustrate this *self-stabilization hypothesis of cooperation* beginning under anarchy, Wendt refers to the ongoing discussion about the future of the European security institutions. Whereas a number of prominent realists such as Mearsheimer (1990) and Waltz (1993) warned about a process propelling Europe "back to the future" – a future overshadowed by the re-emergence of the traditional balance-of-power politics that characterized the pre-1939 European state system - Wendt (1992a: 417f.) does not expect the old behavioral patterns to return, as the European states of the 1990s are no longer those of 1949 when they, together with the United States, founded NATO in order to balance the Soviet Union.

> Even if egoistic reasons were its starting point, the process of cooperating tends to redefine those reasons by reconstituting identities and interests in terms of new intersubjective understandings and commitments. Changes in the distribution of power during the late twentieth century are undoubtedly a challenge to these new understandings, but it is not as if West European states have some inherent, exogenously given interest in abandoning collective security if the price is right. (Wendt 1992a: 417f.)

Thus, it may be that NATO will undergo some transformation adapting to the new security environment. Yet, after decades of cooperation the Western European states now form a sort of Deutschean "pluralistic security community" which by itself is enough to make it an unlikely event that the future will look very much like the past.

Wendt (1992a: 393; 1994: 384f.; see also Onuf 1989; Koslowski and

Kratochwil 1994: 225) derives the self-stabilization hypothesis of international cooperation from a more encompassing theoretical framework which he refers to as *constructivism*.[16] As a distinct perspective on international relations, constructivism adopts a "systemic communitarian ontology" (Wendt 1992a: 425) focusing on the social construction of world politics and state identities (Wendt 1992a: 393; 1995: 71). The central tenet of this approach might be summarized as follows: the international reality, i.e. the fundamental structures of the international system, the self-understandings of states, and states' intentional behavior, is constituted by intersubjective knowledge which is itself dependent on the process of international interaction (see also Kohler-Koch 1989b: 53–6). In fact, it can be argued that constructivism dissolves systemic structures and identities into the "distribution of knowledge" in the international system. Intentional behavior is interpreted both as a *consequence* of knowledge: action presupposes knowledge – and as a *modifier* of knowledge: action can create new situations which lead to a re-evaluation of traditional cognitions. In other words: action and knowledge are mutually constitutive and, in the final analysis, irreducible to each other.

According to constructivism, foreign policy decisions are governed by both the meanings that states attribute to social objects and their self-understandings. (As do most students of regimes, Wendt [1994: 385; see also 1992a: 396f.] explicitly adopts a statist position, assuming that "states are the principal units of analysis for international political theory.") Behavior is thus dependent on what the world appears to be (i.e. on actors' perceptions) and how individual states conceive of their own role in this world (i.e. on actors' self-understandings). Such meanings are not idiosyncratic and subjective, though, but are organized by overarching intersubjective structures which consist of the "shared understandings, expectations, and social knowledge embedded in *international institutions*" (Wendt 1994: 389 [emphasis added]). These intersubjective structures and the institutions which embody them enable states to calculate the benefits and costs of different behavioral options and to make rational choices with regard to their individual goals (Wendt 1992a: 396f.; Dessler 1989: 454).

At the same time, interests are dependent on the self-understandings

[16] In this book, we reserve the term "constructivism" for Wendt's specific approach. It should be noted, therefore, that the term is often used with a somewhat broader meaning, covering the whole range of approaches that we refer to as "strong cognitivism."

of states which are also conceptualized as being deeply affected by the social knowledge structuring the international system. In this sense, identities are defined as "relatively stable, role-specific understandings and expectations about the self" that are "grounded in the *theories* which actors collectively hold about themselves and one another and which constitute the structure of the social world" (Wendt 1992a: 397, 398 [emphasis added]). Identities are "at once cognitive schemes that enable actors to determine 'who I am/we are' in a situation and positions in a social role structure of shared understandings and expectations" (Wendt 1994: 385). Identities are acquired by socialization into the intersubjective structures of the international system, or as Wendt (1992a: 397) puts it, "actors acquire identities . . . by participating in . . . collective meanings."

While socialization into intersubjective structures constitutes actors and forms identities, changes of these identities might at least in the long run transform structures and thereby reorientate international practices owing to the disappearance of old interests related to the former structures and the emergence of new ones. To account for this process of identity transformation, Wendt (1994: 389; see also Koslowski and Kratochwil 1994: 216) argues that the "distribution of knowledge" which forms the basic structure of the international system basically depends for its existence on its reproduction in the practice of states. Only as long as this structure actually shapes international behavior can it be considered to be in existence. In this sense, Wendt (1992: 406; see also 1995: 74) talks about the "ontological dependence of structure on process." And elsewhere he writes: "[I]n the last analysis, agents and structures are produced or reproduced by what actors do" (Wendt 1994: 390). According to this point of view, the choices of states are not determined by structural preconditions. There is always a margin of freedom which can be used in an unforeseeable way bringing about structural change. As Wendt (1992a: 419) has put it, "roles are not played in mechanical fashion according to precise scripts, . . . but are 'taken' and adapted in idiosyncratic ways by each actor." In this sense, micro-behavior can change macrostructures, since neither social structures nor social identities exist independently of interaction.

This dependence of identity on both structure and interaction makes it possible for more collective understandings of self and other to emerge from repeated cooperation as a generic form of strategic interaction in international politics. The emergence of rule-governed cooperation under the structural conditions of a (Hobbesian) state of nature may lead the involved actors to gradually change their beliefs about who they are. They become habituated to cooperation and, in the process, develop more collective identities (Wendt 1994: 390). The emergence of collective identities, in turn, strengthens the readiness of the actors to cooperate even in cases where the dominant strategy of a self-interested actor is to defect. Indeed, the interplay of cooperation and identity formation might trigger a sort of "positive echo-effect," which, since at least in the long run the deeper structures of the international system and the identitites acquired through interaction must be compatible, may culminate in structural transformation (Wendt and Duvall 1989: 64–6; Wendt 1994: 391–3; see also Dessler 1989: 469).

Wendt's critique of the rationalist mainstream in international relations theory and his formulation of an alternative research program drawing heavily on the work of sociologists such as Peter Berger and Thomas Luckmann (1967) as well as social psychologists such as George Herbert Mead (1934) is intriguing. We agree with him, though, that meta-theory should not gain the upper hand over substantive theory and also that it is time scholars sought to make good the theoretical promise of constructivism by demonstrating its ability to shed light on concrete empirical puzzles. This said, we believe that there are a number of issues in the abstract constructivist argument that deserve further scrutiny and efforts at clarification – efforts which are likely to bring rewards when it comes to probing the empirical merits of constructivism more thoroughly and systematically.

(1) The relationship between actors' identities and their interaction is ambiguous, because the concept of identity is used to account for both change and stability of practice. On the one hand, partially recast identities help to explain the decay of international structures such as the institution of self-help; on the other, the identity-shaping effects of rule-based cooperation are adduced as an important factor securing the robustness of international institutions such as regimes. We do not argue that there is anything fundamentally inconsistent about that; our point is, however, that many questions are left open this way. Perhaps it would be helpful to distinguish different social identities in the international system and to relate different behavioral regularities to these types of identity in order to come to a closer understanding of what kind of identity would be more prone to regime change than others. Additionally, Wendt (1992a: 398) argues that state actors usually have more than one identity and that the "commitment to and the salience of particular identities vary." This variation basically depends on "how deeply the social structures . . . [that these identities] instantiate pene-

trate conceptions of self" (Wendt 1994: 386). In order to assess the salience of particular identities, therefore, one would need to consider inter-identity relationships. One should also know how to measure the varying impact of structures on actors' conceptions of self. In other words, one needs an identity-ranking as well as a comparison of different identity-forming institutions. This points to the need to analyze in more detail possible role conflicts and the means states have at their disposal of solving them (Barnett 1993; 1995; Young 1996).

(2) The relationship between identity and actor requires clarification. On the one hand, an actor's self-understanding is considered constitutive for his interests and as such a prerequisite for rational decisionmaking. On the other hand, Wendt acknowledges a certain distance between state actors as subjects of international politics and their identities. They have the capacity to engage in "character planning" (Wendt 1992a: 419). This appears to re-open the floor for instrumental ("choice-centric") perspectives which Wendt orginally sought to overcome in favor of a more "institution-centric approach." By allowing for "self-transformation" (Wendt 1994: 390) and "self-conscious efforts to change structures of identity and interests" (Wendt 1992a: 418), the question arises how such efforts may be motivated. Rather surprisingly, Wendt (1992a: 411, 419), in this context, points to the *costs* of maintaining or changing certain self-understandings in a dynamic social world. But if so, must this criterion not undermine constructivism's premise that social actors cannot be reduced to utility-maximizers?

(3) A third problem refers to a central claim of constructivism which might be called the "congruence assumption." This assumption states that the fundamental structures of the international system, the actors' identities and more issue-area specific normative arrangements such as international regimes always tend towards an internal balance or harmony (Dessler 1989: 469; Wendt and Duvall 1989: 63–6). When one component changes, the other two sooner or later will have to change as well. This assumption immediately provokes the question of what induces the first component to change. Constructivists usually point to the practices of actors or their interactions as the ultimate source of transformation. We have already quoted Wendt's (1994: 390) sententious remark: "In the last analysis, agents and structures are produced or reproduced by what actors do." But this leaves open the crucial question of when do (or when can) actors decide to act against existing structures and when do they keep reproducing them. In other words: when does the identity-forming capacity of structures triumph over the

structure-transforming power of agents and *vice versa*? It is this indeterminacy of constructivism as a social theory which Hollis and Smith (1991: 406) refer to when they suggest that "it is more a description of social life than a basis for explanation." In fact, it seems as though the agent – structure problem, which has driven constructivist theory-building to such a large extent (Wendt 1987), has not been solved but has merely re-emerged in a different (though certainly fascinating) guise.

(4) Finally, more attention should be given to the largely implict role of ethics in Wendt's approach. Wendt makes a distinction between self-regarding and other-regarding identities, but also recognizes that collective (i.e. other-regarding) identities in real-world international politics are far from pure. States are no self-sacrificing units. As Wendt (1994: 387) puts it: "Identification is a continuum along which actors normally fall between the extremes, motivated by both egoistic and solidaristic loyalities." International life, even in a community of states, is not harmonious. There are always conflicts of interests to be dealt with. Therefore, if we accept that collective identities have at least some impact on conflict settlement, this implies that states have to come to terms with the question of who should respect whose interests under what circumstances. This, however, is basically what ethics is all about (Steigleder 1992: 82). In other words: states – when they act solidaristically under real-world conditions – do not only consider the legitimate interests of others but also their own. In order to decide in cases of conflict, states need a common moral code to weigh the different claims and they have to engage in argumentation in order to convince others of their interpretation of the moral situation. Hence, any community of states worthy of its name relies on some form of ethics defining the rights and duties of its members. If this is true, theorists taking a communitarian perspective on international relations should be more explicitly concerned with the content, reach, and impact of morality at the international level.

The historical-dialectical approach, or the power of history

On the preceding pages, we have discussed strong cognitivist approaches to international regimes, a common feature of which has been an emphasis on issues of institutional effectiveness and robustness. Moreover, in one way or another, all of the authors we have considered so far are concerned with the impact or the development of international communities which form the backdrop against which international regimes are analyzed. Thus, Franck and Hurrell argue that the correspondence of individual regimes with the normative necessities of an international society enhances their reliability as guides to state behavior. Kratochwil and Müller make the additional point that mutual respect is a precondition for practical discourses, which, in turn, are a prerequisite of stable regimes. It is the presence of an international community that makes the permanent renegotiation of the meaning of regime injunctions possible, since states know that their legitimate interests will be taken into account by other states. Finally, Wendt addresses the *evolution* of international communities. He argues that actors' internal dispositions to respect others' legitimate interests are positively affected by the enduring practice of rule-governed cooperation. Consequently, international communities arise from, and are deepened as a result of, ongoing mutually beneficial policy coordination (see also Buzan 1993). Paradoxically, Wendt thereby suggests that change produces stability: identities that have become less egoistical over time make for more robust regimes. The decline of the international self-help system at least in some regions of the world is accompanied by the emergence of a new structure which makes international institutions more resilient because actors start to identify positively with the welfare of others (Wendt 1994: 386).

If these scholars are concerned with the sources of the stability of international institutions, Robert Cox is more interested in what might cause their breakdown (and replacement). In Cox's view, contemporary international institutions have unjust distributive consequences which reinforce the rule of the advanced capitalist states over the rest of the world. His theory sets out to analyze the possibilities of historic change in international relations involving an unraveling of existing regimes and organizations. For this purpose, Cox seeks insights into the contradictions of the existing world order that might be used by social movements to revolt effectively against international and transnational exploitation and to bring about a just global order. The fact that Cox's cognitive interests are hostile to the institutional status quo does not mean that he is silent on issues of regime robustness and effectiveness. On the contrary, acquiring knowledge about the conditions of regime strength is an essential part of his agenda, as such knowledge – at least in principle – can be converted into knowledge about how to weaken the prevailing order of things.

For Cox, the international institutions of the postwar era are part of an encompassing hegemonic world order controlled by the United States together with other OECD nations. They reflect the interests and values of the ruling Western elites and help form a liberal world society. Their main function is to ensure optimal conditions – political as well as economic – for the global exploitation of private capital, i.e. the possibility to make use of comparative advantages, fairly stable exchange rates, a steadily growing world economy, the international protection of private property, as well as sufficient social stability in the areas of production.

According to Cox, the hegemonic order of the postwar era is rooted in the social conflicts of the nineteenth century. In these conflicts, the bourgeoisie prevailed as the ruling class in Europe and the United States. It succeeded in shaping the political and economic relations within these countries according to its economic interests and to defend the new order against attempts to enforce revolutionary change. With regard to international relations, the bourgeoisie pursued a liberal foreign trade policy. It promoted the global expansion of the capitalist mode of production and attempted to guarantee the free movement of goods, capital, and technology. During the course of the twentieth century it became obvious in the most advanced capitalist countries that the liberal ownership structure and thus the capitalist mode of production could only be maintained if social peace was guaranteed. Thus the bourgeoisie entered into a historic compromise with the industrial workers, resulting in the modern welfare state which ensures social minimum standards to the population. According to Cox (1996: 198), "it had become accepted wisdom that society would not tolerate high unemployment or any dismantling of the welfare state. If these things were to occur, it would, it was said, cost the state the loss of legitimacy."

This historic compromise radiated into international politics. The relations between states were newly organized according to the welfare state principle of "embedded liberalism" (Ruggie 1983). It became the main function of international institutions

> to reconcile domestic social pressures with the requirements of a world economy. The International Monetary Fund was set up to provide loans to countries with balance of payments deficits in order to provide time in which they could make adjustments, and to avoid the sharp deflationary consequences of an automatic gold standard. The World Bank was to be a vehicle for longer term financial assistance. Economically weak countries were to be given assistance by the system itself either directly through the system's institutions or by other states after the system's institutions had certified their conformity to the system's rules. (Cox 1986: 230)

Thus, as far as the Third World is concerned, the purpose of these institutions is to promote the capitalist mode of production and to secure the integration of these economies into the world market.

In a way similar to neorealism, the concepts of power and conflict occupy key positions in Cox's critical approach to hegemonic orders. These orders emerge in historical conflicts and manifest themselves in international institutions which are upheld by political power. Behavioral patterns are thus dependent on a particular configuration of forces. In contrast to the neorealist paradigm, however, Cox (1983: 164; 1996: 77) employs a broader concept of power which combines physical coercion with ideological manipulation. He endorses Machiavelli's simile of power as a centaur: half man, half beast. In his usage, "power" does not only refer to the external control of actors' decisions through the manipulation of strategic constraints (the "beast"), but also to their internal control through the dissemination of values and interpretations of reality (the "man"). Power in this sense "frames thought and thereby circumscribes action" (Cox 1992a: 179); it involves a direct grasp on the minds of actors. In addition to this broadened understanding of power, there are two further ways in which Cox's approach differs from the neorealist paradigm: (1) he gives ontological primacy to societal over governmental actors, and (2) – partly as a corollary of his power concept – he adopts a more encompassing understanding of hegemony. We consider each of these in turn.

In his analysis of international politics Cox asserts the *ontological primacy of societal actors*. Thus, he departs from the framework of systemic and state-centric theorizing common to virtually all theories of regimes we have looked at so far. More specifically, he claims that hegemonic world orders rest on the expansion of a dominant national class across borders (Cox 1983: 171; 1992b: 140; 1996: 246). In historic conflicts societal actors – such as the bourgeoisie in the nineteenth century – manage to gain control over the state and to consolidate their rule by gradually reshaping national key institutions such as judiciary, education, the press, and religion. Control over these institutions helps them to "create in people certain modes of behavior and expectations" (Cox 1983: 164), consistent with both the prevailing mode of accumulation and the structure of dominance. In a second step, the new ruling class extends its conception of social and political order to the international and transnational level, the major aim being to build up a homogeneous international system in which it is able to realize its profit and power interests. In order to achieve this goal, the ruling class in one country attempts to export its model of society and then to socialize the elites of the target countries via their integration into international organizations and regimes. In other words: the social relations in other countries are manipulated so as to create in the local elites an interest in cooperating with an external ally in order to consolidate their own power position. In contrast to neoliberal cooperation theory, in Cox's approach the actors are not simply given. Rather a dominant class in one country creates its partners abroad, controlling their interest formation both by influencing their domestic environment and by socializing them into a particular worldview. Hence, in Cox's account of international relations, intervention (in the broad sense of interfering with the domestic affairs of another state) is not a specific tool of statecraft actors sometimes resort to: foreign policy and intervention become virtually indistinguishable.

If Cox emphazises the ontological primacy of societal actors both in national and international politics, this does not mean that he is unaware of the fallacy of seeking to give a single-factor explanation of a complex social phenomenon (Cox 1986: 246). His approach is deliberately non-reductionist, taking into account the interdependencies which exist between the strategies of societal actors, national institutions, and the international system. Thus, to give one example, he observes that "Stalinism was, at least in part, a response to a sense of threat to the existence of the Soviet state from a hostile world order" (Cox 1986: 221). Similarly, Cox is aware that social conflicts in certain countries are crucially shaped by the state of the world economy. Yet, in the final analysis, he insists that social forces are the fundamental movers in politics, and that domestic politics, more so than vice versa, shapes international politics. Consequently, Cox (1983: 173f.) rejects all attempts to reform the international system top-down. By contrast, he argues that "we must shift the problem of changing world order back from international institutions to national societies." In his view the national context remains the only place where effective opposition to the prevailing order can be organized, "although world-economy and world-political conditions materially influence the prospects for such an enterprise."

The domestic constellation of social forces, in turn, is crucially affected by the production process. According to Cox (1986: 216), "the production of goods and services, which creates both the wealth of a society and the basis for a state's ability to mobilize power behind its foreign policy, takes place through a power relationship between those who control and those who execute the task of production." But this power relationship is precarious. It is constantly challenged by the evolution of new modes of production which generate new social forces. These new forces bring about changes in the form of the state and in its foreign policy orientation. If similar social processes are released in a plurality of countries due to similar changes in the economic sphere, a new international order may be the result. In other words: the nature of the state is determined by the domestic constellation of social forces, which is crucially affected by the production process. The structure of the international system, in turn, is dependent on the nature of the most powerful states.

To illustrate these ontological dependencies, Cox points to the ongoing globalization in the world economy. He argues that this trend reflects a fundamental shift in the previously nationalistic and state-orientated mode of production in the advanced capitalist countries. The core of this trend is that the economy starts to free itself from state control and intervention. The key words of the emerging production process are global competitiveness, deregulation, and privatization. The gradual replacement of the postwar international economy by a global economy creates new social forces, "a transnational managerial class" (Cox 1986: 234), which seeks to establish a truly global market. These forces challenge the traditional model of the welfare state and hence the corresponding international institutions of "embedded liberalism." Provided that these forces succeed and take over the capitalist core regions, one has to reckon with a completely new structure of international relations which might be described as a "new medievalism": "a multi-level system of political authorities with micro- and macro-regionalisms and transborder identities interacting in a more complex political process" (Cox 1992a: 179; see also Bull 1977: 254f., 264–76).

As with his concept of power and in connection to it, Cox employs – again compared to neorealist theorizing – a broader *concept of hegemony*. Hegemonic orders are stationary equilibria of history in a political space. They arise from social conflicts and represent a compromise between opposed social forces, which, at least for a certain time, is not seriously challenged. In this sense, Cox (1986: 224) defines hegemonic orders as "historical structures" which are maintained by "a fit between power, ideas and institutions." The interdependence of these three factors creates a framework of action which shapes social behavior channeling it in predefined ways such that the pre-existing power relations tend to be reproduced. At the same time, Cox, in a way similar to Wendt's, emphasizes that historical structures do not determine actors' behavior in any mechanical sense, but should be understood as stable constellations of forces that shape the "context of habits, pressures, expectations and constraints within which action takes place" (Cox 1986: 217).

For Cox (1996: 364) "hegemony" is an analytical construct. It "is invisible, a latent force that can be seized only intellectually." What can be observed, however, is the impact of a hegemonic order on social behavior via institutions. The effective operation of institutions thus becomes an indicator of an existing hegemony, or as Cox (1996: 364) has put it, "hegemony is the secret of the viability of institutions." In international politics hegemonic orders manifest themselves in international regimes and organizations which implement the conception of rule, as held by the transnationally dominant social class and its allies, in different issue-areas. International institutions organize international as well as transnational relations in accordance with the interests of the ruling class, in particular its interests in maximizing capital returns. In Cox's (1996: xi) words: "international organization has contributed to particular structures of world order by reflecting and reinforcing dominant forms of state and preeminent social forces." As in neorealist and neoliberal theory, hegemonic institutions thus mirror power relationships which, at the same time, they help to stabilize.

Although international hegemonic orders are in line with the interests of a dominant class, they must be distinguished from purely coercive forms of rule. While, in the latter, material power is the crucial medium of social coordination, in hegemonic orders consensus and compromise play an indispensible role. Uncoerced conformity of behavior by most states and non-state actors most of the time is an essential characteristic of hegemony in Cox's sense. Social deviation is only a marginal phenomenon. According to Cox (1986: 251, n. 16; 1992a: 179; 1992b: 140), this voluntary acceptance of hegemonic orders is mainly the result of a common ideology. The majority of the relevant governmental and private actors are convinced they live in the best of all possible worlds and are quite willing to support the international institutions expressing the existing world order. In other words: the maintenance of the hegemonic institutions seems to be a matter of general interest, and their norms and rules are observed largely by virtue of the belief that they are legitimate. Only in exceptional cases are external sanctions to enforce compliance necessary. The possibility of the use of force to punish non-conforming behavior recedes to the background. As a result, institutions acquire a measure of independence from their material power basis

(Cox 1986: 219). The socialization of national elites is an important function of international organizations and regimes (Cox 1983: 172f.). Simultaneously, its dependence on a common ideology makes the hegemonic order potentially vulnerable to intellectual criticism. The role of ideology is thus ambivalent, or, in Cox's preferred terminology, dialectical. It makes governance without government easier (as compared to a realist world) but, at the same time, may become a seed of destruction.

Another constitutive element of a hegemonic order is the ability of the dominant class to impose positive as well as negative sanctions. The weight attached to ideological factors notwithstanding, enforcement capacities are important, because the degree of voluntary support for a hegemonic order decreases from the center to the periphery. The greater the distance of an actor from the center, the more likely he is aware that *he* does not live in the best of all possible worlds, but rather belongs to the disadvantaged, if not the suppressed. In these areas, hegemonic institutions can be maintained only by force. This is why the ruling class must have a sufficient number of instruments of coercion at its disposal. Since their use is expensive, however, it will employ them as rarely as possible. Simultaneously, conflicts of interest which cannot be defused by a common ideology might also occur in the center. In these cases the ruling class has to make compromises with strategically important actors whom it can neither force nor manipulate to act as it desires. Apart from the ideology-based social consensus, compromises are the second pillar of voluntary support for a hegemonic order. Compromises presuppose sufficient distributive margins on the part of the ruling class, however, as allies need to be given a share in the net profits from the order. Thus, a hegemonic order always comprises winners and losers. The winners who are interested in upholding the hegemonic order must compensate and thus appease some of the losers up to a point where they can suppress the resistance of the rest of the losers by force. The winners, i.e. the dominant or ruling class, join with the compensated losers, who become the ruling class's allies, to form a so-called "historic bloc" (Cox 1983: 167–9). A historic bloc comprises those actors who think that they would lose if a particular order should fail. Its coherence is necessary in order to maintain the rule of the advantaged over those who reject the current order and thus might attempt to form an oppositional bloc.

A hegemonic world order is an order at the margins of power. The ruling class tries to pursue its interests as far as possible and to convert them into institutions. Its leeway is circumscribed by the negative as well as positive sanctions at its disposal and the persuasiveness of its ideology. On the one hand, the ruling class has to marginalize oppositional social forces and, if necessary, to use force to prevent them from organizing themselves to become a serious challenge to the existing order. On the other hand, it has to ensure, via compromise and consensus, the necessary support of a critical mass of subjects. The ruling class, thus, must be careful to avoid tensions between the three components which constitute the historical structure. *Material power* must be large enough to make it possible successfully to deter and impose sanctions on deviant behavior. It is equally important, though, that the persuasiveness of the legitimizing *ideology* be upheld since otherwise the capacity of the ruling class for sanctioning and compromising is likely to be rapidly exhausted. Finally, it is essential that the net return that the ruling class receives from the *institutions* of the hegemonic order does not dwindle to an extent which would make it impossible to maintain the coherence of the historic bloc.[17]

Cox draws two conclusions from his analysis of the complex and precarious nature of hegemonic orders. The first implication that he points to is the subversive potential of critical intellectuals who might delegitimize capitalism's model of order by unveiling contradictions in its ideological underpinnings and by coming up with alternative conceptions of social order (Cox 1983: 168). Contradictions, once understood, weaken the coherence of the historic bloc while new ideas, at the same time, may give greater coherence to counter-hegemonic forces. Both can lead to a change in the social constellation of forces which, in turn, may eventually cause the unraveling of existing institutions. Second, neoliberal regime theory turns out to be research "at the service of big-power management of the international system" (Cox 1986: 248). Its cardinal sin is that it "takes the existing order as given, as something to be made to work more smoothly, not as something to be criticized and changed" (Cox 1992a: 173). By analyzing the reproduction problems of the international system and by exploring the possibilities of peaceful conflict management via the formation and maintenance of international institutions, neoliberal regime theory contributes to preserving the efficiency of the present American hegemony. It helps the ruling

[17] To Cox (1986: 223) the realist theory of hegemonic stability (see sect. 4.1 above) is flawed precisely because it focuses exclusively on material power ("dominance"). Instead he advocates a formulation "in which state power ceases to be the sole explanatory factor and becomes part of what is to be explained."

capitalist class to uphold its distributive margins and to stabilize the historic bloc.

Paradoxically, Cox criticizes neoliberal regime theory for its technical success.[18] Its insights are real (if limited), but conservative in their political implications. For Cox (1986: 208), neoliberalism comes under the category of *problem-solving theory*. Such theory takes "the present as given and reasons about how to deal with particular problems within the existing order of things" (Cox 1996: 525). Problem-solving theory is contrasted with *critical theory*, which aims at uncovering the historical structure of a society thus providing opportunities for its critique. Critical theory

> stands apart from the prevailing order of the world and asks how that order came about. Critical theory, unlike problem-solving theory, does not take institutions and social and power relations for granted but calls them into question by concerning itself with their origins and how and whether they might be in the process of changing... Critical theory is directed to the social and political complex as a whole rather than to the separate parts. (Cox 1986: 208)

According to Cox, any attempt to change the existing hegemonic order is doomed to failure without a deep understanding of the existing historical structure as the product of a complex interaction of ideas, material power, and institutions. Change, if it is to occur, has to be brought about through the purposive formation of an oppositional power bloc and by providing a convincing intellectual alternative to the existing order.

Cox suggests that the blindness of neoliberal regime theory to its rule-stabilizing function can be put down to its positivist epistemology which concentrates on the exploration of regularities and endorses a historical separation of subject and object. By virtue of its concern with the search for law-like patterns (operative, for example, in the formation and demise of regimes), regime theory is incapable of moving beyond the present historical structure. This is because regularities do not exist except within a stable configuration of power. As a result, regime theory can make reliable statements about the behavior of states in international relations only with regard to periods of relative structural stability (Cox

[18] The paradox is that here one of the most radical critics of mainstream international relations theories (including neoliberal regime theory) grants these theories a measure of success (by their own criteria), which the authors of these theories have seldom, if ever, claimed (see, for example, Keohane 1986b: 5).

1986: 210). This stability, however, is contingent on the successful management of social conflicts by the ruling class. In other words, the presupposed historical structure within which positivist research methods can be successfully applied is permanently contested such that those who search for "immutable" regularities lose sight of the possibility of historic change and hence are bound to be caught by surprise when it occurs. For this reason, positivist explanations turn out useless as soon as historical structures alter (Cox 1986: 243). Because of new modes of production, new knowledge, and new institutions, actors behave differently and patterns of explanation developed with a view to a (now) past epoch have become obsolete. The tendency inherent in theories such as neoliberalism to stabilize the existing order is reinforced by the positivist ideal of the separation of subject and object, that is, the separation of the scientific community from its objects of investigation (Cox 1986: 209f.). This notion is illusory, though, and, as a result, knowledge turns into ideology: it appears as objective truth, when, in fact, it cannot exist independently of, and is necessarily shaped by, the position of the observer, which is both historically and socially defined.

In line with authors such as Kratochwil, Ruggie, and Müller, Cox calls for a stronger consideration of interpretative approaches in the analysis of international politics as an alternative to positivist research. This is necessary since the historical structures on which knowledge is always dependent are both unique and in constant change. Comparative methodology is inappropriate in this connection, as it presupposes regularities as well as the identity of recurring social phenomena. As Cox (1986: 243f.) puts it: "both human nature and the structures of human interaction change, if only very slowly. History is the process of their changing. One cannot therefore speak of 'laws' in any generally valid sense transcending historical eras, nor of structures as outside or prior to history." Furthermore, historical structures must not be studied as though they were completely independent of the scientific community that does the research. They must not be objectified. Rather, subject and object, the community of scientists and its object of research, are inextricably interwoven. This is why, according to Cox, the methods of interpretation that aim at understanding unique features evolving through time from within the historical subjects provide an appropriate access to the reality of historical structures. The aim must be to gain knowledge of the "outside" in the light of the "inside." In addition, the knowledge gained has to be re-examined continually. It has to be applied to a changing reality and correspondingly modified. It is here that the image of science as a permanent court may be helpful. Judges apply existing laws to a changing social reality. Individual laws not only form the basis for the juridical evaluation of a case. In a sense, they themselves have to stand up to the cases to which they claim to be applicable. Society and hence the nature of these cases change over time, though, and therefore the law, too, needs adjusting from time to time. Similarly, Cox (1986: 207) argues in regard to the social sciences that "as reality changes, old concepts have to be adjusted or rejected and new concepts forged in an initial dialogue between the theorist and the particular world he tries to comprehend."

In his work, Cox once more lays bare two deficits of regime theory which have often been pointed to by critics and adherents of regime analysis: (1) the relative neglect of domestic factors; and (2) the paucity of systematic reflection on the moral status of contemporary international institutions. With regard to the first issue, Cox makes the important point that the postwar international order cannot be understood except as the (nearly) worldwide institutionalization of the specifically *American* conception of social order. He is not the only one to have made this observation, though. Thus, Ruggie (1983; 1993b: 24–31), Anne-Marie [Slaughter] Burley (1993: 141–9), Gilpin (1987: 72f.), and Stephen Gill and David Law (1993: 96) have all noted the parallels between central domestic regulations in the United States and the multilateral principles of postwar international institutions. For the analysis of international relations, this means that a focus on constellations of power and interests is not sufficient. Very much also depends on who it is that possesses an overwhelming amount of power and has those interests, since different states make different use of their power and pursue their interests with different means. "[I]t was the fact of an *American* hegemony that was decisive after World War II, not merely American *hegemony.*" (Ruggie 1993b: 31)

Furthermore, attention is increasingly being drawn to the fact that differences in states' polities appear to be associated with differences in their willingness to establish and support international institutions. For example, Slaughter Burley (1993: 233) put forward the hypothesis that regimes involving liberal democracies are in general more robust than comparable regimes of which the membership is composed of *either* liberal and non-liberal *or* exclusively non-liberal states. In this connection, it is noteworthy that it is becoming increasingly common among liberal states to convert international agreements into national law and that this is likely to strengthen their commitment to such agreements

(Chayes and Chayes 1993: 185; Müller 1993b; Kratochwil 1993a). Additionally, authors such as Peter Cowhey (1993: 186) and Kurt Taylor Gaubatz (1996: 110) provide evidence that institutional as well as cultural factors contribute to democracies exhibiting a greater reliability in fulfilling their international commitments. This finding is strengthened by an observation frequently made (e.g. Rittberger 1987; Buzan 1993), according to which the "OECD world" exhibits a particularly high proportion of stable regimes. Finally, Robert Keohane, Peter Haas, and Marc Levy (1993: 14, 24) report an observation which indirectly points to the importance of domestic structures for the effectiveness of international environmental institutions: such institutions generally possess particularly limited means of sanctioning. In order to further their cause, they, therefore, often resort to encouraging the formation of transnational networks and to mobilizing the support of societal actors. Obviously, however, democracies are particularly sensitive to societal demands for action.

Important and provocative as such findings doubtlessly are, they must not be confounded with theoretical progress. Indeed, the integration into a theory of domestic factors is still in an embryonic state. That is, not only do many of the unit-level hypotheses that have been thrown out lack systematic empirical corroboration,[19] but also it is unclear how the insights they confer might be integrated with the established systemic theories of international regimes. In other words, scholars once again confront the levels-of-analysis problem (Singer 1961). The good news, however, is that students of regimes and international negotiation have come up with at least two models which appear to be capable of guiding such integrative efforts. One is associated with the name of Robert Putnam (1988) who has suggested analyzing international negotiations – including instances of what Young has called "institutional bargaining" (i.e. attempts at regime-building) – as "two-level games." Governments (or their representatives in international negotiations) are pictured as playing at two boards simultaneously: one is international, where their partners are other governments (or their agents); the other is domestic, where their partners are those groups and actors who are in a position to reject any agreement that has been negotiated at the international level. Putnam refers to the set of agreements that would be ratified domestically as the "win-set" of a govern-

[19] For example, the question is not settled as to the extent societal relations correlate with the mode of production as Cox contends.

ment (or negotiator). This concept plays a pivotal role in his formulation which progresses by exploring two sets of questions: (1) how does the size of the win-sets affect the outcome of international negotiations (both in terms of the likelihood of success and in terms of distributional aspects)? and (2) how do structures and processes (both at the domestic and the international level) influence the size of the win-sets? In the meantime, a set of structured and focused case studies have been conducted to probe the analytical power of Putnam's intriguing model (Evans, Jacobson, and Putnam 1993). Although this endeavor has produced important insights, plenty of work seems to be left for those who wish to exhaust fully the theoretical potential of the two-level approach, especially with a view to gaining a deeper understanding of the formation and maintenance of international regimes (Kydd and Snidal 1993: 130–4).[20]

The other model has been proposed by Michael Zürn (1993a) who has argued that the best way to bridge the domestic and international levels in the study of international regime formation is to explore the nature of what he calls a "regime-conducive foreign policy" and, subsequently, to seek to identify those unit-level attributes that dispose states to engage in such policies. On the basis of a literature review and an exploratory empirical study (based on issue-areas in pre-1989 East – West politics), Zürn arrives at three main conclusions:

> First, a state actor's foreign policy will result in regime formation when the state tries to correct dissatisfying outcomes in an issue area by utilizing economic and informational resources, and when it displays an orientation toward reciprocity accompanied by the readiness to make one-sided concessions. Second, such a regime-conducive foreign policy is most likely to emerge in states with a corporatist domestic structure. Third, this is most likely to happen in such states after a change in domestic power constellation has taken place, and when the routinization of the pre-established policy is not very high. (Zürn 1993a: 283)

Zürn (1993a: 293, 301, 310) himself emphasizes the preliminary character of his results, admitting that he could do little to preclude the possibility of selection bias in the empirical part of his study. To our mind, however, this only increases the desirability of more research being conducted along these lines.

[20] For an interesting attempt to combine situation-structuralism with Putnam's two-level approach, see Zangl (1994) and Wolf and Zangl (1996).

The moral status of international institutions is a second problem that Cox's work highlights and which, although it has attracted some attention in the literature (Keohane 1984: 247–51; Breitmeier and Wolf 1993: 341f.; Rittberger 1995: 350–3), is clearly understudied. For Cox (1996: ixf.), the international institutions of the postwar period manifest a hegemonic world order which he regards as reprehensible. Consequently, he demands their alteration according to moral principles such as equity and justice. By contrast, Keohane (1984: 79f.; 1988: 393), takes a more favorable view. Although he concedes that present-day international regimes do not in general have morally positive consequences, he regards them as justified by virtue of the fact that, without these institutions (or politically feasible alternative ones, which are not likely to be more just, though), the prospects of humanity would be even dimmer: there would be no robust cooperation in the face of international anarchy; without cooperation, however, the problems that mankind faces at the turn of the twenty-first century cannot be solved. In the background of these divergent assessments of contemporary international institutions lurks the age-old, but still unresolved question of the relation between justice and order: when and under what conditions may an unjust but stable social order be challenged in the name of justice? When and under what conditions are the moral risks of an attempted transformation higher than the moral costs of its toleration? Can the international institutions of our day be justified as the lesser evil in light of their possible alternatives?

With these questions two clusters of problems are touched: one is purely ethical, the other primarily analytical (although it has immediate implications for the moral issue). From an ethical perspective, the question of what the appropriate moral principles are to assess international politics stands in the foreground. It reaches far into the ongoing controversy between state-centric and cosmopolitan conceptions of international ethics.[21] The difficulties from an analytical perspective are hitherto similarly insoluble. Here, the problem is the empirical estima-

[21] Walzer (1985) is presumably the most prominent contemporary representative of a more state-centric approach, assuming that political communities and hence the states through which they exert their right to self-determination are endowed with fundamental rights and duties. Beitz (1979), Luban (1980), and Pogge (1994) are among those who advocate a cosmopolitan ethics. They argue that states either do not possess rights at all or only to the extent that they are internally just (see also Hoffmann 1994). For a remarkable attempt to reconcile communitarian perspectives with an approach based on the notion of inviolable and inalienable human rights, see Gewirth (1988, 1996) and Steigleder (1992).

tion of the probable consequences of alternative courses of action. Without knowledge of these probable consequences, even well-reasoned ethical criteria remain futile. Yet, in the area of research into the effects of international institutions and possible alternatives, little progress has been made so far – and for weighty methodological reasons (Biersteker 1993).

It is remarkable how vehemently Cox argues that a change of international institutions is necessary, when, at the same time, he is admittedly unable to estimate analytically in which direction such change is likely to lead. Although he puts social conflicts into the center of his historic-analytical approach, portraying them as the engine of history, he makes no effort to understand the conditions under which these conflicts are dealt with peacefully. Apparently, he hopes that the crucial actors, in the crucial moment, will realize how unproductive a military resolution would be (Cox 1992a: 186; 1992b: 142). Thus, while conflicts are at the heart of his analysis, the course these conflicts are likely to take (including the mode of conflict management that is likely to prevail) remains without theoretical consideration. This is most unsatisfactory in the face of the destructive force of modern weaponry, which accentuates the moral dilemma associated with a revolutionary change of existing structures.

In addition, although Cox offers an explanation for social developments in the twentieth century which often appears highly plausible, his account lacks analytical precision and, as a result, is hard to verify empirically. He does not offer any theoretically grounded predictions about who will use which strategies in a historical conflict. Nor does he investigate the determinants that condition the outcome of those conflicts. Finally, he remains vague on crucial issues such as how social contradictions arise and become politically relevant, how and under what conditions counter-hegemonic forces will be formed, or how exploitative structures can be overcome. Though he emphasizes the necessity of forming a strong opposition (1983: 174; 1992b: 144; 1996: 534), he is silent about how possible forms of organization might look given that the interests of the suppressed are likely to be mixed. Cox seems to assume a harmony of interests within social classes, while inter-class interaction appears either as a zero-sum conflict or as marked by the extended bargaining and compromise-building that is typical of Battle of the Sexes or similar non-pure coordination games. By contrast, much more often studied problems of collective action – such as those associated with the famous Prisoner's Dilemma - which are likely to plague attempts at *intra-class collaboration* as well (Olson 1965: ch. 4) do not seem to be considered at all by Cox.

The criticism made by members of the realist camp (Waltz 1986: 337–42; Mearsheimer 1995: 43f.) that Cox's critical theory cannot say whether the future order is really more desirable than the existing one is thus justified. As long as this question remains unanswered, taking sides in historic conflicts will remain arbitrary. Yet, at the same time, the realist criticism is somewhat hypocritical since realists, too, as representatives of a status-quo orientated problem-solving strategy, cannot know whether their choice is justified. Furthermore, they often overshoot the mark with their polemics. Mearsheimer (1995: 42f.), for example, claims that critical theorists overestimate the power of discourse and underestimate or even ignore the power of material conditions. This is not very accurate, however. Cox, in particular, never tires of emphasizing the *interaction* of discourse and historical experience. Whether he has succeeded in reconstructing this interaction in an analytically satisfactory manner is another question. Yet, to maintain that critical theory ignores historical experiences is beside the point and fails to do justice to both its innovative potential and the provocative questions it raises.

5.2.3 *The critics of the critics*

Strong cognitivism has attracted criticism from both sides. Some critics, arguing from a radically anti-positivist position, hold that strong cognitivists fail to take their own basic insights seriously enough, while others, who are committed to the rationalist agenda in international relations theory, question the value of precisely these insights (or at least their relevance for international politics). We briefly address these criticisms in turn.

Many strong cognitivists admit that rationalism as a paradigm for the study of international regimes is not altogether useless. They concede that, *under certain conditions*, positivist approaches can yield valuable insights into the dynamics of international cooperation. When interpretations of actions are unproblematic, abstracting away communicative action may not be detrimental to understanding collective behavior (Kratochwil and Ruggie 1986: 774; Kratochwil 1989: 261). Similarly, when identities and cognitive structures are relatively stable, treating them as exogenously given makes little difference for the concrete analysis of some process or event (Cox 1986: 209f.; 1992b: 135; Wendt 1992a: 423; 1994: 387). Therefore, strong cognitivists acknowledge that studies designed along rationalist lines are capable of improving our understanding of state behavior (although they insist that there are social *prerequisites* of rationality which, as such, cannot be accounted for by rationalism without circularity).

The first group of critics takes issue with strong cognitivism precisely on these concessions to positivism, arguing that they are incompatible with "the main insights of interpretive social science – namely that all social practices . . . are constituted through intersubjective meanings; that all social activity requires interpretation both by immediate participants and by those seeking to analyze that activity in a systematic fashion" (Neufeld 1993: 55). A second reason for dissatisfaction with the "mainstream [!] interpretive theorists" (Neufeld 1993: 59) whom we have dealt with under the heading of "strong cognitivism" is that they have failed to give up the goal of trying to *explain* international behavior. As Richard Price (1994: 204) has put it, "their interpretivist ontological convictions are wedded to a commitment to causal explanation, which leaves them with one foot in interpretativism (understanding) and the other in the legacy of positivism (explanation)."

The question of how "pure" interpretativism must be in order to avoid the pitfalls of positivism is contested among students of international relations critical of the prevailing epistemology of their discipline. Moreover, the debate is further complicated by the fact that there are strong cognitivists such as Wendt (1991: 391; see also Haussmann 1991) who criticize the very distinction between interpretative and positivist approaches as being itself a legacy of positivist conceptions of explanation which forces an ultimately meaningless choice upon students of international relations. This tricky problem is one of the core issues of the "the third debate" in international relations theory (Lapid 1989; Schaber and Ulbert 1994). This debate revolves around a number of meta-theoretical questions: what are the criteria for intersubjectively valid knowledge? To what extent can theory be liberated from observation? What distinguishes interpretation from analysis? Yet for all the differences on meta-theoretical issues such as the precise relationship between interpretative and empiricist science that may cause fissures in the post-positivist camp, they all agree that international institutions matter in a much more fundamental way than rationalist assumptions lead us to think, that intersubjective meanings are of crucial importance at all levels of social life including international politics, and that, consequently, interpretative approaches are needed to cope with the phenomenon of rule-based cooperation among states.

The second group of critics of strong cognitivism questions precisely this common denominator. They argue that strong cognitivists exaggerate the autonomous impact of international institutions on state policy. These critics hold that the level of institutionalization of international politics is still, by far, too low to significantly affect the identities and interests of the actors (Stein 1990: 26, n. 1). The norms and rules that exist are usually so vague that interpretation becomes almost arbitrary and there is hardly a foreign policy decision that could not be justified by smart advocates (Hollis and Smith 1990: 184). Critics of this persuasion warn about the risks of uncritically importing into International Relations theoretical concepts which were developed in view of domestic society. Although they recognize that there are constitutive institutions which enable state actors to play the international game, they stress that this game includes rule compliance as well as rule violation. Moreover, *both* kinds of acts are perfectly comprehensible to the involved decisionmakers. The issue is not interpretation, but when calculations of costs and benefits induce states to play the game in this way rather than the other. In other words, the decision to follow rules can be sufficiently (though not perfectly) explained in the framework of an individualistic ontology. Thus, Keohane (1989c: 6) warns against the pretensions of an international communitarianism: "the pressures from domestic interests, and those generated by the competitiveness of the state system, exert much stronger effects on state policy than do international institutions, even broadly defined."

Most scholars inclined towards strong cognitivism would probably admit that institutionalization at the international level is comparatively underdeveloped, that "the international arena is still but a 'negative community'" (Kratochwil 1989: 68). Nevertheless, they would insist on the irreducible impact on state policy of the existing web of institutions. The question whether state identities are shaped mainly by domestic factors or by international structures cannot be decided but on the basis of empirical research (Kratochwil 1989: 261; Wendt 1992a: 423; 1992b: 185; 1994: 391). It is doubtful, though, that a meaningful comparison of the merits of the two approaches is already possible. Not only the cognitivist concept of "identity," but also concepts fundamental to the rationalist argument such as "reputation" still await their operationalization (Keohane 1988: 387f.; Wendt 1994: 391).

6 Conclusion: prospects for synthesis

In this book we have argued that three schools of thought coexist in the study of international regimes. Each of these schools focuses on a specific variable, which helps to define its identity. *Neoliberals* stress (self-) interest as a motive for cooperation among states and likewise for the creation of, and compliance with, international regimes. *Realists* emphasize how power and considerations of relative power position affect the content, and circumscribe the effectiveness and robustness, of international regimes. *Cognitivists* point out that both the perception of interests and the meaning of power capabilities is dependent on actors' causal and social knowledge. In recent years, vigorous debates have been conducted between realists and neoliberals (Baldwin 1993b; Kegley 1995) as well as between cognitivists and rationalists (Kratochwil and Mansfield 1994; Der Derian 1995). This suggests that juxtaposing these three schools of thought is not only a convenient way of classifying the ever-growing literature about international institutions, but is faithful to an intersubjective reality as well.

The reality of this paradigmatic pluralism does not entail its desirability, though. To the extent that power, interests, and knowledge *interact* in the production of international regimes, continuing to invest large amounts of each school's intellectual resources into sharpening differences and demonstrating superiority over competitors may hamper rather than further progress in our understanding of international institutions. Kenneth Boulding (1978) once argued that order at any level of societal aggregation including the international system results from the interplay of three social mechanisms: exchange relations, threat systems, and image integration. Given the strong affinities of these mechanisms with the respective explanatory variables that guide neoliberals, realists, and cognitivists in their research into international regimes, Boulding's thesis suggests that none of these schools of thought alone is capable of capturing all essential dimensions of regimes. At the same time, it implies that, if the present school-based competition can be replaced by some sort of division of labor or synthesis, they may well do so together.[1] However, even if everyone agreed that Boulding's general model reflects an important truth about social order including order at the international level, such an inter-paradigmatic division of labor (however desirable in the abstract) would not necessarily be feasible. There is no *a priori* guarantee that the specific perspectives of power-, interest-, and knowledge-based theories really add up to a coherent whole: both (ontological) assumptions about the nature of actors and the international system and epistemological orientations might simply be too disparate to permit a meaningful combination of two or more of these accounts. Resuming and elaborating on observations we have made in the preceding chapters, we therefore conclude this study with some considerations about the prospects for synthesis of two or even all three schools of thought in contemporary regime analysis.

Realism and neoliberalism: synthesis through contextualization?

Realists and neoliberals have recently been engaged in an intense, at times almost bitter, dispute about which of the two schools is better equipped to analyze and explain international regimes and other phenomena in world politics. Contributors to this debate have always been aware of the close relationship of these two variants of *rationalist* theorizing about international politics. This may help to explain why efforts to demonstrate the distinctness and the priority of one's favored approach have dominated this debate. At the same time, this intellectual kinship has permitted both realists and neoliberals to suggest that the members of the other camp are not altogether wrong but that their theoretical propositions can be seen as a *special case* of one's own account of international politics and regimes. Realists have implied that their theory subsumes neoliberalism, and neoliberals have made the inverse claim. Thus, Grieco (1988a: 503) has pointed out that, by virtue of its recognition of states' concerns for *both* absolute and relative gains,

[1] Baldwin (1993a: 15) has drawn attention to the correspondence between the three social mechanisms which, according to Boulding, are responsible for social order and the phenomena studied by neoliberals, realists, and cognitivists.

"realism provides a more comprehensive theory of the problem of cooperation than does neoliberal institutionalism" (see also Mearsheimer 1995: 24);[2] and Keohane (1989c: 15) is even more outspoken: "In comparing neoliberal institutionalism with neorealism, we must understand that neoliberal institutionalism is not simply an alternative to neorealism, but, in fact, claims to subsume it" (see also Keohane and Martin 1995: 41f.; Keck 1991; 1993).

As claims about priority and subordination among theoretical positions these statements are in sharp opposition to one another. There is, however, a notable common denominator, and we would argue that students of regimes who adhere to a rationalist mode of analysis are likely to make more progress on their project by seeking to enlarge and exploit these commonalities than by going for full victory. Neoliberals and realists concede to one another that the other side's arguments and predictions are valid *provided* that certain conditions hold which their opponents have failed to acknowledge and to specify so far. To our mind, future theoretical and empirical research along rationalist lines should build upon this limited mutual recognition and aim at establishing the conditions or *contexts* in which "neoliberal" (i.e. optimistic) rather than "realist" (i.e. pessimistic) expectations about international regimes are likely to apply and vice versa. Serious efforts towards this end might not only further our understanding of international regimes but also reveal a broader zone of agreement between these two schools than has been perceived and acknowledged so far.[3]

[2] Grieco does not explicitly refer to neoliberalism as a special case of realism. He argues, however, that the extent to which states are concerned with relative gains (i.e. his sensitivity coefficient *k*) varies and he recognizes that states do care for absolute gains (as neoliberals assume). It follows that, in situations where absolute gains are large compared to relative ones or where intolerance for relative losses is low, realism offers a prediction for cooperation which is no different from neoliberalism's.

[3] We have already quoted with approval Snidal's (1993: 741) call for steps "towards a contextually richer theory that is able to explain international politics better than either vulgar realism or vulgar liberalism in isolation." Similarly, Keohane (1993b: 293, 297), referring to the same two schools of thought, has bemoaned the "artificial barriers between academicians' doctrines" and speculated about a "new synthesis of these views." Of the protagonists of the recent debate Grieco seems least willing to give up the competitive approach, even though he not only acknowledges that neoliberalism has made "important contributions to the study of world politics" (Grieco 1993b: 312) but also, by way of his discussion of the sources of variation in states' sensitivity to relative losses, has begun an investigation which may be regarded as leading directly to a specification of the conditions which govern the respective validity of "vulgar" realist and "vulgar" neoliberal claims about regimes. Apparently, realists, not unlike the actors in their models, prefer to go it alone.

Much of the recent debate between realists and neoliberals has centered on the significance of relative gains orientations in international politics. There are two issues here: (1) what difference (if any) does relative gains seeking make for international interaction (including cooperation) and for the nature and efficacy of international regimes?; and (2) when are states concerned with relative gains? With regard to the *first issue* we have pointed to a remarkable convergence in the views of the realist Grieco and the neoliberal Keck who have both suggested that, in a situation where states are unwilling to put up with gaps in gains from cooperation in favor of their partners, international regimes need not be irrelevant, but may in fact assume additional functions (e.g. facilitating side-payments and providing "voice opportunities" to disadvantaged states) (see also Keohane and Martin 1995: 45f.). Owing to the competitive approach that has dominated the scholarly discussion so far, insufficient attention has been paid to this somewhat surprising turn of the debate. Surely, empirical research has yet to establish whether (and when) regimes may indeed serve the purpose of helping states to manage relative gains concerns and how this function is reflected in their normative and procedural content. Yet, for the time being, this can be regarded as an excellent example of "how the different arguments [as provided by neoliberals and realists] work together" (Snidal 1993: 741) to produce interesting new hypotheses about international institutions.

Although several of his critics have been slow to recognize it, from the onset of this debate Grieco (1988a: 501; 1988b: 610–13) has taken the position that relative gains concerns are not a constant but vary over relationships and across issue-areas, even though he stressed that they never completely disappear. The *second issue* therefore is under what conditions relative gains concerns are severe. Knowing these conditions might provide us with an important clue as to when "realist" and "neoliberal" hypotheses about international regimes are in force, respectively, and, thus, how *both* theoretical perspectives might offer valid insights into the nature and efficacy of international regimes[4] if only we are prepared to recognize that their predictions presuppose different, indeed complementary, contexts of action. An approach very much in

[4] As the above discussion shows, the content of the "realist" hypothesis has recently been in flux. Orthodox realists would argue that concerns with relative gains must undermine the effectiveness of international institutions, whereas the strand of "modern realism" represented by Grieco expects international regimes to have at least some impact under these circumstances as well.

this spirit has been suggested by Robert Powell (1991) who proposes to focus on *constraints* on action rather than on *motivations*. Constructing a simple game-theoretic model, which, however, is complex enough to mirror both realist and neoliberal concerns, Powell shows how under certain external conditions (e.g. when the efficiency of force is high) states will act *as if* they were concerned with relative gains such that the realist expectations are warranted. By contrast, other constraints are demonstrated to induce (or permit) the sort of behavior that liberals have described: states try to maximize their absolute gains apparently with no consideration of how well others do. Not surprisingly, Powell (1991: 1304, 1311) explicitly developed this model with a view to outlining a *synthesis* of the two competing schools of thought.[5]

To sum up, while we certainly do not mean to argue that all differences between the interest- and the power-based schools of thought in regime analysis are illusory, we believe that, in the recent debate, these differences have tended to be overstated and that there is a considerable potential for a fruitful combination of ideas so far associated with alternative perspectives on international institutions. More specifically, the possibility of a unified but contextualized rationalist theory of international regimes seems to be emerging, where predictions (and explanations) are conditional on situational attributes. Presumably, this theory would be built on a distinction between three types of contexts:

(1) non-problematic social situations (e.g. constant-sum and harmony situations), where rationalists expect regimes either to be absent or to have no consequences
(2) mixed-motive situations with weak concerns about relative gains (the standard case of neoliberals)
(3) mixed-motive situations with strong concerns about relative gains (the standard case of realists).

From this vantage point, future theoretical and empirical research should focus on two questions. First, what makes a mixed-motive

[5] Powell (1991: 1304) is critical of the tendency for participants to the neoliberal–realist debate to frame their argument in terms of opposing assumptions about states' fundamental motivations (i.e. in terms of behavioral models), because it unnecessarily precludes a "third-image unification" of the two approaches. Thus, he assumes with neoliberalism that states are absolute gains maximizers but points out that this motivation – depending on the characteristics of the situation in which states interact – is perfectly compatible with an intolerance for relative losses which may keep states from cooperating for mutual gain. In a recent article, Keohane (1993b: 275f.) has endorsed this conception of state motivation.

situation (in terms of absolute gains) one of type (3) rather than type (2)? And second, how does the situation being one of type (3) rather than type (2) affect international regimes, including their propensity to emerge in the first place, their content, their effectiveness, and their robustness?[6]

Rationalism and weak cognitivism: complementary explanations?

A synthesis or fruitful division of labor should be possible not only between the two rationalist schools of thought in regime analysis, neoliberalism and realism, but between rationalist explanations of international institutions and weak cognitivism as well. The form of this synthesis is likely to be different, though. While power- and interest-based approaches to international regimes can apparently be made compatible by specifying the conditions of validity of each, i.e. by theorizing the contexts in which realist and neoliberal predictions apply, respectively, rationalist and weakly cognitivist arguments appear to be working together best when they are seen as addressing subsequent links in one causal chain. Perhaps more to the point, weakly cognitivist theories may be used to fill – frequently admitted – gaps in rationalist explanations of international regimes.

There are at least two ways in which weakly cognitivist theories may supplement rationalist accounts of international institutions. The *first* is straightforward, at least in principle: while rationalist theories of regimes treat actors' preferences as exogenously given, cognitivists, by studying phenomena such as complex learning or normative change, seek to illuminate precisely how actors come to choose certain *goals* in a particular situation. Similarly, when situation-structuralists analyze choice-situations which may or may not give rise to regimes with particular institutional features they do not inquire into the origins of the *options* that actors perceive themselves to have in this situation, but, again, use them as their unexplained point of departure. Here, studies

[6] Building on an analysis of Krasner's (1991) critique of contractualism, Powell (1994: 338–43) argues that the main difference between realist and neoliberal accounts of regimes is to be found in divergent assessments of the robustness of regimes: adducing arguments about sunk costs and reputational concerns, neoliberals claim that institutional history matters, whereas realists remain skeptical in this regard. Students of regimes inclined towards the kind of synthetic approach we have just outlined may derive from this observation the hypothesis that regime robustness is low if states' sensitivity for relative gains is high.

of the role of epistemic communities which supply decisionmakers with new policy-relevant causal knowledge promise important additional insights complementing the game-theoretic analysis.

Rationalists have acknowledged the potential value of a division of labor between game theory on the one hand and "theories of the pay-offs" such as weak cognitivism on the other. Thus, Snidal (1986: 42f.) has noted that such theories "enable game theory to be constructively and complementarily linked to other approaches to international politics – even, in some cases, to theories that may be viewed as alternatives to rational models" (see also Oye 1986b: 5f.). He also emphasizes the methodological advantages of theory-based derivations of pay-offs over inductive procedures, which not only yield incomplete results, but are also highly vulnerable to circular reasoning (Snidal 1986: 40–4). So there is definitely a potential for cognitivist "theories of the pay-offs" to complement productively the game-theoretic analyses that the mainstream approach to regimes has been drawing upon. Much work remains to be done, though, to realize this possibility (at least in the field of regime analysis). Moreover, the resulting mixed theories are not likely to be nearly as neat, transparent, and well-specified as the rational-choice models that form part of them (Simon 1985).

While, in this first model, interests and cognitive factors are combined such that the latter precede the former in the causal chain, in the *second* type of synthesis of rationalist and cognitivist approaches that we regard as promising the sequence is reversed: here ideas, rather than helping to explain preferences and perceived options (which, in turn, explain outcomes), *intervene* between preferences (which may or may not be accounted for in cognitivistic terms) and outcomes such as regime formation. This approach to a rationalist-cognitivist synthesis, where ideas operate as "focal points" (Schelling 1960), is exemplified by Garrett and Weingast's (1993) study of the completion of the EC's internal market. Explicitly rejecting the perception of a "stark divide between 'rationalists' and 'reflectivists'" (cognitivists) and convinced that these approaches "may very fruitfully be integrated" (Garrett and Weingast 1993: 176, 185), these authors show how attention to – institutionally constructed – common belief systems or focal points (such as the principle of "mutual recognition" of national standards in the EC case) can remedy an important deficiency in the functional argument (see sect. 5.1.1 above).

The problem with conventional interest-based (functional) explanations of cooperation, according to Garrett and Weingast, is that they fail to take into account that actors in a mixed-motive situation usually face several possibilities for cooperating (i.e. multiple equilibria) which cannot easily be distinguished in terms of efficiency and self-interest (see also Bates 1988). It is only because of the *post hoc* character of functional explanations (Keohane 1984: 80) that this fact – the strong underdetermination, from a purely interest-oriented perspective, of most problematic social situations – is often overlooked. Often deliberately propagated ideas which create convergent expectations permit actors to coordinate their behavior in a mutually beneficial way and, at the same time, explain the specific content of the resulting regime.

Ideas are also important when the available equilibria vary in their distributional outcomes, i.e. in situations akin to Battle of the Sexes. In this case, as Krasner (1991) has convincingly argued, relative power enters the stage as an alternative coordinating device (see sect. 4.2 above). Garrett and Weingast concede this point. What is more, they come up with an interesting attempt to extend their proposed synthesis of functional and cognitivist approaches to include specifically power-based arguments. In so doing, they make use of the contextual approach to synthesis we have described above. In particular, Garrett and Weingast (1993: 186) hypothesize that

> [t]he lesser the distributional asymmetries between contending cooperative equilibria and the smaller the disparities in the power resources of actors, the more important will be ideational factors. Similarly, the effects of focal points will increase with the actors' uncertainty about the consequences of agreements[7] or about relative capabilities. Thus, both power and ideas can be expected significantly to influence the resolution of multiple-equilibria problems, *but the relative explanatory power of each is likely to vary significantly with the context*. [emphasis added]

[7] As we have seen above (sect. 3.4), for Young uncertainty of this kind is *typical* of real-world processes of institutional bargaining, which he sees as taking place under a "veil of uncertainty." Consequently, he attaches no restricting condition to the hypothesis that the existence of salient solutions or focal points increases the likelihood of regime formation. Incidentally, the fact that Young advances this *ideational* hypothesis underscores the assessment made earlier in this book (ch. 3, n. 39) that there is a significant overlap zone between his particular variant of interest-based theorizing and the knowledge-based approach to international regimes. Indeed, although Young himself refers to his approach to regime formation as interest-based (Young and Osherenko 1993d), it would not be completely off the mark to describe his model as an attempt to bridge neoliberal and cognitivist and – recall his concept of structural leadership – perhaps even realist concerns within the study of international regimes.

It seems to us that this approach to specifying the interrelationship between power, interests, and knowledge in the emergence and continuation of rule-based cooperation holds considerable promise and should certainly be followed up and further developed.

Rationalism and strong cognitivism: no synthesis but a fruitful dialogue?

Up to this point we have discussed two possible syntheses of extant theories about regimes: one unifying the two predominant rationalist approaches, neoliberalism and realism, and another which would also include the less radical form of knowledge-based theorizing which we have labeled "weak cognitivism." The fact that such inter-paradigmatic syntheses appear possible does not imply that all the differences between the three schools of thought we have identified in the study of regimes are illusory: neoliberals, realists, and cognitivists do stress different variables in their respective attempts to grasp the phenomenon of international regimes. Nor does it imply that the more complex multivariate theories that could result from such syntheses are *necessarily* better than each of their components: the gain in explanatory power achieved this way may be too slight to make up for the sacrifice in parsimony and coherence that comes with adding variables. We do contend, however, that the prospects for an integration (along the lines indicated above) which would indeed provide students of regimes with considerably greater explanatory leverage than they command so far are good enough to warrant greater efforts towards this goal in the future.

The prospects for a productive synthesis among rationalist approaches or between rationalism and weak cognitivism are sizeable, not only because the component theories enjoy *prima facie* plausibility. Just as important in this connection, their core assumptions (though not their theoretical emphases) are largely compatible with one another. This prerequisite, however, does *not* seem to be met with regard to mainstream rationalist and strongly cognitivist approaches to regimes. Thus, we believe that a fruitful dialogue can be, and is already being, entertained among "economists" (rationalists) and "sociologists" (strong cognitivists) in the study of international regimes; but it is much more difficult if not impossible to imagine at this stage a "grand rationalist-cognitivist synthesis" which would preserve the identities (i.e. the most fundamental assumptions and concerns) of both *synthesanda*.

In the preceding chapter (sect. 5.2), we extensively discussed the deeply rooted differences between rationalist and strongly cognitivist approaches to international regimes. Thus, it may suffice, as a justification for our skepticism, to point out once again two very conspicuous obstacles that stand in the way of an integration of these two perspectives. The *first* one is methodological and results from the fact that at least some strong cognitivists hold the positivism to which mainstream regime analysis is committed responsible for a flawed analysis of international norms and argue the necessity of an interpretivist treatment of this subject (Kratochwil and Ruggie 1986; Cox 1986; see also ch. 2 and sect. 5.2.1 above). Rationalists, in turn, have re-affirmed their allegiance to a "sophisticated positivistic" explanation of international institutions including the formulation and empirical testing of causal hypotheses (Keohane 1993a: 24–6). To be sure, philosophers of science have seriously challenged the traditional distinction between *Erklären* (explaining) and *Verstehen* (understanding) as basic methods of social research (Haussmann 1991), although others insist that there are indeed "two stories" to tell – one from the outside, the other from the inside – neither of which ultimately can replace the other (Hollis and Smith 1991). Moreover, by no means all cognitivists identify with the post-modernist denial of objective knowledge (Wendt 1992a: 393f.), and rationalists who have begun to study the role of ideas have admitted that interpretation cannot be ignored in such an endeavor (Goldstein and Keohane 1993a: 26–9). Nevertheless, for all the uncertainty that surrounds this issue at the moment, the claim made by some in the strongly cognitivist camp that a serious study of the convincing force of arguments or of the intersubjective knowledge that constitutes state identities requires methodological tools and suggests epistemological standards fundamentally different from those valid in mainstream analyses, may well delay and tightly circumscribe the potential for a fruitful collaboration between rationalists and strong cognitivists in the study of international regimes.

Presumably, the more formidable obstacle inhibiting a grand synthesis, however, is not methodological but substantive (Risse-Kappen 1995). Rationalists and strong cognitivists make fundamentally different heuristic assumptions concerning the "logic" that shapes the behavior of the actors they study. In the words of March and Olson (1989), the former study state behavior under the premise of a "logic of consequentiality," whereas the latter reject this premise arguing that states, as other social actors, follow a "logic of appropriateness." To put it differently, rationalists scrutinze a "system" which is composed of a group of interacting utility-maximizers, whereas strong cognitivists try to illuminate a "society" which is formed by (as much as it forms) a community of role-players (Wendt and Duvall 1989). Again, the point may seem to be overstated and many qualifications could rightly be added. Thus, rationalists have maintained that their approach does not presuppose a denial of international society and admitted the context-dependence of rational choice models (Keohane 1984: 73f.; 1988: 388, 390). At the same time, as we have noted, few strong cognitivists contest that the rationalist perspective is capable of providing insights into the behavior of states in the international arena. However, neither the mutual recognition that one's preferred mode of analysis is inherently limited nor the mutual acknowledgment that the respective alternative has its merits, too, must be confused with evidence that the approaches in question can work together productively. In fact, if our assessment of the obstacles that such a cooperation would confront is correct, evidence of this kind is not likely to be produced. This is not to say that such cautious and respectful attitudes are insignificant. They enhance the prospects for an open and fruitful scholarly dialogue from which both sides can benefit.

For all the cross-fertilizing impact such an inter-paradigmatic dialogue might have, it is likely to remain one between competitors. A competition requires an arena in which it can unfold. We suggest that the most suitable one in this case is the issue of *regime robustness*. Both rationalists and strong cognitivists agree that international regimes are not "up for grabs" (to appropriate Krasner's pithy expression): regimes do not collapse as a result of, or adapt smoothly to, any change in the external environment that prompted their creation in the first place; they develop a life of their own. Scholarly agreement breaks down, however, when it comes to explaining this phenomenon. While rationalists point to various cost factors, particularly those associated with a damaged reputation as a cooperation partner and with the (re-)creation of international institutions, strong cognitivists bring in a sense of community which apparently operates at the international level as well and develop fascinating, but so far largely speculative arguments about the way in which cooperation stabilizes itself through the processes of identity (re-)formation that it triggers.

The lack of compelling empirical demonstrations is not specific to the strong cognitivist interpretation of regime robustness, though. Rationalists, too, have failed so far to subject their hypotheses to carefully designed empirical tests or to provide systematic evidence for the working of the causal mechanisms (e.g. reputational concerns) they have credited with the generation of the phenonomen at issue (i.e. regime robustness). To be sure, testing these divergent explanations is far from straightforward and requires solving numerous difficult problems of research design and operationalization, but, given the importance of this issue for the study of international regimes, evasion of these difficulties would hardly be justifiable.

At least two approaches suggest themselves in this connection. The first one attempts to tackle the problem *directly* by carefully tracing actual decisionmaking processes (George and McKeown 1985). When the structural underpinnings of a regime change and compliance becomes more inconvenient, what considerations inform the choices of governments? Do they actually and consciously trade off long-term gains against short-term sacrifices? And do they therefore seek to avoid action that may damage their reputation as a reliable cooperation partner? Or can we observe that the range of options actors take into account during the life-cycle of a given regime progressively diminishes, as we should expect it to if socialization is taking place? And do we find evidence of communicative action and argumentation altering the collective understanding of the situation at hand?

The methodological uncertainties of this approach are extensive and obvious. A second, *indirect*, approach should therefore be taken into consideration as well. It can come in many variants. One is to inquire into the determinants of *regime robustness*, treating the resilience of international institutions as a variable rather than a constant. If it is possible to derive non-congruent rationalist and strongly cognitivist hypotheses about those determinants, a comparative test based upon a carefully selected set of cases may be feasible helping us to assess the relative explanatory power of rationalist and strongly cognitivist accounts of international regimes.[8]

Another variant of this indirect approach to sorting out the relative merits of rationalist and strong cognitivist perspectives takes the levels-of-analysis problem as its point of departure. Regime analysis has often been criticized for its systemic bias and its neglect of *domestic factors* (Haggard and Simmons 1987; Junne 1990; Milner 1992). We agree with this criticism. However, rather than echoing the complaints about regime theory's subsystemic blinders, we would like to draw attention to an aspect of this issue which is rarely mentioned but gains impor-

[8] This is *in nuce* the approach that we are pursuing in our own research (Hasenclever, Mayer, and Rittberger 1996).

tance in the light of the preceding discussion. So far (with the notable exception of Cox), both rationalists and strong cognitivists in the study of regimes have been rather silent on the role of domestic factors. It could be argued, however, that this silence is more justified in one case than in the other. More specifically, those strong cognitivists who argue that states' interests and identities are to a large extent the products of international interaction should *expect* domestic factors to matter little. Consequently, they would not seem to be liable to the criticism that they disregard domestic politics. Wendt (1992a: 395, 425; 1992b: 183; 1994: 391), who has repeatedly referred to his position as *international communitarianism*, is certainly a case in point.

By contrast, rationalists have not been willing to commit themselves to such an extreme position. Some situation-structuralists have emphasized the variability of state preferences, suggesting that at least part of this variation is due to unit-level structural factors. Even those neoliberals (such as Keohane) who have opted for a strongly systemic theory in the Waltzian tradition (see ch. 3 above) have made it clear that they regard this only as a first cut and that ultimately domestic factors would have to be reintroduced somehow (Keohane 1988: 392). Proponents of a power-based approach to international regimes have articulated similar views (Grieco 1990: 24f.; Krasner 1993a: 141). Thus, those observers of regime theory who charge it with a systemic bias that must reduce its explanatory power may have a valid point with regard to these mainstream approaches but less so as far as strong cognitivism is concerned.[9]

Meanwhile, if the communitarianism to which some strong cognitivists (such as Wendt) subscribe justifies their neglect of domestic politics as consistent with their basic assumptions, this must not be mistaken for a confirmation of these assumptions. For the time being, these theorists enjoy the advantage of being less vulnerable to a widespread criticism of regime analysis than their utilitarian competitors (particularly neoliberals) who have more difficulty "rationalizing" their preoccupation with system-level variables. However, this advantage for strong cognitivism would immediately turn into a considerable liability if it were shown that domestic variables do indeed exert a major influence on state behavior under international regimes. Wendt (1994: 391) is

[9] It would not be quite correct, though, to claim that neoliberals have nothing to say whatsoever about the domestic dimension of regimes. In particular, both Putnam's and Zürn's models of the interaction of domestic and international politics (which we have briefly discussed in the preceding chapter) are more readily subsumed under rationalism than under strong cognitivism.

keenly aware of what is at stake for his approach: "My rival hypothesis is not merely that states might acquire collective interests (which dissents from realism) but that they might do so through processes at the systemic level – which dissents from rationalist versions of systemic theory, realist *or* liberal" (since both versions of rationalism assume that states' preferences over outcomes are not, or only marginally, affected by systemic variables). Thus, the theory competition between rationalist and strongly cognitivist approaches provides another reason for students of international institutions to devote a greater share of their attention to possible unit-level determinants of international behavior.

These possibilities for pitting rationalism against strong cognitivism notwithstanding, there is no guarantee that the contest can be decided on empirical grounds. Nor is it beyond reasonable doubt that students of regimes are on the right track when they attempt to establish one of the two paradigms as the winner at the expense of the other. Perhaps a supposition Young (1989a: 213) once made is much more to the point: the situation may not be unlike that in optics where two incompatible accounts of light, a wave theory and a particle theory, apparently coexist very fruitfully. Each explains different aspects of the phenomenon under consideration, and, consequently, neither one is dispensible. The logical incompatibility of the two theories remains, though, and, for this reason, they cannot simply be combined in an all-encompassing synthesis. Yet, without either of them our understanding of the phenomenon would be poorer and more limited. What if the same kind of relationship existed between rationalist and strongly cognitivist accounts of international regimes? Could it not be be that, as Hollis and Smith (1990: 7) have emphasized in a closely related context, there are always "two stories to tell," each representing an independent view on international politics, one focusing on the sociality of choices, the other emphasizing their rationality? We believe that there is more than just one promising way in which to pursue theoretical progress in the study of international regimes and cooperation.

References

Adler, Emanuel 1992, "The Emergence of Cooperation: National Epistemic Communities and the International Evolution of the Idea of Nuclear Arms Control," in P. Haas (ed.) 1992c, 101–46.

Adler, Emanuel, and Haas, Peter M. 1992, "Epistemic Communities, World Order, and the Creation of a Reflective Research Program," in P. Haas (ed.) 1992c, 367–90.

Aggarwal, Vinod K. 1985, *Liberal Protectionism: The International Politics of Organized Textile Trade*, Berkeley: University of California Press.

Alt, James E., Calvert, Randell L., and Humes, Brian D. 1988, "Reputation and Hegemonic Stability: A Game-Theoretic Analysis," *American Political Science Review* 82: 445–66.

Ashley, Richard K. 1984, "The Poverty of Neorealism," *International Organization* 38: 225–86.

Aubert, Vilhelm 1963, "Competition and Dissensus: Two Types of Conflict and Conflict Resolution," *Journal of Conflict Resolution* 7: 26–42.

Austin, J. L. 1975, *How to Do Things with Words*, 2nd edn., Oxford: Clarendon Press.

Axelrod, Robert 1984, *The Evolution of Cooperation*, New York: Basic Books.

1986, "An Evolutionary Approach to Norms," *American Political Science Review* 80: 1095–111.

Axelrod, Robert, and Keohane, Robert O. 1986, "Achieving Cooperation under Anarchy: Strategies and Institutions," in Oye (ed.) 1986a, 226–54.

Baldwin, David A. 1993a, "Neoliberalism, Neorealism, and World Politics," in Baldwin (ed.) 1993b, 3–25.

(ed.) 1993b, *Neorealism and Neoliberalism: The Contemporary Debate*, New York: Columbia University Press.

Barnett, Michael 1993, "Institutions, Roles, and Disorder: The Case of the Arab States System," *International Studies Quarterly* 37: 271–96.

1995, "Sovereignty, Nationalism, and Regional Order in the Arab States System," *International Organization* 49: 479–510.

Bates, Robert 1988, "Contra Contractarianism: Some Reflections on the New Institutionalism," *Politics and Society* 16: 387–401.

Behnke, Andreas 1993, *Structuration, Institutions, and Regimes: The Case of the CSBM,* Stockholm International Studies 93:1, International Graduate School, Stockholm University.

Beitz, Charles R. 1979, *Political Theory and International Relations,* Princeton University Press.

Beller, Ekkehard, Efinger, Manfred, Marx, Katja, Mayer, Peter, and Zürn, Michael 1990, *Die Tübinger Datenbank der Konflikte in den Ost-West-Beziehungen,* Tübinger Arbeitspapiere zur internationalen Politik und Friedensforschung 13, University of Tübingen.

Berger, Peter L., and Luckmann, Thomas 1967, *The Social Construction of Reality: A Treatise in the Sociology of Knowledge,* Garden City, N.Y.: Doubleday Anchor.

Bernstein, Richard J. 1985, "Introduction," in Bernstein (ed.), *Habermas and Modernity,* Cambridge: Polity Press, 1–32.

Biersteker, Thomas J. 1993, "Constructing Historical Counterfactuals to Assess the Consequences of International Regimes: The Global Debt Regime and the Course of the Debt Crisis of the 1980s," in Rittberger (ed.) 1993a, 315–38.

Boulding, Kenneth E. 1962, *Conflict and Defense: A General Theory,* London: Harper Torchbooks.

1978, *Ecodynamics: A New Theory of Social Evolution,* London: Sage.

Breitmeier, Helmut 1996, *Wie entstehen globale Umweltregime? Der Konfliktaustrag zum Schutz der Ozonschicht und des globalen Klimas,* Opladen: Leske & Budrich.

Breitmeier, Helmut, Levy, Marc A., Young, Oran R., and Zürn, Michael 1996a, *International Regimes Database: Data Protocol,* IIASA Working Paper, 96–154 Laxenburg, Austria.

1996b, *The International Regimes Database as a Tool for the Study of International Cooperation,* IIASA Working Paper 96–160, Laxenburg, Austria.

Breitmeier, Helmut, and Wolf, Klaus Dieter 1993, "Analysing Regime Consequences: Conceptual Outlines and Environmental Explorations," in Rittberger (ed.) 1993a, 339–60.

Brennan, Geoffrey, and Buchanan, James M. 1985, *The Reason of Rules: Constitutional Political Economy,* Cambridge University Press.

Brzoska, Michael 1991, "Warum gibt es so wenige Atomwaffenstaaten? Zum Erklärungswert verschiedener theoretischer Ansätze," *Politische Vierteljahresschrift* 32: 24– 55.

Bull, Hedley 1977, *The Anarchical Society: A Study of Order in World Politics,* Basingstoke: Macmillan.

Burley, Anne-Marie 1993, "Regulating the World: Multilateralism, International Law, and the Protection of the New Deal Regulatory State," in Ruggie (ed.) 1993a, 125–56.

Buzan, Barry 1993, "From International System to International Society: Structural Realism and Regime Theory Meet the English School," *International Organization* 47: 327–52.

Caporaso, James 1993, "International Relations Theory and Multilateralism: The Search for Foundations," in Ruggie (ed.) 1993a, 51–90.

Chayes, Abram, and Chayes, Antonia Handler 1993, "On Compliance," *International Organization* 47: 175–205.
Collier, David 1995, "Translating Quantitative Methods for Qualitative Researchers: The Case of Selection Bias," American Political Science Review 89: 461–6.
Conybeare, John A. C. 1984, "Public Goods, Prisoners' Dilemmas and the International Political Economy," *International Studies Quarterly* 28: 5–22.
1987, *Trade Wars: The Theory and Practice of International Commercial Rivalry*, New York: Columbia University Press.
Cowhey, Peter F. 1993, "Elect Locally – Order Globally: Domestic Politics and Multilateral Cooperation," in Ruggie (ed.) 1993a, 157–200.
Cox, Robert W. 1983, "Gramsci, Hegemony and International Relations: An Essay in Method," *Millennium* 12: 162–75.
1986, "Social Forces, States and World Orders: Beyond International Relations Theory," in Keohane (ed.) 1986a, 204–55.
1992a, "Multilateralism and World Order," *Review of International Studies* 18: 161–180.
1992b, "Towards a Post-Hegemonic Conceptualization of World Order: Reflections on the Relevancy of Ibn Khaldun," in Rosenau and Czempiel (eds.) 1992, 132–59.
Cox, Robert W. (with Timothy J. Sinclair) 1996, *Approaches to World Order*, Cambridge University Press.
Czempiel, Ernst-Otto 1981, *Internationale Politik: Ein Konfliktmodell*, Paderborn: Schöningh.
Der Derian, James (ed.) 1995, *International Theory: Critical Investigations*, Basingstoke: Macmillan.
Dessler, David 1989, "What's at Stake in the Agent – Structure Debate," *International Organization* 43: 441–73.
1991, "Beyond Correlations: Toward a Causal Theory of War," *International Studies Quarterly* 35: 337–55.
Deutsch, Karl W. 1963, *The Nerves of Government: Models of Political Communication and Control*, London: Free Press of Glencoe.
Drake, William J. and Nicolaïdis, Kalypso 1992, "Ideas, Interests and Institutionalization: "Trade in Services' and the Uruguay Round," in P. Haas (ed.) 1992c, 37–100.
Duffield, John 1992, "International Regimes and Alliance Behavior: Explaining NATO Conventional Force Levels," *International Organization* 46: 819–55.
Eckstein, Harry 1975, "Case Study and Theory in Political Science," in F. I. Greenstein, and N. W. Polsby, (eds.), *Handbook of Political Science*, vol. VII, Reading: Addison- Wesley, 79–138.
Efinger, Manfred, Mayer, Peter, and Schwarzer, Gudrun 1993, "Integrating and Contextualizing Hypotheses: Alternative Paths to Better Explanations of Regime Formation," in Rittberger (ed.) 1993a, 252–82.
Efinger, Manfred, Rittberger, Volker, and Zürn, Michael 1988, *Internationale Regime in den Ost-West-Beziehungen: Ein Beitrag zur Erforschung der friedlichen Behandlung internationaler Konflikte*, Frankfurt a.M.: Haag & Herchen.

Efinger, Manfred, and Zürn, Michael 1990, "Explaining Conflict Management in East–West Relations: A Quantitative Test of Problem-Structural Typologies," in Rittberger (ed.) 1990b, 64–89.

Elster, Jon 1989, *The Cement of Society: A Study of Social Order*, Cambridge University Press.

Evans, Peter B., Jacobson, Harold K., and Putnam, Robert D. (eds.) 1993, *Double-Edged Diplomacy: International Bargaining and Domestic Politics*, Berkeley: University of California Press.

Evans, Tony, and Wilson, Peter 1992, "Regime Theory and the English School of International Relations: A Comparison," *Millennium* 21: 329–51.

Franck, Thomas M. 1990, *The Power of Legitimacy Among Nations*, New York: Oxford University Press.

Garrett, Geoffrey 1993, "International Cooperation and Institutional Choice: The European Community's Internal Market," in Ruggie (ed.) 1993a, 365–98.

Garrett, Geoffrey, and Weingast, Barry R. 1993, "Ideas, Interests, and Institutions: Constructing the European Community's Internal Market," in Goldstein and Keohane (eds.) 1993b, 173–206.

Gaubatz, Kurt Taylor 1996, "Democratic States and Commitment in International Relations," *International Organization* 50: 109–39.

Gehring, Thomas 1994, *Dynamic International Regimes: Institutions for International Environmental Governance*, Frankfurt a.M.: Lang.

George, Alexander L., and McKeown, Timothy J. 1985, "Case Studies and Theories of Organizational Decision Making," in L. S. Sproull, and P. D. Larke (eds.), *Advances in Information Processing in Organizations*, vol. II, Greenwich, Conn.: JAI Press, 21–58.

Gewirth, Alan 1988, "Ethical Universalism and Particularism," *The Journal of Philosophy* 85: 283–302.

1996, *The Community of Rights*, The University of Chicago Press.

Giddens, Anthony 1982, *Profiles and Critiques in Social Theory*, Berkeley: University of California Press.

Gill, Stephen, and Law, David 1993, "Global Hegemony and the Structural Power of Capital," in Stephen Gill (ed.), *Gramsci, Historical Materialism, and International Relations*, Cambridge University Press, 93–124.

Gilpin, Robert 1972, "The Politics of Transnational Economic Relations," in Robert O. Keohane and Joseph S. Nye, Jr. (eds.), *Transnational Relations and World Politics*, Cambridge, Mass.: Harvard University Press, 48–69.

1975, *U.S. Power and the Multinational Corporation: The Political Economy of Foreign Direct Investment*, New York: Basic Books.

1981, *War and Change in World Politics*, Cambridge University Press.

1987, *The Political Economy of International Relations*, Princeton University Press.

Goldstein, Judith 1989, "The Impact of Ideas on Trade Policy: The Origins of U.S. Agricultural and Manufacturing Policies," *International Organization* 43: 31–71.

Goldstein, Judith, and Keohane, Robert O. 1993a, "Ideas and Foreign Policy: An Analytical Framework," in Goldstein and Keohane (eds.) 1993b, 3–30.

(eds.) 1993b, *Ideas and Foreign Policy: Beliefs, Institutions, and Political Change,*

Ithaca: Cornell University Press.
Gowa, Joanne 1986, "Anarchy, Egoism, and Third Images: 'The Evolution of Cooperation' and International Relations," *International Organization* 40: 167–86.
1989a, "Bipolarity, Multipolarity, and Free Trade," *American Political Science Review* 83: 1245–56.
1989b, "Rational Hegemons, Excludable Goods, and Small Groups: An Epitaph for Hegemonic Stability Theory?" *World Politics* 41: 307–24.
Gowa, Joanne, and Mansfield, Edward D. 1993, "Power Politics and International Trade," *American Political Science Review* 87: 408–20.
Grieco, Joseph M. 1988a, "Anarchy and the Limits of Cooperation: A Realist Critique of the Newest Liberal Institutionalism," *International Organization* 42: 485–507.
1988b, "Realist Theory and the Problem of International Cooperation: Analysis with an Amended Prisoner's Dilemma," *Journal of Politics* 50: 600–24.
1990, *Cooperation among Nations: Europe, America, and Non-Tariff Barriers to Trade*, Ithaca: Cornell University Press.
1993a, "The Relative-Gains Problem for International Cooperation: Comment," in *American Political Science Review* 87: 729–35.
1993b, "Understanding the Problem of International Cooperation: The Limits of Neoliberal Institutionalism and the Future of Realist Theory," in Baldwin (ed.) 1993b, 301–38.
1995, "The Maastricht Treaty, Economic and Monetary Union and the Neo-Realist Research Programme," *Review of International Studies* 21: 21–40.
Haas, Ernst B. 1964, *Beyond the Nation–State: Functionalism and International Organization*, Stanford University Press.
1975, "Is There a Hole in the Whole? Knowledge, Technology, Interdependence and the Construction of International Regimes," *International Organization* 29: 827–76.
1980, "Why Collaborate? Issue-Linkage and International Regimes," *World Politics* 32: 357–402.
1990, *When Knowledge is Power*, Berkeley: University of California Press.
Haas, Peter M. 1989, "Do Regimes Matter? Epistemic Communities and Mediterranean Pollution Control," *International Organization* 43: 377–403.
1990, *Saving the Mediterranean: The Politics of International Environmental Cooperation*, New York: Columbia University Press.
1992a: "Banning Chlorofluorocarbons: Epistemic Community Efforts to Protect Stratospheric Ozone," in P. Haas (ed.) 1992c, 187–225.
1992b: "Introduction: Epistemic Communities and International Policy Coordination," in P. Haas (ed.) 1992c, 1–35.
(ed.) 1992c, "Knowledge, Power, and International Policy Coordination," special issue of *International Organization* 46, no. 1.
1993, "Epistemic Communites and the Dynamics of International Environmental Co-operation," in Rittberger (ed.) 1993a, 168–201.
Habermas, Jürgen 1981, *Theorie des kommunikativen Handelns:* vol. I:

Handlungsrationalität und gesellschaftliche Rationalisierung; vol. II: *Zur Kritik der funktionalistischen Vernunft*, Frankfurt a.M.: Suhrkamp.

1983, *Moralbewußtsein und kommunikatives Handeln*, Frankfurt a.M.: Suhrkamp.

Haggard, Stephan, and Simmons, Beth A. 1987, "Theories of International Regimes," *International Organization* 41: 491–517.

Hall, John A. 1993, "Ideas in the Social Sciences," in Goldstein and Keohane (eds.) 1993b, 31–54.

Hardin, Russell 1971, "Collective Action as an Agreeable *n*-Prisoners' Dilemma," *Behavioral Science* 16: 472–81.

1982, *Collective Action*, Baltimore: Johns Hopkins University Press/Resources for the Future.

Harsanyi, John 1969, "Rational Choice Models of Political Behavior vs. Functionalist and Conformist Theories," *World Politics* 21: 513–36.

Hasenclever, Andreas, Mayer, Peter, and Rittberger, Volker 1996, *Justice, Equality, and the Robustness of International Regimes: A Research Design*, Tübinger Arbeitspapiere zur Internationalen Politik und Friedensforschung 25, University of Tübingen.

Haussmann, Thomas 1991, *Erklären und Verstehen: Zur Theorie und Pragmatik der Geschichtswissenschaft*, Frankfurt a.M.: Suhrkamp.

Hempel, Carl Gustav, and Oppenheim, Paul 1948, "Studies in the Logic of Explanation," *Philosophy of Science* 15, 135–75.

Henkin, Louis 1968, *How Nations Behave: Law and Foreign Policy*, New York: Praeger.

Herz, John H. 1950, "Idealist Internationalism and the Security Dilemma," *World Politics* 2: 157–80.

Heymann, Philip B. 1973, "The Problem of Coordination: Bargaining and Rules," *Harvard Law Review* 86: 797–877.

Hirsch, Fred 1976, *Social Limits to Growth*, London: Routledge & Kegan Paul.

Hirschman, Albert O. 1945, *National Power and the Structure of Foreign Trade*, Berkeley: University of California Press.

Höffe, Otfried 1987, *Politische Gerechtigkeit: Grundlegung einer Philosophie von Recht und Staat*, Frankfurt a.M.: Suhrkamp.

Hoffmann, Mark 1987, "Critical Theory and the Inter-Paradigm Debate," *Millennium* 16: 231–49.

1994, "Normative International Theory: Approaches and Issues," in A. J. R. Groom, and Margot Light (eds.), *Contemporary International Relations: A Guide to Theory*, London: Pinter, 27–47.

Hoffmann, Stanley, Keohane, Robert O., and Mearsheimer, John J. 1990, "Correspondence: Back to the Future, Part II: International Relations Theory and Post-Cold War Europe," *International Security* 15: 191–9.

Hollis, Martin, and Smith, Steve 1990, *Explaining and Understanding International Relations*, Oxford: Clarendon Press.

1991, "Beware of Gurus: Structure and Action in International Relations," *Review of International Studies* 17: 393–410.

1992, "Structure and Action: Further Comment," *Review of International Studies* 18: 187–8.
Hurrell, Andrew 1993, "International Society and the Study of Regimes," in Rittberger (ed.) 1993a, 49–72.
Ikenberry, John G. 1993, "Creating Yesterday's New World Order: Keynesian 'New Thinking' and the Anglo-American Postwar Settlement," in Goldstein and Keohane (eds.) 1993b, 57–86.
Jackson, Robert H. 1993, "The Weight of Ideas in Decolonization: Normative Change in International Relations," in Goldstein and Keohane (eds.) 1993b, 111–38.
Johnson, Harry G. 1954, "Optimum Tariffs and Retaliation," *Review of Economic Studies* 21: 142–53.
Jervis, Robert 1978, "Cooperation under the Security Dilemma," *World Politics* 30: 167–214.
Jönsson, Christer 1993, "Cognitive Factors in Explaining Regime Dynamics," in Rittberger (ed.) 1993a, 202–22.
Junne, Gerd 1990, "Theorien über Konflikte zwischen kapitalistischen Industrieländern," in Rittberger (ed.) 1990c, 353–71.
1992, "Beyond Regime Theory," *Acta Politica* 27: 9–21.
Keck, Otto 1991, "Der neue Institutionalismus in der Theorie der Internationalen Politik," *Politische Vierteljahresschrift* 32: 635–53.
1993, "The New Institutionalism and the Relative-Gains-Debate," in Pfetsch 1993 (ed.), 35–62.
Kegley, Charles W., Jr. (ed.) 1995, *Controversies in International Relations Theory: Realism and the Neoliberal Challenge*, New York: St. Martin's Press.
Keohane, Robert 1980, "The Theory of Hegemonic Stability and Changes in International Economic Regimes 1967–1977," in Ole R. Holsti, Randolph M. Siverson, and Alexander L. George (eds.), *Change in the International System*, Boulder, Colo.: Westview Press, 131–62.
1983, "The Demand for International Regimes," in Krasner (ed.) 1983a, 141–71.
1984, *After Hegemony: Cooperation and Discord in the World Political Economy*, Princeton University Press.
(ed.) 1986a, *Neorealism and Its Critics*, New York: Columbia University Press.
1986b, "Realism, Neorealism and the Study of World Politics," in Keohane (ed.) 1986a, 1–26.
1986c, "Reciprocity in World Politics," *International Organization* 40: 1–27.
1988, "International Institutions: Two Approaches," *International Studies Quarterly* 32: 379–96.
1989a, "Closing the Fairness–Practice Gap," *Ethics and International Affairs* 3: 101–16.
1989b, *International Institutions and State Power: Essays in International Relations Theory*, Boulder, Colo.: Westview Press.
1989c, "Neoliberal Institutionalism: A Perspective on World Politics," in Keohane 1989b, 1–20.

1989d, "Theory of World Politics: Structural Realism and Beyond," in Keohane 1989b, 35–73.

1990, "International Liberalism Reconsidered," in John Dunn, (ed.), *The Economic Limits to Modern Politics*, Cambridge University Press, 165–94.

1993a, "The Analysis of International Regimes: Towards a European-American Research Programme," in Rittberger (ed.) 1993a, 23–45.

1993b, "Institutionalist Theory and the Realist Challenge After the Cold War," in Baldwin (ed.) 1993b, 269–300.

Keohane, Robert O., Haas, Peter M., and Levy, Marc A. 1993, "The Effectiveness of International Environmental Institutions," in Peter M. Haas, Robert O. Keohane, and Marc A. Levy (eds.), *Institutions for the Earth: Sources of Effective International Environmental Protection*, Cambridge, Mass.: MIT Press, 3–24.

Keohane, Robert O., and Martin, Lisa L. 1995, "The Promise of Institutionalist Theory," *International Security* 20: 39–51.

Keohane, Robert O., and Nye, Joseph S., Jr. 1977, *Power and Interdependence: World Politics in Transition*, Boston: Little, Brown.

Kindleberger, Charles P. 1973, *The World in Depression 1929–1939*, London: Allen Lane, The Penguin Press.

1976, "Systems of International Economic Organization," in David P. Calleo, (ed.), *Money and the Coming World Order*, New York University Press, 15–39.

1981, "Dominance and Leadership in the International Economy: Exploitation, Public Goods, and Free Rides," *International Studies Quarterly* 25: 242–54.

1986, "Hierarchy Versus Inertial Cooperation," *International Organization* 40: 841–7.

King, Gary, Keohane, Robert O., and Verba, Sidney 1994, *Designing Social Inquiry: Scientific Inference in Qualitative Research*, Princeton University Press.

Kohler-Koch, Beate (ed.) 1989a, *Regime in den internationalen Beziehungen*, Baden-Baden: Nomos.

1989b, "Zur Empirie und Theorie internationaler Regime," in Kohler-Koch (ed.) 1989a, 17–85.

Koslowski, Rey, and Kratochwil, Friedrich V. 1994, "Understanding Change in International Politics: The Soviet Empire's Demise and the International System," *International Organization* 48: 215–47.

Krasner, Stephen D. 1976, "State Power and the Structure of International Trade," *World Politics* 28: 317–47.

(ed.) 1983a, *International Regimes*, Ithaca: Cornell University Press.

1983b, "Regimes and the Limits of Realism: Regimes as Autonomous Variables," in Krasner (ed.) 1983a, 355–68.

1983c, "Structural Causes and Regime Consequences: Regimes as Intervening Variables," in Krasner (ed.) 1983a, 1–21.

1985, *Structural Conflict: The Third World Against Global Liberalism*, Berkeley: University of California Press.

1988, "Sovereignty: An Institutional Perspective," *Comparative Political Studies* 21: 66–94.

1991, "Global Communications and National Power: Life on the Pareto Frontier," *World Politics* 43: 336–66.

1993a, "Sovereignty, Regimes, and Human Rights," in Rittberger (ed.) 1993a, 139–67.

1993b, "Westphalia and All That," in Goldstein and Keohane (eds.) 1993b, 235–65.

Kratochwil, Friedrich V. 1984, "The Force of Prescriptions," *International Organization* 38: 685–708.

1988, "Regimes, Interpretation, and the 'Science' of Politics: A Reappraisal," *Millennium* 17: 263–84.

1989, *Rules, Norms, and Decisions: On the Conditions of Practical and Legal Reasoning in International Relations and Domestic Affairs*, Cambridge University Press.

1993a, "Contract and Regimes: Do Issue Specificity and Variations of Formality Matter?" in Rittberger (ed.) 1993a, 73–93.

1993b, "Norms Versus Numbers. Multilateralism and the Rationalist and Reflexist Approaches to Institutions – A Unilateral Plea for Communicative Rationality," in Ruggie (ed.) 1993a, 443–74.

Kratochwil, Friedrich V., and Mansfield, Edward D. (eds.) 1994, *International Organization: A Reader*, Glasgow: HarperCollins.

Kratochwil, Friedrich V., and Ruggie, John Gerard 1986, "International Organization: A State of the Art on an Art of the State," *International Organization* 40: 753–75.

Kriesberg, Louis 1982, *Social Conflicts*, 2nd edn., Englewood Cliffs, N.J.: Prentice-Hall.

Kupchan, Charles A., and Kupchan, Clifford A. 1995, "The Promise of Collective Security," *International Security* 20: 52–61.

Kydd, Andrew, and Snidal, Duncan 1993, "Progress in Game-Theoretical Analysis of International Regimes," in Rittberger (ed.) 1993a, 112–35.

Lake, David A. 1993, "Leadership, Hegemony, and the International Economy: Naked Emperor or Tattered Monarch with Potential?" *International Studies Quarterly* 37: 459–89.

Lapid, Yosef 1989, "The Third Debate: On the Prospects of International Theory in a Post-Positivist Era," *International Studies Quarterly* 33: 235–54.

Levy, Jack S. 1994, "Learning and Foreign Policy: Sweeping a Conceptual Minefield," *International Organization* 48: 279–312.

Levy, Marc A., Young, Oran R., and Zürn, Michael 1995, "The Study of International Regimes," *European Journal of International Relations* 1: 267–330.

Lipson, Charles 1984, "International Cooperation in Economic and Security Affairs," *World Politics* 37: 1–23.

List, Martin 1991, *Umweltschutz in zwei Meeren: Vergleich der internationalen Zusammenarbeit zum Schutz der Meeresumwelt in Nord- und Ostsee*, München: tuduv.

1992, "Rechtsstaatlichkeit in (West)Europa: eine regimeanalytische Betrachtung," *Politische Vierteljahresschrift* 33: 622–42.

Luban, David 1980, "Just War and Human Rights," *Philosophy and Public Affairs* 9: 161–81.

Lumsdaine, David Halloran 1993, *Moral Vision in International Politics: The Foreign Aid Regime, 1949–1989*, Princeton University Press.

Mansbach, Richard W., and Vasquez, John A. 1981, *In Search of Theory: A New Paradigm for Global Politics*, New York: Columbia University Press.

March, James G., and Olsen, Johan P. 1989, *Rediscovering Institutions: The Organizational Basis of Politics*, New York: Free Press.

Martin, Lisa L. 1993, "The Rational State Choice of Multilateralism," in Ruggie (ed.) 1993a, 91–121.

Mayer, Peter, Rittberger, Volker, and Zürn, Michael 1993, "Regime Theory: State of the Art and Perspectives," in Rittberger (ed.) 1993a, 391–430.

McKeown, Timothy J. 1983, "Hegemonic Stability Theory and 19th Century Tariff Levels in Europe," *International Organization* 37: 73–91.

Mead, George Herbert 1934, *Mind, Self, and Society: From the Standpoint of a Social Behaviorist*, The University of Chicago Press.

Mearsheimer, John J. 1990, "Back to the Future: Instability in Europe After the Cold War," *International Security* 15: 5–56.

1995, "The False Promise of International Institutions," *International Security* 19: 5–49.

Mercer, Jonathan 1996, *Reputation and International Politics*, Ithaca: Cornell University Press.

Milner, Helen 1992, "International Theories of Cooperation: Strengths and Weaknesses," *World Politics* 44: 466–96.

1993, "International Regimes and World Politics: Comments on the Articles by Smouts, de Senarclens and Jönsson," *International Social Science Journal* 45: 491–7.

Moravcsik, Andrew 1992, "Liberalism and International Relations Theory," Working Paper Series 92–6, The Center for International Affairs, Harvard University, Cambridge, Mass.

Müller, Harald 1989, "Regimeanalyse und Sicherheitspolitik: das Beispiel Nonproliferation," in Kohler-Koch (ed.) 1989a, 277–313.

1993a, *Die Chance der Kooperation: Regime in den internationalen Beziehungen*, Darmstadt: Wissenschaftliche Buchgesellschaft.

1993b, "The Internalization of Principles, Norms, and Rules by Governments: The Case of Security Regimes," in Rittberger (ed.) 1993a, 361–88.

1994, "Internationale Beziehungen als kommunikatives Handeln: Zur Kritik der utilitaristischen Handlungstheorien," *Zeitschrift für Internationale Beziehungen* 1: 15–44.

Neufeld, Mark 1993, "Interpretation and the 'Science' of International Relations," *Review of International Studies* 19: 39–61.

1994, "Reflexivity and International Relations Theory," in Claire Turenne Sjolander and Wayne S. Cox (eds.), *Beyond Positivism: Critical Reflections on International Relations*, Boulder, Colo.: Lynne Rienner, 11–35.

Noehrenberg, Eric H. 1995, *Multilateral Export Controls and International Regime Theory: The Effectiveness of COCOM*, Sinzheim: Pro Universitate.

Nollkaemper, André 1992, "On the Effectiveness of International Rules," *Acta Politica* 27: 49–70.

Nye, Joseph S., Jr. 1987, "Nuclear Learning and U.S. – Soviet Security Regimes," *International Organization* 41: 371–402.

1988, "Neorealism and Neoliberalism," *World Politics* 40: 235–51.

1993, *Understanding International Conflicts: An Introduction to Theory and History*, New York: HarperCollins.

Olson, Mancur, Jr. 1965, *The Logic of Collective Action: Public Goods and the Theory of Groups*, Cambridge, Mass.: Harvard University Press.

Onuf, Nicholas Greenwood 1989, *World of Our Making: Rules and Rule in Social Theory and International Relations*, Columbia, University of South Carolina Press.

Ostrom, Elinor 1990, *Governing the Commons: The Evolution of Institutions for Collective Action*, Cambridge University Press.

Oye, Kenneth A. (ed.) 1986a, *Cooperation under Anarchy*, Princeton University Press.

1986b, "Explaining Cooperation under Anarchy: Hypotheses and Strategies," in Oye (ed.) 1986a, 1–24.

Peterson, M. J. 1992, "Whalers, Cetologists, Environmentalists, and the International Management of Whaling," in P. Haas (ed.) 1992c, 147–86.

Pfetsch, Frank R. (ed.) 1993, *International Relations and Pan-Europe: Theoretical Approaches and Empirical Findings*, Münster: Lit.

Pogge, Thomas W. 1994, "An Egalitarian Law of the People," *Philosophy and Public Affairs* 23: 195–224.

Powell, Robert 1991, "Absolute and Relative Gains in International Relations Theory," *American Political Science Review* 85: 1303–20.

1994, "Anarchy in International Relations Theory: The Neorealist – Neoliberal Debate," *International Organization* 48: 313–44.

Price, Richard 1994, "Interpretation and Disciplinary Orthodoxy in International Relations," *Review of International Studies* 20: 201–4.

Putnam, Robert D. 1988, "Diplomacy and Domestic Politics: The Logic of Two-Level Games," *International Organization* 42: 427–60.

Raub, Werner, and Voss, Thomas 1986, "Conditions for Cooperation in Problematic Social Situations," in Andreas Diekmann and Peter Mitter (eds.), *Paradoxical Effects of Social Behavior: Essays in Honor of Anatol Rapoport*, Heidelberg: Physica-Verlag, 85–103.

Rawls, John 1955, "Two Concepts of Rules," *Philosophical Review* 64: 3–32.

1971, *A Theory of Justice*, Cambridge, Mass.: Harvard University Press.

Risse-Kappen, Thomas 1994, "Ideas Do Not Float Freely: Transnational Coalitions, Domestic Structures, and the End of the Cold War," *International Organization* 48: 185–214.

1995, "Reden ist nicht billig: Zur Debatte um Kommunikation und Rationalität," *Zeitschrift für Internationale Beziehungen* 2: 171–84.

Rittberger, Volker 1987, "Zur Friedensfähigkeit von Demokratien:

Betrachtungen zur politischen Theorie des Friedens," Aus Politik und Zeitgeschichte [no volume number], 3–12.

1990a, "Editor's Introduction," in Rittberger (ed.) 1990b, 1–8.

(ed.) 1990b, *International Regimes in East – West Politics*, London: Pinter.

(ed.) 1990c, *Theorien der Internationalen Beziehungen: Bestandsaufnahme und Forschungsperspektiven* (PVS Sonderheft 21), Opladen: Westdeutscher Verlag.

Rittberger, Volker (with the assistance of Peter Mayer) (ed.) 1993a, *Regime Theory and International Relations*, Oxford: Clarendon Press.

1993b, "Research on International Regimes in Germany: The Adaptive Internalization of an American Social Science Concept," in Rittberger (ed.) 1993a, 3–22.

1995, "Über die Friedensleistung internationaler Regime," in Dieter Senghaas (ed.), *Den Frieden denken*, Frankfurt a.M.: Suhrkamp, 341–362.

Rittberger, Volker, and Zürn, Michael 1990, "Towards Regulated Anarchy in East–West Relations," in Rittberger (ed.) 1990b, 9–63.

1991, "Regime Theory: Findings From the Study of 'East–West Regimes'," *Cooperation and Conflict* 26: 165–83.

1992, "Transformation of Conflicts in East–West Relations: Towards an Institutionalist Inventory," *Law and State* 45: 7–36.

Rosenau, James N., and Czempiel, Ernst-Otto (eds.) 1992, *Governance Without Government: Order and Change in World Politics*, Cambridge University Press

Ruggie, John Gerard 1975, "International Responses to Technology: Concepts and Trends," *International Organization* 29: 557–83.

1983, "International Regimes, Transactions, and Change: Embedded Liberalism in the Postwar Economic Order," in Krasner (ed.) 1983a, 195–231.

1986, "Continuity and Transformation in the World Polity: Toward a Neorealist Synthesis," in Keohane (ed.) 1986a, 131–57.

(ed.) 1993a, *Multilateralism Matters: The Theory and Praxis of an Institutional Form*, New York: Columbia University Press.

1993b, "Multilateralism: The Anatomy of an Institution," in Ruggie (ed.) 1993a, 3–47.

1995, "The False Premise of Realism," *International Security* 20: 62– 70.

Russett, Bruce 1983, *Prisoners of Insecurity: Nuclear Deterrence, the Arms Race, and Arms Control*, San Francisco: Freeman.

Schaber, Thomas, and Ulbert, Cornelia 1994, "Reflexivität in den Internationalen Beziehungen: Literaturbericht zum Beitrag kognitiver, reflexiver und interpretativer Ansätze zur dritten Theoriedebatte," *Zeitschrift für Internationale Beziehungen* 1: 139–69.

Scharpf, Fritz W. 1989, "Decision Rules, Decision Styles and Policy Choices," *Journal of Theoretical Politics* 1: 149–76.

Schelling, Thomas C. 1960, *The Strategy of Conflict*, Cambridge, Mass.: Harvard University Press.

1973, "Hockey Helmets, Concealed Weapons, and Daylight Saving: A Study of Binary Choices with Externalities," *Journal of Conflict Resolution* 17: 381–428.

Schimmelfennig, Frank 1995, *Debatten zwischen Staaten: Eine Argumentationstheorie internationaler Systemkonflikte*, Opladen: Leske & Budrich.

Schrogl, Kai-Uwe 1990, *Die Begrenzung konventioneller Rüstung in Europa: Ein regimeanalytisches Konfliktmodell*, Tübinger Arbeitspapiere zur internationalen Politik und Friedensforschung 14, University of Tübingen.

1993, *Zivile Satellitennutzung in internationaler Zusammenarbeit*, Cologne: Carl Heymanns Verlag.

Schwarzer, Gudrun 1990a, "The Berlin Regime," in Rittberger (ed.) 1990b, 189–215.

1990b, *Weiträumige grenzüberschreitende Luftverschmutzung: Konfliktanalyse eines internationalen Umweltproblems*, Tübinger Arbeitspapiere zur internationalen Politik und Friedensforschung 15, University of Tübingen.

1994, *Friedliche Konfliktregulierung: Saarland – Österreich – Berlin: Eine vergleichende Untersuchung territorialer Machtkonflikte*, Tübingen: Universitas.

Searle, John R. 1969, *Speech Acts: An Essay in the Philosophy of Language*, Cambridge University Press.

Sebenius, James K. 1992, "Challenging Conventional Explanations of International Cooperation: Negotiation Analysis and the Case of Epistemic Communities," in P. Haas (ed.) 1992c, 323–65.

Simon, Herbert A. 1972, "Theories of Bounded Rationality," in C. B. Radner and R. Radner (eds.), *Decision and Organization*, Amsterdam: North-Holland, 161–76.

1985, "Human Nature in Politics: The Dialogue of Psychology with Political Science," *American Political Science Review* 79: 293–304.

Singer, J. David 1961, "The Level-of-Analysis Problem in International Relations," *World Politics* 14, 77–92.

Slaughter Burley, Anne-Marie 1993, "International Law and International Relations Theory: A Dual Agenda," *American Journal of International Law* 87, 205–39.

Smith, Roger K. 1987, "Explaining the Non-Proliferation Regime: Anomalies for Contemporary International Relations Theory," *International Organization* 41: 253–82.

1989, "Institutionalization as a Measure of Regime Stability: Insights for International Regime Analysis from the Study of Domestic Politics," *Journal of International Studies* 18: 227–44.

Snidal, Duncan 1985a, "Coordination Versus Prisoners' Dilemma: Implications for International Cooperation and Regimes," *American Political Science Review* 79: 923–42.

1985b, "The Limits of Hegemonic Stability Theory," *International Organization* 39: 579–614.

1986, "The Game *Theory* of International Politics," in Oye (ed.) 1986a, 25– 57.

1991a, "International Cooperation Among Relative Gains Maximizers," *International Studies Quarterly* 35: 387–402.

1991b, "Relative Gains and the Pattern of International Cooperation," *American Political Science Review* 85: 701–26.

1993, "The Relative-Gains Problem for International Cooperation: Response, *American Political Science Review* 87: 738–42.

Snyder, Glenn H., and Diesing, Paul 1977, *Conflict among Nations: Bargaining, Decision Making, and System Structure in International Crisis*, Princeton University Press.

Soroos, Marvin S. 1993, "Arctic Haze and Transboundary Air Pollution: Conditions Governing Success and Failure," in Young and Osherenko (eds.) 1993c, 186–222.

Steigleder, Klaus 1992, *Die Begründung des moralischen Sollens: Studien zur Möglichkeit einer normativen Ethik*, Tübingen: Attempto.

Stein, Arthur A. 1983, "Coordination and Collaboration: Regimes in an Anarchic World," in Krasner (ed.) 1983a, 115–40.

1990, *Why Nations Cooperate: Circumstances and Choice in International Relations*, Ithaca: Cornell University Press.

Stinchcombe, Arthur L. 1968, *Constructing Social Theories*, New York: Harcourt, Brace and World.

Strange, Susan 1983: "*Cave! Hic Dragones*: A Critique of Regime Analysis," in Krasner (ed.) 1983a, 337–54.

Taylor, Charles 1985, "Interpretation and the Sciences of Man," in *Philosophy and the Human Sciences* (Philosophical Papers, vol. II), Cambridge University Press, 15–57.

Taylor, Michael 1976, *Anarchy and Cooperation*, London: Wiley.

Underdal, Arild 1992, "The Concept of 'Regime Effectiveness'," *Cooperation and Conflict* 27: 227–40.

1995, "The Study of International Regimes," *Journal of Peace Research* 32: 113–19.

van Ham, Peter 1992, "The Lack of a Big Bully: Hegemonic Stability Theory and Regimes in the Study of International Relations," *Acta Politica* 27: 29–48.

Vasquez, John A., and Mansbach, Richard W. 1984, "The Role of Issues in Global Co-operation and Conflict," *British Journal of Political Science* 14: 411–33.

Wallerstein, Immanuel 1974, *The Modern World System I: Capitalist Agriculture and the Origins of the European World-Economy in the Sixteenth Century*, New York: Academic Press.

1980, *The Modern World System II: Mercantilism and the Consolidation of the European World-Economy, 1600–1750*, New York: Academic Press.

1989, *The Modern World System III: The Second Era of Great Expansion of the Capitalist World-Economy, 1730–1840s*, San Diego: Academic Press.

Waltz, Kenneth N. 1964, "The Stability of a Bipolar World," *Daedalus* 93: 881–909.

1979, *Theory of International Politics*, New York: Random House.

1986, "Reflections on *Theory of International Politics*: A Response to My Critics," in Keohane (ed.) 1986a, 322–45.

1993, "The New World Order," *Millennium* 22: 187–95.

Walzer, Michael 1985, "The Moral Standing of States: A Response to Four Critics," in Charles R. Beitz *et al.* (eds.) *International Ethics*, Princeton University Press, 215–37.

Webb, Michael C., and Krasner, Stephen D. 1989, "Hegemonic Stability Theory: An Empirical Assessment," *Review of International Studies* 15: 183–98.

Weber, Max 1949, "'Objectivity' in Social Science and Social Policy," in *The Methodology of the Social Sciences* (ed. and trans. by E. A. Shils and H. A. Finch), New York: Free Press, 49–112.

Wendt, Alexander 1987, "The Agent – Structure Problem in International Relations Theory," *International Organization* 41: 335–70.

1991, "Bridging the Theory/Meta-theory Gap in International Relations," *Review of International Studies* 17: 383–92.

1992a, "Anarchy is What States Make of It: The Social Construction of Power Politics," *International Organization* 46: 391–425.

1992b, "Levels of Analysis vs. Agents and Structures: Part III," *Review of International Studies* 18: 181–85.

1994, "Collective Identity Formation and the International State," *American Political Science Review* 88: 384–96.

1995, "Constructing International Politics," *International Security* 20: 71–81.

Wendt, Alexander, and Duvall, Raymond 1989, "Institutions and International Order," in Ernst-Otto Czempiel and James N. Rosenau (eds.), *Global Changes and Theoretical Challenges: Approaches to the World Politics for the 1990s*, Lexington, Mass.: Lexington Books, 51–73.

Wettestad, Jørgen, and Andresen, Steinar 1991, *The Effectiveness of International Resource Cooperation: Some Preliminary Findings*, Lysaker: Fridtjof Nansen Institute.

Wolf, Dieter, and Zangl, Bernhard 1996, "The European Economic and Monetary Union: 'Two-level Games' and the Formation of International Institutions," *European Journal of International Relations* 2: 355–93.

Wolf, Klaus Dieter 1991, *Internationale Regime zur Verteilung globaler Ressourcen: Eine vergleichende Analyse ihrer Entstehung am Beispiel der Regelung des Zugangs zur wirtschaftlichen Nutzung des Meeresbodens, des geostationären Orbits, der Antarktis und zu Wissenschaft und Technologie*, Baden-Baden: Nomos.

Wolf, Klaus Dieter, and Zürn, Michael 1986, "'International Regimes' und Theorien der Internationalen Politik," *Politische Vierteljahresschrift* 27: 201–21.

Yarbrough, Beth V. and Yarbrough, Robert M. 1987, "Cooperation and the Liberalization of International Trade: After Hegemony, What?" *International Organization* 41: 1–26.

Young, Oran R. 1977, *Resource Management at the International Level: The Case of the North Pacific*, London/New York: Pinter and Nichols.

1980, "International Regimes: Problems of Concept Formation," *World Politics* 32: 331–56.

1982, *Resource Regimes: Natural Resources and Social Institutions*, Berkeley: University of California Press.

1983, "Regime Dynamics: The Rise and Fall of International Regimes," in Krasner (ed.) 1983a, 93–113.

(ed.) 1985, *Bargaining: Formal Theories of Negotiation*, Urbana: University of Illinois Press.

1986, "International Regimes: Toward a New Theory of Institutions," *World Politics* 39: 104–22.

1989a, *International Cooperation: Building Regimes for Natural Resources and the Environment*, Ithaca: Cornell University Press.

1989b, "The Politics of International Regime Formation: Managing Natural Resources and the Environment," *International Organization* 43: 349–76.

1991, "Political Leadership and Regime Formation: On the Development of Institutions in International Society," *International Organization* 45: 281–308.

1992, "The Effectiveness of International Institutions: Hard Cases and Critical Variables," in Rosenau and Czempiel (eds.) 1992, 160–94.

1994, *International Governance: Protecting the Environment in a Stateless Society*, Ithaca: Cornell University Press.

1996, "Institutional Linkages in International Society: Polar Perspectives," *Global Governance* 2: 1–23.

Young, Oran R. and Osherenko, Gail 1993a, "The Formation of International Regimes: Hypotheses and Cases," in Young and Osherenko (eds.) 1993c, 1–21.

1993b, "International Regime Formation: Findings, Research Priorities, and Applications," in Young and Osherenko (eds.) 1993c, 223–61.

(eds.) 1993c, *Polar Politics: Creating International Environmental Regimes*, Ithaca: Cornell University Press.

1993d, "Testing Theories of Regime Formation: Findings from a Large Collaborative Research Project," in Rittberger (ed.) 1993a, 223–50.

Zacher, Mark W. 1987, "Trade Gaps, Analytical Gaps: Regime Analysis and International Commodity Trade Regulation," *International Organization* 41: 173–202.

Zacher, Mark W., and Matthew, Richard A. 1995, "Liberal International Theory: Common Threads, Divergent Strands," in Kegley (ed.) 1995, 107–50.

Zacher, Mark W. (with Brent A. Sutton) 1996, *Governing Global Networks: International Regimes for Transportation and Communication*, Cambridge University Press.

Zangl, Bernhard 1994, "Politik auf zwei Ebenen: Hypothesen zur Bildung internationaler Regime," *Zeitschrift für Internationale Beziehungen* 1: 279–312.

Zartman, I. William, and Berman, Maureen R. 1982, *The Practical Negotiator*, New Haven, Conn.: Yale University Press.

Zürn, Michael 1990, "Intra-German Trade: An Early East – West Regime," in Rittberger (ed.) 1990b, 151–88.

1992, *Interessen und Institutionen in der internationalen Politik: Grundlegung und Anwendung des situationsstrukturellen Ansatzes*, Opladen: Leske & Budrich.

1993a, "Bringing the Second Image (Back) in: About the Domestic Sources of Regime Formation," in Rittberger (ed.) 1993a, 282–311.

1993b, "Problematic Social Situations and International Institutions: On the Use of Game Theory in International Politics," in Pfetsch (ed.) 1993, 63–84.

Zürn, Michael, Wolf, Klaus Dieter, and Efinger, Manfred 1990, "Problemfelder und Situationsstrukturen in der Analyse internationaler Politik: eine Brücke zwischen den Polen?" in Rittberger (ed.) 1990c, 151–74.

Index

CAMBRIDGE STUDIES IN INTERNATIONAL RELATIONS

43 *Mark Neufeld*
The restructuring of international relations theory

42 *Thomas Risse-Kappen (ed.)*
Bringing transnational relations back in
Non-state actors, domestic structures and international institutions

41 *Hayward R. Alker*
Rediscoveries and reformulations
Humanistic methodologies for international studies

40 *Robert W. Cox with Timothy J. Sinclair*
Approaches to world order

39 *Jens Bartelson*
A genealogy of sovereignty

38 *Mark Rupert*
Producing hegemony
The politics of mass production and American global power

37 *Cynthia Weber*
Simulating sovereignty
Intervention, the state and symbolic exchange

36 *Gary Goertz*
Contexts of international politics

35 *James L. Richardson*
Crisis diplomacy
The Great Powers since the mid-nineteenth century

34 *Bradley S. Klein*
Strategic studies and world order
The global politics of deterrence

33 *T. V. Paul*
Asymmetric conflicts: war initiation by weaker powers

32 *Christine Sylvester*
Feminist theory and international relations in a postmodern era

31 *Peter J. Schraeder*
US foreign policy toward Africa
Incrementalism, crisis and change

30 *Graham Spinardi*
From Polaris to Trident: the development of US Fleet Ballistic Missile technology

29 *David A. Welch*
Justice and the genesis of war

28 *Russell J. Leng*
Interstate crisis behavior, 1816–1980: realism versus reciprocity

27 *John A. Vasquez*
The war puzzle

26 *Stephen Gill (ed.)*
Gramsci, historical materialism and international relations

25 *Mike Bowker and Robin Brown (eds.)*
From Cold War to collapse: theory and world politics in the 1980s

24 *R. B. J. Walker*
Inside/outside: international relations as political theory

23 *Edward Reiss*
The Strategic Defense Initiative

22 *Keith Krause*
Arms and the state: patterns of military production and trade

21 *Roger Buckley*
US–Japan alliance diplomacy 1945–1990

20 *James N. Rosenau and Ernst-Otto Czempiel (eds.)*
Governance without government: order and change in world politics

19 *Michael Nicholson*
Rationality and the analysis of international conflict

18 *John Stopford and Susan Strange*
Rival states, rival firms
Competition for world market shares

17 *Terry Nardin and David R. Mapel (eds.)*
Traditions of international ethics

16 *Charles F. Doran*
Systems in crisis
New imperatives of high politics at century's end

15 *Deon Geldenhuys*
Isolated states: a comparative analysis

14 *Kalevi J. Holsti*
Peace and war: armed conflicts and international order 1648–1989

13 *Saki Dockrill*
Britain's policy for West German rearmament 1950–1955

12 *Robert H. Jackson*
Quasi-states: sovereignty, international relations and the Third World

11 *James Barber and John Barratt*
South Africa's foreign policy
The search for status and security 1945–1988

10 *James Mayall*
Nationalism and international society

9 *William Bloom*
Personal identity, national identity and international relations

8 *Zeev Maoz*
National choices and international processes

7 *Ian Clark*
The hierarchy of states
Reform and resistance in the international order

6 *Hidemi Suganami*
The domestic analogy and world order proposals

5 *Stephen Gill*
American hegemony and the Trilateral Commission

4 *Michael C. Pugh*
The ANZUS crisis, nuclear visiting and deterrence

3 *Michael Nicholson*
Formal theories in international relations

2 *Friedrich V. Kratochwil*
Rules, norms, and decisions
On the conditions of practical and legal reasoning in international relations and domestic affairs

1 *Myles L. C. Robertson*
Soviet policy towards Japan
An analysis of trends in the 1970s and 1980s